MIRACLE AT KITTY HAWK

Isn't it astonishing that all these secrets
have been preserved for so many years
just so that we could discover them!!

Orville Wright, June 7, 1903

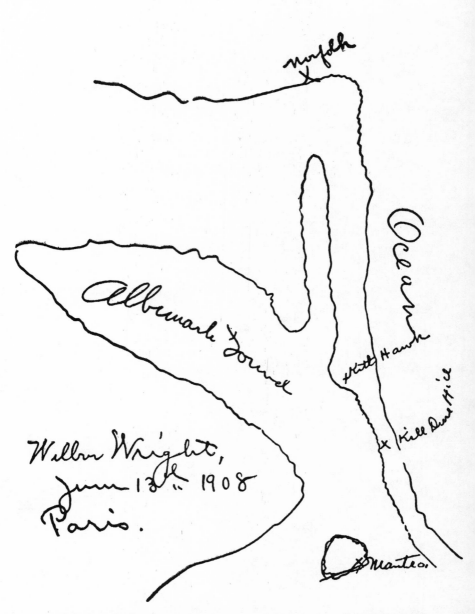

Sketch by Wilbur Wright showing the position of Kitty Hawk and Kill Devil Hill. Drawn from Memory.

MIRACLE AT
KITTY HAWK

The Letters of Wilbur and Orville Wright

EDITED BY

FRED C. KELLY

AUTHORIZED BIOGRAPHER OF THE WRIGHT BROTHERS

. . . .

DA CAPO PRESS
A Member of the Perseus Books Group

This Da Capo Press paperback edition of *Miracle at Kitty Hawk* is an unabridged republication of the edition published in New York in 1951. It is reprinted by arrangement with Farrar, Strauss & Giroux, Inc.

Cataloging in Publication data is available from the Library of Congress.

ISBN 0-306-81203-7

First Da Capo Press edition 1996; second Da Capo Press edition 2002

Published by Da Capo Press
A Member of the Perseus Books Group
http://www.dacapopress.com

1 2 3 4 5 6 7 8 9 10——06 05 04 03 02

Contents

1. Boyhood   1

2. From Bicycle Shop to Kitty Hawk   13

3. Secrets from a Wind Tunnel   49

4. Power Flight   101

5. What Next with a Flying Machine   125

6. A Miracle Hard to Believe   157

7. Two Yankees and Europe   201

8. World Recognition   253

9. The Cost of Pre-eminence   357

10. Elder Statesman of Aviation   393

11. Back from Exile   467

    Index   471

EDITOR'S PREFACE

In the Manuscript Division of the Library of Congress, where the executors of Orville Wright deposited the Wright brothers' papers, there are about thirty thousand items in the Wright files; but as there were many letters *to* the Wrights that they never bothered to answer, probably not more than ten thousand of the letters preserved were written by the brothers themselves. To put into the confines of a single volume the letters that tell the story of the Wrights' achievements and reveal their personalities, to provide a record approaching the equivalent of autobiography—the purpose of this book—obviously called for much elimination. Since this book is aimed at the general reader, it seemed best to omit letters dealing with highly technical aerodynamic problems, as well as those relating to patent suits and to routine business transactions. Hundreds of others having possible historic value, replies to requests to attend dinners and meetings, or to grant favors of some kind, did not fit into this project. I believe these less than six hundred letters finally selected are not only representative but may be considered the cream, as to both interest and importance.

I have favored letters that are self-explanatory; but it became evident that many interpretative notes were needed. In a few places, in the interest of strict accuracy, I have used paragraphs that had been approved by Orville Wright himself for use in my biography, *The Wright Brothers*.

The temptation was strong at times to explain an event by

shoving forward letters written long afterward. Chronological order, however, proved in general to be most suitable.

One may wonder how so many letters written long before the Wrights had gained fame happened to be saved. One explanation is that their father had a streak of squirrel in him, was saving by nature and also felt much family sentiment. Any letter from Wilbur or Orville, no matter to which member of the family, that came into his hands he put away, not for its historic value but simply because it was from one of "the boys."

Then Orville himself gathered in a great many letters that he and Wilbur had written long before they began to keep copies. Orville did this intending eventually to yield to the constant pressure upon him from various publishers to prepare an autobiography. He procrastinated about undertaking that job and never did consciously make a start on it, for he did not like to write. Wilbur wrote many letters for the fun of it, Orville almost never, though when he did write, Orville could express himself with the same clarity so characteristic of Wilbur. Over the years, in spite of his disinclination to write, he sent out many letters that make up probably more autobiographical material than he realized.

In preparing these letters for publication, I have spelled out in full the names of months in datelines, to give uniformity, and have italicized names of newspapers and magazines. Once or twice I have corrected spelling of proper names. Except for such slight changes, the material selected is presented as it was written. I have become indebted to a number of persons who gave aid and comfort. Most of all, I must express gratitude to John Jameson of Northfield, Illinois, who had shown the good taste to marry a niece of Wilbur and Orville Wright and knew what treasure is in these letters. It was he who first proposed that a book of them should be published; and, after Orville Wright's death, he contributed much of his time to classifying the material to make editing easier. He has been a frequent source of wise suggestions. I am grateful to Harold Miller and Harold Steeper, Orville Wright's executors, for their courtesy in making available to me, in the Library of Congress, the Wright papers not accessible to students generally until the year 1960. All those I have dealt with at the library have gone far beyond ordinary official duties to be helpful, especially Arthur G. Renstrom and Marvin McFarland in the Division of Aeronautics. Edward Weeks, of the *Atlantic Monthly*, and F. G. Fassett, Jr., director of publications for the Carnegie Institution of Washington have given valuable editorial suggestions, as did Lester Gardner, former head of the Institute of Aeronautical Sciences. Again and again, I have felt gratitude to Miss Mabel Beck, Orville Wright's secretary for many years, for the excellent order in which all the Wright papers had been kept. I must express appreciation to Mrs. Elsa M. Ellifritz of Akron, Ohio, who has typed nearly every line in this book, always painstakingly.

I

BOYHOOD

The earliest communication to be found from either Wilbur or Orville Wright is a post card written by Orville, aged nine, to his father in Omaha when the Wright family was living in Cedar Rapids, Iowa. It will be noted that even then Orville was trying to satisfy his curiosity by scientific experiment.

April 1, 1881

Dear Father,—I got your letter today. My teacher said I was a good boy today. We have 45 in our room. The other day I took a machine can and filled it with water then I put it on the stove I waited a little while and the water came squirting out of the top about a foot. . . . The old cat is dead.

.   .   .   .

Orville Wright often said afterward that he and Wilbur owed much to an upbringing that gave them "exceptional advantages." These were not from wealth. When the family had to get along on the income of the father, his salary from the United Brethren Church was never more than $900 a year. He sometimes got a little additional income from an

3

Indiana farm, and he managed to pay for his daughter Katharine's education at Oberlin College, including two years
in the preparatory department. But luxury money was scarce.
Whatever Wilbur and Orville spent on hobbies they had to
earn. All the money anyone needs, their father would say,
is just enough to keep from being a burden to others. The
advantages Orville had in mind were a home environment
where the children were encouraged to pursue intellectual
interests; to investigate whatever aroused curiosity.

Bishop Milton Wright, dignified and kindly, with a patri-
archal beard, commanded the respect of his children and
they obeyed him because they liked to please him. In later
years, when public exhibitions of their flying machine on
Sunday would have been most profitable, Wilbur and Orville
refused to permit Sunday flights, out of consideration for
their father.

Strict though he was in close adherence to his own ideals
and principles, Bishop Wright was broad-minded and tolerant and did not set rigid rules of conduct for his children.
He disapproved of card playing not because he considered
it wicked, but because he thought it was a waste of time.

In every way he could, Bishop Wright aimed to stimulate
his children's thinking. An independent thinker himself, he
encouraged independence in others. In his theological library were books by Robert Ingersoll and other agnostics.
Before they were through high school Wilbur and Orville
had methodically gone through these works and were much
influenced by them; but their father never sought to divert
them from such reading.

If Wilbur and Orville got any of their mechanical genius
by inheritance it was from their mother, Susan Koerner
Wright, daughter of a German-born wagon maker. She had

a knack, whenever a needed appliance was lacking, for turning some other household device to unintended use; and the children often said that "mother could mend anything." Once when money was scarce she made her sons Reuchlin and Lorin a sled.

Mrs. Wright died in 1889. Wilbur, himself in poor health at this time, as a result of an accident while skating, had undertaken much of the care of his mother. As Bishop Wright wrote afterward, "Her life was probably lengthened, at least two years, by his skill and assiduity." *

Though both Wilbur and Orville stuck to bachelorhood, they had plenty of experience with children. Their brother Lorin lived only three blocks away and his four children put in much of their time at 7 Hawthorne Street, in Dayton.

Orville never seemed to tire of playing with them. If they tired of games, he would make candy. Wilbur would amuse them in an equally wholehearted way, but not for so long at one time. When he had enough of children on his lap, he would straighten out his long legs to make them slide off. Both uncles, Wilbur especially, liked to read to them. Wilbur's favorite books for this purpose were *The Chatterbox* or, for moral uplift, the Gelett Burgess *Goop Book*.

Orville was four years younger than Wilbur, and three years older, to the day, than his sister, each born in Dayton on August 19. Blue-eyed, dark-haired, quick-moving and smiling, Katharine was always ready to joke about something. She was much more talkative than either Wilbur or

* From letter published Nov. 5, 1908, to New Castle (Indiana) *Daily Tribune*. The Wrights were a Hoosier family. Bishop Wright was born in Indiana, and his wife was brought there from Virginia in infancy; three of the four sons—all except Orville—were born in three different Indiana counties, Wilbur eight miles from New Castle,

Orville, more interested in all kinds of people and more
concerned with appearances.

Ever since the mother's death, when Katharine was only
fifteen years old, and Reuchlin and Lorin were in homes of
their own, those still under the parental roof had been more
closely drawn together; what one was doing intensely interested all.

.   .   .   .

*Orville Wright, at age twenty, to his father—in which Orville
makes political comment*

Dayton, Ohio, October 16, 1891

We had a great time here yesterday. McKinley, Sherman
& Foraker* were all here and spoke at the fair grounds. . . .
Sherman spoke in the morning and I did not get to hear him.
McKinley followed in the afternoon with an able speech, so
they say, but if I were to listen to many more like it I am
afraid I would soon be a free trader. Of course the speech
was intended to catch the crowd and on this point it was an
admirable success. McKinley is a fine-looking man, has a
large head and a very pleasant face. He looks like an honest
man. Foraker followed him in a humorous speech which was

---

* William McKinley, afterward President, then campaigning for election as Governor of Ohio, had, as Chairman of the Ways and Means
Committee in Congress, sponsored the "McKinley Bill" for a high pro-
tective tariff; John Sherman was United States Senator from Ohio;
Joseph B. Foraker, afterward United States Senator, had been defeated
at the previous election for a third term as Governor of Ohio.

enjoyed more by the crowd than was McKinley's but the speech was far inferior. A few minutes' look at Foraker and I was satisfied and left. If he is an honest man he ought to sue his face for slander.

. . . .

Wilbur and Orville had become enthusiasts, in 1892, over the new European type of bicycle called the "safety," with both wheels the same size. Orville even did some track racing. They began to do repairing for other boys and soon opened their own shop to sell bicycles, including those of their own manufacture. By this time Katharine had entered the preparatory department at Oberlin and, as Bishop Wright made frequent trips on church business, the brothers were often at home alone, preparing their own meals as they later would at Kitty Hawk.

Wilbur Wright, at Dayton, Ohio, to his sister Katharine

September 18, 1892

We have been living fine since you left. Orville cooks one week and I cook the next. Orville's week we have bread and butter and meat and gravy and coffee three times a day. My week I give him more variety. You see that by the end of his week there is a big lot of cold meat stored up, so the first half of my week we have bread and butter and "hash" and coffee, and the last half we have bread and butter and eggs and sweet potatoes and coffee. We don't fuss a bit about whose week it is to cook. Perhaps the reason is evident. If Mrs. Jack Spratt had undertaken to cook all fat, I guess Jack wouldn't have kicked on cooking every other week either.

. . . .

Five feet ten and a quarter inches in height, Wilbur was an inch and a half taller than Orville. Both were slender. Wilbur usually weighed about 140 pounds and Orville five pounds more.

The brothers were thoroughly congenial and, soon after they started the Wright Cycle Company, kept a joint bank account. Each drew out whatever he needed and neither paid the slightest attention to what the other spent. They enjoyed working together. Long afterward, Orville remarked: "I can remember when Wilbur and I could hardly wait for morning to come to get at something that interested us. *That's* happiness!"

But there were two things for which Orville often chided Wilbur: for talking down to him as if he were still a "kid"; and his habit of saying or writing "I" when he meant "we."

At the time he wrote the letter which follows, Wilbur looked older than his twenty-seven years, for he was already bald.

Wilbur Wright to his father

September 12, 1894

The bicycle business is fair. Selling new wneels is about done for this year but the repairing business is good and we are getting about $20 a month from the rent of three wheels. We get $8 a month for one, $6.50 for another, and the third we rent by the hour or day. We have done so well renting them that we have held on to them instead of disposing of them at once, although we really need the money invested in them. Could you let us have about $150 for a while? We think we could have it nearly all ready to pay back by the time you get home.

I have been thinking for some time of the advisability of my taking a college course. I have thought about it more or less for a number of years but my health has been such that I was afraid that it might be time and money wasted to do so, but I have felt so much better for a year or so that I have thought more seriously of it and have decided to see what you think of it and would advise.

I do not think I am specially fitted for success in any commercial pursuit even if I had the proper personal and business influences to assist me. I might make a living but I doubt whether I would ever do much more than this. Intellectual effort is a pleasure to me and I think I would be better fitted for reasonable success in some of the professions than in business.

I have always thought I would like to be a teacher. Although there is no hope of attaining such financial success as might be attained in some of the other professions or in commercial pursuits, yet it is an honorable pursuit, the pay is sufficient to enable one to live comfortably and happily, and [teaching] is less subject to uncertainties than almost any other occupation. It would be congenial to my tastes, and I think with proper training I could be reasonably successful.

Of course I could not attempt a college course unless you

are able and willing to help me some. I think that by keeping a couple of bicycles to rent and by doing some repairing, and possibly a few sales, enough could be made to meet the greater part of the expense, or at least enough to help along quite a good bit. I think with six or eight hundred dollars I could complete the course, which would probably take about four years. I would be glad to have you think the matter over and give me your advice on it.

. . . .

Bishop Wright's reply

September 15, 1894

I received your letter. Yes, I will help you what I can in a collegiate course. I do not think a commercial life will suit you well. Probably you may not be able to go through college without some intermissions. I will loan you boys the $150 you ask.

. . . .

Wilbur gave up the idea of going to college. Neither his nor Orville's formal education went beyond high school, and though each spent the time for a full course, neither ever received a diploma. The Wright family moved to Dayton, Ohio, from Richmond, Indiana, just before the commencement exercises in Wilbur's final year and he did not bother to go back. Orville took special studies in his senior year in place of other work required for graduation.

In 1895 the Wright brothers read about the gliding experiments of Otto Lilienthal in Germany. (Lilienthal was far in advance of all others who ever worked on the flying problem before the Wrights.) They were fascinated by what little they could learn about Lilienthal, for it seemed to them that gliding through the air must be the king of sports. When they read in 1896 that Lilienthal had been killed in one of his experiments, they wondered if they could go on from where he and others had left off.

They read everything they could find about attempts to fly; but the Dayton Public Library did not provide much, and in May, 1899, Wilbur wrote to the Smithsonian Institution* in Washington for suggestions about reading matter.

. . . .

---

* Dr. Samuel P. Langley, Director and Secretary of the Smithsonian Institution, had been making aeronautical studies and experiments and succeeded in building power-driven models that flew. Later he built and attempted to fly a full size, man-carrying machine; but in this he failed.

II

FROM BICYCLE SHOP TO KITTY HAWK

Wilbur Wright to the Smithsonian Institution

Dayton, Ohio, May 30, 1899

I have been interested in the problem of mechanical and human flight ever since as a boy I constructed a number of bats of various sizes after the style of Cayley's and Pénaud's machines. My observations since have only convinced me more firmly that human flight is possible and practicable. It is only a question of knowledge and skill just as in all acrobatic feats. Birds are the most perfectly trained gymnasts in the world and are specially well fitted for their work, and it may be that man will never equal them, but no one who has watched a bird chasing an insect or another bird can doubt that feats are performed which require three or four times the effort required in ordinary flight. I believe that simple flight at least is possible to man and that the experiments and investigations of a large number of independent workers will result in the accumulation of information and knowledge and skill which will finally lead to accomplished flight.

The works on the subject to which I have had access are Marey's and Jamieson's books . . . and various magazine and cyclopaedic articles. I am about to begin a systematic study of the subject in preparation for practical work to which I expect to devote what time I can spare from my regular business. I wish to obtain such papers as the Smithsonian Institution has published on this subject, and if possible a list of other works in print in the English language. I am an enthusiast, but not a crank in the sense that I have some pet theories as to the proper construction of a flying machine. I wish to avail myself of all that is already known and then if possible add my mite to help on the future worker who will attain final success.

. . . .

The Smithsonian sent them some pamphlets, one of them by Lilienthal on gliding, and a list of titles including Octave Chanute's *Progress in Flying Machines*. Chanute, a successful construction engineer living in Chicago, had directed experiments with gliders of his own design, but these had not shown great promise. As a historian and bibliographer of man's attempt to fly, however, Chanute was the best.

Some of the impressions they got from their reading Wilbur described years later.*

. . . .

When we came to examine these books we were astonished to learn what an immense amount of time and money had been expended in futile attempts to solve the problem of

---

* In a deposition before the United States Court of Appeals, in the infringement suit of the Wright Company *vs.* the Herring-Curtiss Company and Glenn Curtiss.

human flight. Contrary to our previous impression, we found that men of the very highest standing in the professions of science and invention had attempted the problem. Among them were such men as Leonardo da Vinci, the greatest universal genius the world has ever known; Sir George Cayley, one of the first men to suggest the idea of the explosion motor; Professor Langley, secretary and head of the Smithsonian Institution; Dr. Bell, inventor of the telephone; Sir Hiram Maxim, inventor of the automatic gun; Mr. O Chanute, the past president of the American Society of Civil Engineers; Mr. Chas. Parsons, the inventor of the steam turbine; Mr. Thomas A. Edison, Herr Lilienthal, M. Ader, Mr. Phillips, and a host of others.

The period from 1889 to 1897 we found had been one of exceptional activity, during which Langley, Lilienthal, Chanute, Maxim, and Phillips had been feverishly at work, each hoping to win the honor of having solved the problem; but one by one they had been compelled to confess themselves beaten, and had discontinued their efforts. In studying their failures we found many points of interest to us.

. . . .

By the time Wilbur and Orville became interested in aviation, Katharine Wright had finished college at Oberlin and was teaching Latin and history at Steele High School in Dayton. Occupied by her teaching, she employed Carrie Kayler, in February, 1900, as helper at 7 Hawthorne Street. Carrie, only fourteen years old, was so small for her age that she had to stand on a chair to reach the gaslight in the kitchen. Orville loved to tease people and, next to Katharine,

Carrie was soon his favorite victim. He wondered if she'd ever be tall enough to be much account, and he'd have her stand up to be measured against a set of marks on the frame of the kitchen door. One day Carrie discovered that she could reach the light by standing tiptoe. She rushed to the dining room to tell the news. Orville immediately got up from the table and led her to the door-casing. Yes, he said, she really *had* grown half an inch; she should be allowed to remain in the Wright home. She was to stay, as it turned out, for nearly half a century, until after Orville's death in January, 1948. And when this book was in preparation, Carrie Kayler Grumbach was the one living person who knew at first hand what went on in the Wright home during and after the time the flying machine was being invented.

Most of Mr. Orville's teasing was fun, Carrie reported, but at times he would keep it up until he would almost have a person in tears. Then you could count on a word from Mr. Will. When he saw things were getting close to the breaking point, he'd say, "I guess that's about enough, Orv." And Mr. Orville would stop instantly. Mr. Orville always listened to Mr. Will, but *never* to anyone else.

Carrie soon discovered that all the Wrights, simple as their tastes were, liked their food prepared well, and Mr. Orville was the most particular of all. He and Mr. Will were good cooks and always willing to help one just learning. One of Mr. Orville's weaknesses was for gravy, and he showed a violent prejudice against what he called white lump gravy. Miss Katharine warned Carrie about lumps in the gravy before she had been there a day. Carrie had no luck with gravy until one day Mr. Will came into the kitchen and peered into the pan as she anxiously stirred flour into a mixture. He reached over and gently took the pan from her.

"Now then, Carrie," he said cheerfully, "let's just pour this out and start over." He rolled back his sleeves and went to work. While Carrie looked on, fascinated, he made the smoothest, savoriest gravy, without a lump.

In later years Orville would say, "No wonder Carrie makes such good gravy. Wilbur taught her."

Mr. Will was always more methodical than Mr. Orville, Carrie felt sure. When he came home from the bicycle shop at noon and for supper he would *always* do these things and in this order: come through the back door into the kitchen and drop his hat on the nearest chair; reach to the top of the cupboard where he kept a comb and carefully smooth down his fringe of hair; and then cross to the sink to wash his hands. After that he would go directly to a cracker box on the dining room sideboard, pick out one cracker and nibble it as he went to the front of the house. That was a signal to set food on the table.

Promptly, when the noon hour was over, Mr. Will would come through the kitchen, looking straight ahead and saying nothing. He'd go out the back door and down the alley. But in a minute he'd come back, with a queer little one-sided smile, for his hat. Mr. Orville, on the other hand, never once forgot his hat; and no matter how absorbed he was in what he was doing or thinking, he always knew what was going on around him.

After they began their studies of aviation, the brothers argued vehemently every night. Carrie Grumbach said the arguments would start in the living room about the time she was doing the supper dishes. At first their voices would go along quietly and evenly, and then would become louder. Suddenly all would be quiet and she'd think maybe they had gone too far. But each was just thinking over what the other had said. If Carrie happened to go into the dining room she could see the two of them on each side of the living room fireplace. Mr. Orville would be sitting straight in his chair with arms folded; but Mr. Will was more likely to be sitting on the small of his back with legs stretched out, his hands clasped behind his head and elbows spread wide. After a while one of them would say, " 'Tisn't either"; and the other would say, " 'Tis too." After keeping that up for a time, they'd swing back into the full-size argument. Carrie could see they were enjoying themselves. It was in these discussions that they invented the airplane!

When they came to the problem of propellers, their arguments were sometimes so persuasive that each would convert the other; Orville would come to Wilbur's point of view, and Wilbur to Orville's, and they would still be as far apart as ever.

However much they argued, there were times when their minds seemed to act as one. One night after they had been working late at their shop, Orville returned home ahead of Wilbur. He was in bed when Wilbur came in. A surprising thing was that Wilbur, contrary to his invariable habit, forgot to bolt the front door. Orville, nearly asleep, reminded him of his oversight. Then when Wilbur went back to put on the lock, Orville thought to himself, "I'll bet he does something else peculiar. He'll blow out the gas in his room." Why he thought Wilbur would blow out the gas, instead of turning it off, he never could explain. Fearing he would drop off to sleep, he sat up in bed until the light in Wilbur's room was off. Then he went to investigate and found the gas was still turned on. Wilbur had blown out the flame. Except for Orville's presentiment, both could have been asphyxiated.

After reading Chanute's book, *Progress in Flying Machines,* Wilbur Wright, thinking Chanute would be interested, wrote to him. (There was a small desk in the living room at the Hawthorne street home where Wilbur did all his writing.) This was the beginning of a correspondence that was to continue for ten years.

The intimate relationship between the Wrights and Chanute, started by that first letter from Wilbur, became important to all three. Several years earlier,* Chanute had suggested:

Success might be much hastened by an *association* of searchers in this field of inquiry [flight], for no one man is likely to be simultaneously an inventor to imagine new shapes and new motors, a mechanical engineer to design the arrangement of the apparatus, a mathematician to calculate its strength and stresses, a practical mechanic to construct the parts, and a syndicate of capitalists to furnish the needed funds. It is probably because the working out of a complete invention requires so great a variety of talent that progress has been so slow.

And now here he was unexpectedly making contact with just such an association as he had said was needed: inventors, mechanical engineers, mathematicians, practical mechanics, and, if not exactly capitalists, men able to finance their experiments—all in the persons of the two Wright brothers.

From Chanute the Wrights learned much of what their predecessors had done; and Chanute was to learn from the Wrights how the problem of flight could be solved.

Because he early recognized that the Wrights were far ahead of their predecessors, Chanute prodded them into continuing their experiments when they might have quit. His

---

* In a lecture at Sibley College, Cornell University, May 2, 1890.

encouragement to the two brothers was Chanute's great contribution and it placed them deeply in his debt.

From the first letter of Wilbur Wright to Octave Chanute

Dayton, Ohio, May 13, 1900

For some years I have been afflicted with the belief that flight is possible to man. My disease has increased in severity and I feel that it will soon cost me an increased amount of money if not my life. I have been trying to arrange my affairs in such a way that I can devote my entire time for a few months to experiment in this field.

My general ideas of the subject are similar [to] those held by most practical experimenters, to wit: that what is chiefly needed is skill rather than machinery. The flight of the buzzard and similar sailors is a convincing demonstration of the value of skill and the partial needlessness of motors.

It is possible to fly without motors, but not without knowledge and skill. This I conceive to be fortunate, for man, by reason of his greater intellect, can more reasonably hope to equal birds in knowledge than to equal nature in the perfection of her machinery.

Assuming then that Lilienthal was correct in his ideas of the principles on which man should proceed, I conceive that his failure was due chiefly to the inadequacy of his method and of his apparatus. As to his method, the fact that in five years' time he spent only about five hours, altogether, in actual flight is sufficient to show that his method was inadequate. Even the simplest intellectual or acrobatic feats could never be learned with so short practice; and even Methuselah could never have become an expert stenographer with one hour per year for practice. . . .

My observation of the flight of buzzards leads me to believe that they regain their lateral balance when partly overturned by a gust of wind, by a torsion of the tips of the wings. If the rear edge of the right wing tip is twisted upward and the left downward the bird becomes an animated windmill and instantly begins to turn, a line from its head to its tail being the axis. It thus regains its level even if thrown on its beam's end, so to speak, as I have frequently seen them. I think the bird also in general retains its lateral equilibrium, partly by presenting its two wings at different angles to the wind, and partly by drawing in one wing, thus reducing its area. I incline to the belief that the first is the more important and usual method. . . .

My business [the bicycle shop] requires that my experimental work be confined to the months between September and January and I would be particularly thankful for advice as to a suitable locality where I could depend on winds of about 15 miles per hour without rain or too inclement weather. I am certain that such localities are rare.

I have your *Progress in Flying Machines* and your articles in the *Annuals* of '95, '96, and '97, as also your recent articles in the *Independent*. If you can give me information as to where an account of Pilcher's experiments can be obtained I would greatly appreciate your kindness.

. . . .

Wilbur Wright to Octave Chanute

June 1, 1900

I very much approve of your articles in the *Independent* and in *McClure's*. It is very important that more persons should be intelligently interested in this subject. Lilienthal's enthusiastic efforts to arouse others may yet prove his most valuable contribution to the solution of the problem. What one man can do himself directly is but little. If however he can stir up ten others to take up the task he has accomplished much. I know of no man in America so well fitted as yourself to do this missionary work. . . .

. . . .

The brothers soon assembled their first glider, at a cost of $15. It weighed about 52 pounds. Counting the "bows" at the ends of each wing surface, the span was nearly 17½ feet, with a total lifting area of 165 square feet. A space 18 inches wide at the center of the lower surface, where the operator would lie "belly-buster," with feet over the rear spar, was left uncovered. The wing curvature was less than Lilienthal had used.

For their experiments the Wrights wanted a sandy area for soft landings, slopes free of trees or shrubs for gliding, and adequate winds. After getting a letter from the Weather Bureau* at Washington, they decided that Kitty Hawk, North Carolina, seemed to meet their requirements better

---

* Willis L. Moore, Chief of Weather Bureau, to Wright Cycle Co.

December 4, 1899

Replying to your letter . . . I have the honor to inform you that the *Monthly Weather Review* contains a table of average hourly wind velocities at all Weather Bureau stations. I send you copies of the *Review* for August and September, 1899, and will send those for October and November as soon as issued.

than any other place no farther from home. Now to confirm this, they wrote to Kitty Hawk.

Joseph J. Dosher, at weather station, Kitty Hawk,
to Wilbur Wright

August 16, 1900

In reply to yours of the 3rd, I will say the beach here is about one mile wide, clear of trees or high hills and extends for nearly sixty miles same condition. The wind blows mostly from the north and northeast September and October. . . . I am sorry to say you could not rent a house here, so you will have to bring tents. You could obtain board.

.   .   .   .

From William J. Tate at Kitty Hawk, to Wilbur Wright

August 18, 1900

Mr. J. J. Dosher of the Weather Bureau here has asked me to answer your letter to him, relative to the fitness of Kitty Hawk as a place to practice or experiment with a flying machine, etc.*

---

* Dosher had referred the letter to Tate because he was considered the best educated man in the community. After writing his reply, Tate returned Wilbur Wright's letter to Dosher who, not suspecting the Wrights would become famous, failed to preserve it. Tate shrewdly made a copy of the letter a while afterward, as well as he could, from memory. What caught his interest most was the remark at the beginning of the letter, where Wilbur said that he and his brother were contemplating some experiments "in scientific kite flying."

In answering I would say that you would find here nearly any type of ground you could wish; you could, for instance, get a stretch of sandy land one mile by five with a bare hill in center 80 feet high, not a tree or bush anywhere to break the evenness of the wind current. This in my opinion would be a fine place; our winds are always steady, generally from 10 to 20 miles velocity per hour.

You can reach here from Elizabeth City, N. C. (35 miles from here) by boat direct from Manteo 12 miles from here by mail boat every Mon., Wed. & Friday. We have Telegraph communication & daily mails. Climate healthy, you could find good place to pitch tents & get board in private family provided there were not too many in your party; would advise you to come any time from September 15 to October 15. Don't wait until November. The autumn generally gets a little rough by November.

If you decide to try your machine here & come I will take pleasure in doing all I can for your convenience & success & pleasure, & I assure you you will find a hospitable people when you come among us.

.   .   .   .

After reading the letter from Tate, the Wrights did not consider any other place but Kitty Hawk.

Wilbur Wright to his father

September 3, 1900

I am intending to start in a few days for a trip to the coast of North Carolina in the vicinity of Roanoke Island, for the purpose of making some experiments with a flying machine. It is my belief that flight is possible and, while I am taking up the investigation for pleasure rather than profit, I think there is a slight possibility of achieving fame and fortune from it. It is almost the only great problem which has not been pursued by a multitude of investigators, and therefore carried to a point where further progress is very difficult. I am certain I can reach a point much in advance of any previous workers in this field even if complete success is not attained just at present. At any rate, I shall have an outing of several weeks and see a part of the world I have never before visited.

.   .   .   .

Katharine Wright to her father

September 5, 1900

We are in an uproar getting Will off. The trip will do him good. I don't think he will be reckless. If they can arrange it, Orv. will go down as soon as Will gets the machine [the glider] ready.

.   .   .   .

From a memorandum by Wilbur Wright, regarding his first trip to Kitty Hawk

Spent Saturday [in Norfolk] trying to find some spruce for spars of machine, but was unsuccessful. Finally I bought some white pine and had it sawed up at J. E. Etheridge Co.'s mill. [A sales slip attached, dated Sept. 8, 1900, shows that the lumber for the spars cost $2.70!] . . . Left for Elizabeth City and put up at the Arlington where I spent several days waiting for a boat to Kitty Hawk. No one seemed to know anything about the place or how to get there.

. . . .

Wilbur Wright to his father

Elizabeth City, N. C., September 9, 1900

I am at this place waiting for a boat to take me across Albemarle Sound to Kitty Hawk, North Carolina, which will be my address for the present. I supposed you knew that I was studying up the flying question with a view to making some practical experiments.

I chose Kitty Hawk because it seemed the place which most clearly met the required conditions. In order to obtain support from the air it is necessary, with wings of reasonable size, to move through it at the rate of 15 or 20 miles per hour. If there is no wind movement, your speed with reference to the ground must be the same. If the wind blows with proper speed, support can be obtained without movement with reference to the ground. It is safer to practice in a wind, provided this is not broken up into eddies and sudden gusts by hills, trees, and so forth.

At Kitty Hawk, which is on the narrow bar separating the Sound from the Ocean, there are neither hills nor trees, so that it offers a safe place for practice. Also the wind there is stronger than any place near home and is almost constant, so that it is not necessary to wait days or weeks for a suitable breeze. It is much cheaper to go to a distant point where practice may be constant than to choose a nearer spot where three days out of four might be wasted.

I have no intention of risking injury to any great extent, and have no expectation of being hurt. I will be careful, and will not attempt new experiments in dangerous situations. I think the danger much less than in most athletic games.

. . . .

Wilbur went to the water front at Elizabeth City to inquire if a boat to Kitty Hawk was available. There he met Israel Perry who lived on his little flat-bottomed schooner. As no other boatman showed any interest, he booked passage with Perry.

It was a leaky boat, and toward the middle of the afternoon they had to seek a smooth water haven in North River where they anchored. Then Wilbur discovered that neither the food on board nor the kitchen met even minimum standards of cleanliness, and he made excuses for not eating. All he had with him was a small jar of jelly Katharine had slipped into his suitcase. The weather did not permit going on until the afternoon of the second day, and they did not reach a wharf on Kitty Hawk bay until nine o'clock that night. Not knowing where to go on shore, Wilbur stayed aboard until the next morning. When he reached Tate's home it was forty-eight hours since he had tasted any food except Katharine's jelly.

He stayed with the Tates for a day or two and then set up a tent to which he dragged the crates containing parts and tools.

Wilbur Wright to his father

Kitty Hawk, September 23, 1900

I have my machine nearly finished. It is not to have a motor and is not expected to fly in any true sense of the word. My idea is merely to experiment and practice with a view to solving the problem of equilibrium. I have plans which I hope to find much in advance of the methods tried by previous experimenters. When once a machine is under proper control under all conditions, the motor problem will be quickly solved. A failure of motor will then simply mean a slow descent and safe landing instead of a disastrous fall.

In my experiments I do not expect to rise many feet from the ground, and in case I am upset there is nothing but soft sand to strike on. I do not intend to take dangerous chances, both because I have no wish to get hurt and because a fall would stop my experimenting, which I would not like at all. The man who wishes to keep at the problem long enough to really learn anything positively cannot take dangerous risks. Carelessness and overconfidence are usually more dangerous than deliberately accepted risks. I am constructing my machine to sustain about five times my weight and am testing every piece. I think there is no possible chance of its breaking while in the air. If it is broken it will be by awkward landing.

My machine will be trussed like a bridge and will be much stronger than that of Lilienthal, which, by the way, was upset through the failure of a movable tail and not by breakage of the machine. The tail of my machine is fixed, and even if my steering arrangement should fail, it would still leave me with the same control that Lilienthal had at best. My machine is more simple in construction and at the same time capable of greater adjustment and control than previous machines.

I have not taken up the problem with the expectation of financial profit. Neither do I have any strong expectation of achieving the solution at the present time or possibly any time. My trip would be no great disappointment if I accomplished practically nothing. I look upon it as a pleasure at the same cost. I am watching my health very closely and expect to return home heavier and stronger than I left. I am taking every precaution about my drinking water.

. . . .

Katharine Wright to her father

September 26, 1900

Orv. went south Monday evening, to join Will. They got a tent and will camp after Orv. gets there, which will be tomorrow morning. They can't buy even tea or coffee or sugar at Kitty Hawk so Orv. took a supply along. They also took cots and Orv. took your trunk. I loaned my trunk to Will.

I was glad to get Orv. off. He had worked so hard and was so run down. They never have had a trip anywhere since the World's Fair.

.   .   .   .

On his way to Kitty Hawk, Orville took time to act on a financial problem.

Orville Wright to his sister

Elizabeth City, September 26, 1900

Tell Harry [an employee at the bicycle shop] to sell those rolls of tire tape in the box back of what he has been selling at 5 cents a roll. They were 10-cent rolls, but we must get rid of them. They are in tin-foil wrappers.

.   .   .   .

Orville Wright to his sister

Kitty Hawk, October 14, 1900

We have been having a fine time. Altogether we have had the machine out three different days, of from two to four hours each time. Monday night and all day Tuesday we had a terrific wind, blowing 36 miles an hour. Wednesday morning the Kitty Hawkers were out early peering around the edge of the woods and out of their upstairs windows to see whether our camp was still in existence. We were all right, however, and though wind continued up to 30 miles, got the machine out to give it another trial. The wind was too strong and unsteady for us to attempt an ascent in it, so we just flew it like a kite, running down a number of strings to the ground, with which to work the steering apparatus. The machine seemed a rather docile thing, and we taught it to behave fairly well. Chains were hung on it to give it work to do, while we took measurements of the "drift" in pounds.

In the afternoon we took the machine to the hill just south of our camp, formerly known as "Look Out Hill," but now as the "Hill of the Wreck."

Well, after erecting a derrick from which to swing our rope with which we fly the machine, we sent it up about 20 feet, at which height we attempt to keep it by the manipulation of the strings to the rudder. The greatest difficulty is in keeping it down. It naturally wants to go higher and higher. When it begins to get too high we give it a pretty strong pull on the ducking string, to which it responds by making a terrific dart for the ground. If nothing is broken we start it up again. This is all practice in the control of the machine. When it comes down we just lay it flat on the ground and the pressure of the wind on the upper surface holds it down so tightly that you can hardly raise it again.

After an hour or so of practice in steering, we laid it down on the ground to change some of the adjustments of the ropes, when, without a sixteenth of a second's notice, the wind caught under one corner and, quicker than thought, it landed 20 feet away, a complete wreck. When it started I was standing at a rear corner holding one of the uprights.

It just took me off my feet and landed me in the heap 20 feet
away.

We had had a number of interesting experiences with it
before, performing some feats which would almost seem an
impossibility. We dragged the pieces back to camp and
began to consider getting home. The next morning we had
cheered up some and began to think there was some hope
of repairing it.

The next three days were spent in repairing, holding the
tent down, and hunting; mostly the last, in which occupation
we have succeeded in killing two large fish hawks each measuring over 5 feet from tip to tip; in chasing a lot of chicken
hawks till we were pretty well winded; and in scaring several
large bald eagles. . . .

This is a great country for fishing and hunting. The fish
are so thick you see dozens of them whenever you look down
into the water. The woods are filled with wild game, they
say; even a few "b'ars" are prowling about the woods not far
away. . . .

But the sand! The sand is the greatest thing in Kitty
Hawk, and soon will be the only thing. The site of our tent
was formerly a fertile valley, cultivated by some ancient
Kitty Hawker. Now only a few rotten limbs, the topmost
branches of trees that then grew in this valley, protrude from
the sand. The sea has washed and the wind blown millions
and millions of tons of sand up in heaps along the coast, completely covering houses and forest. Mr. Tate is now tearing
down the nearest house to our camp to save it from the
sand. . . .

You can't get dirty. Not enough to raise the least bit of
color could be collected under a finger nail. We have a

method of cleaning dishes that has made the dish rag and the tea towel a thing of the past. . . .

We need no introduction in Kitty Hawk. Every place we go we are called Mr. Wright. Our fame has spread far and wide up and down the beach.

. . . .

Orville Wright to his sister

Kitty Hawk, October 18, 1900

We spent half the morning yesterday in getting the machine out of the sand. When we finally did get it free, we took it up the hill, and made a number of experiments in a 25-mile wind. We have not been on the thing since the first time we had it out, but merely experiment with the machine alone, sometimes loaded with 75 pounds of chains. We tried it with tail in front, behind, and every other way. When we got through, Will was so mixed up he couldn't even theorize. It has been with considerable effort that I have succeeded in keeping him in the flying business at all. He likes to chase buzzards, thinking they are eagles, and chicken hawks, much better.

. . . .

Both the Wrights were much interested in observing the flight of birds, and the following unedited comments are from a notebook of Wilbur's in 1900.

The buzzard which uses the dihedral angle finds greater difficulty to maintain equilibrium in strong winds than eagles and hawks which hold their wings level.

The hen hawk can rise faster than the buzzard and its motion is steadier. It displays less effort in maintaining its balance.

Hawks are better soarers than buzzards but more often resort to flapping because they wish greater speed.

A damp day is unfavorable for soaring unless there is a high wind.

No bird soars in a calm.

The object of the tail is to increase the spread of surface in the rear when the wings are moved forward in light winds and thus preserve the centre of pressure at about the same spot. It seems to be used as a rudder very little. In high winds it is folded up very narrow.

All soarers, but especially the buzzard, seem to keep their fore and aft balance more by shifting the center of resistance than by shifting the centre of lift. Thus a buzzard soaring in the normal position will be turned upward by a sudden gust. It immediately lowers its wings much below its body. The momentum of its body now acting above the center of resistance turns the bird downward very quickly.

Viewed from directly beneath, the motion of the wings fore and aft seems very small indeed. Neither do birds appear to draw in one wing more than the other. The raising and lowering of the wings is very perceptible whenever the observer is almost on a level with the bird.

A pigeon moving directly from the observer oscillates very rapidly laterally, especially when moving slowly just before lighting. The wings are not drawn in to any perceptible extent first on one side and then on the other as would be the case if the bird were balancing by increasing or decreasing the area of either wing alternately. Moreover, the oscillations of lateral balance are so rapid that gravity alone could not possibly produce them. The bird certainly twists its wing tips so that the wind strikes one wing on top and the other on its lower side, thus by force changing the birds lateral position.

If a buzzard be soaring to leeward of the observer, at a distance of a thousand feet, and a height of about one hundred feet, the cross section of its wings will be a mere line when the bird is moving from the observer but when it moves toward him the wings will appear broad.

This would indicate that its wings are always inclined upward which seems contrary to reason.

A bird when soaring does not seem to alternately rise and fall as some observers have thought. Any rising or falling is irregular and seems to be due to disturbances of fore and aft equilibrium produced by gusts. In light winds the birds seem to rise constantly without any downward turns.

A bird sailing quartering to the wind seems to always present its wings at a positive angle, although propulsion in such position seems unaccountable.

Birds can not soar to leeward of a descending slope unless high in the air.

Buzzards find it difficult to advance in the face of a wind blowing more than thirty miles per hour. Their soaring speed can not be far from thirty miles.

.   .   .   .

Wilbur Wright at Elizabeth City to his sister

October 23, 1900

We have said "Good bye Kitty, Good bye Hawk, Good bye
Kitty Hawk, we're gwine to leave you now." We reached
here this afternoon, after a pleasant trip from Kitty Hawk of
six hours. It took me forty-five hours going down there and
Orville sixteen hours.

. . . .

Wilbur Wright to Octave Chanute

November 16, 1900

My brother and myself spent a vacation of several weeks
at Kitty Hawk, North Carolina, experimenting with a soaring machine. . . .

The machine had neither horizontal nor vertical tail. Longitudinal balancing and steering were effected by means
of a horizontal rudder projecting in front of the planes.
Lateral balancing and right and left steering were obtained
by increasing the inclination of the wings at one end and
decreasing their inclination at the other. The short time at
our disposal for practice prevented as thorough tests of these
features as we desired, but the results obtained were very
favorable and experiments will be continued along the same
line next year.

. . . .

During the winter of 1900–1901 the Wrights went ahead with plans, determined before they had left Kitty Hawk, that their next experiments would be with a larger glider— large enough to be flown as a kite, with an operator aboard, in the kind of winds they could usually expect. The 1901 glider was of the same general design as the first one, but with considerably more area, for greater lifting power. They increased the curvature of the wings to conform to the shape on which Lilienthal had based his tables of air pressures. The front and rear edges of the wings were about 7 feet apart and the total span 22 feet. With the rear corners of the wings rounded off, and a section 20 inches wide removed from the middle of the lower wing, the lifting area was 290 square feet. The machine weighed 98 pounds, nearly double the earlier one. This was a much larger machine than anyone had ever dared try to fly.

During the experiments of 1901, the brothers were to have company in camp. When their friend Chanute had learned, during a visit to Dayton in June, that no doctor was available near their camp, he thought the brothers were taking big risks. He said he knew a young man in Coatesville, Pennsylvania, George A. Spratt, who had been making studies in aeronautics and who had had medical training. If the Wrights would board him at camp, Chanute said, he would pay Spratt's traveling expenses to Kitty Hawk and would feel compensated by the pleasure given, for Spratt had never seen gliding experiments. Chanute also asked if they would be willing to have with them E. C. Huffaker, a technical man, of Chuckey, Tennessee, who was building a glider for Chanute that he wanted to have tested. The Wrights consented. For a time, too, Chanute himself, on their invitation, was with them.

When Chanute first visited the Wrights they brought him to dinner at 7 Hawthorne Street, and Katherine was nervous, wanting everything to be just right—but the three men were so absorbed in their talk that they scarcely knew what they ate.

Wilbur Wright to Octave Chanute

Kitty Hawk, July 26, 1901

We reached Kitty Hawk [July 10] several days later than we expected owing to the greatest storm in history of the place. Anemometer cups gave way at 83 miles per hour so that is highest speed recorded. After a dry spell of 7 weeks the storm was followed by rains for a full week. This has delayed us beyond expectation, both by preventing us from working at times, and especially by compelling us to devote a large part of our time to fighting mosquitoes which are the worst at this time, (owing to the rains,) the oldest inhabitant has ever experienced. You should by all means bring with you from the north eight yards of the finest meshed mosquito bar you can find, as the bar here is too large to keep them off at night. Except for mosquitoes our camp life has been pleasant but exciting at times.

We expect to have our machine completed today as only a few little details remain to be finished.

Mr. Huffaker arrived a week ago, and Mr. Spratt last night. If convenient it would be well to send down another tent as we find that we will probably be crowded a little.

.   .   .   .

Although several glides on July 27, the day of the machine's first trial, exceeded in distance the best of the year before, it was soon evident that in a number of respects the machine was not as good as the first one. With the wing camber recommended by Lilienthal, it could not glide at a slope as near to level as the 1900 machine had done.*

From Wilbur Wright's Diary

July 30, 1901

The most discouraging features of our experiments so far are these: The lift is not much over one third that indicated by the Lilienthal tables. As we had expected to devote a major portion of our time to experimenting in an 18-mile wind without much motion of the machine, we find that our hopes of obtaining actual practice in the air are decreased to about one fifth what we hoped, as now it is necessary to glide in order to get a sustaining speed. Five minutes' practice in free flight is a good day's record. We have not yet reached so good an average as this even.

The good points as indicated by the experiments already made are these:—

1. The machine is strong. It has suffered no injury although very severely used in some forty landings.

2. With less than an hour's practice we succeeded in get-

---

* In launching the glider it was necessary to run with it about 20 feet at the top of the hill, a man at each end to support it and shove it off. The third man assisting was often William J. Tate or his half-brother Dan; sometimes it was one of the members of the Kill Devil lifesaving crew.

ting a free flight of over 300 feet at an angle of 1 in 6. Many
of our failures in other attempts were due only to the fact
that the hill was not steep enough to really get a fair start.
The machine starting so close to the ground that the least
undulation caused the rear ends of the rib to touch the
ground and thus prevent the machine turning up to sufficient
angle to rise again.

3. We have experimented safely with a machine of over
300 square feet surface in winds as high as 18 miles per hour.
Previous experimenters had pronounced a machine of such
size impracticable to construct and impossible to manage.
It is true that we have found this machine less manageable
than our smaller machine of last year, but we are not sure
that the increased size is responsible for it. The trouble seems
rather in the travel of the center of pressure.

4. The lateral balance of the machine seems all that could
be desired.

. . . .

Wilbur Wright said, on their way home after the 1901
gliding experiments, that he didn't think man would fly in
a thousand years. In a way, though, as Orville Wright said
long afterward, it was encouraging to learn that the work
of predecessors could not be relied upon. It meant that more
knowledge was needed, rather than that flight was impossible.

Octave Chanute to Wilbur Wright

Chicago, Ill., August 23, 1901

I have your welcome letter of the 22nd and am glad to know that you got through your experiments without accident. I think you have performed quite an achievement in sailing with surfaces wider than any which I dared to use, and on which a change of incidence by a wind gust would make so great a difference in the center of pressure.

. . . .

Octave Chanute to Wilbur Wright

Chicago, Ill., August 29, 1901

I have been talking with some members of the Western Society of Engineers. The conclusion is that the members would be very glad to have an address, or a lecture from you, on your gliding experiments.

. . . .

Wilbur Wright to Octave Chanute

Dayton, Ohio, September 2, 1901

I have been rather puzzled to know what answer to make to your kind letter of Aug. 29th. After your kindness in interesting yourself in obtaining an opportunity to address this society, for me, I hardly see how to refuse, although the time set is too short for the preparation of anything elaborate or highly finished.

. . . .

Katharine Wright to her father

September 3, 1901

Through Mr. Chanute, Will has an invitation to make a speech before the Western Society of Engineers, which has a meeting in Chicago in a couple of weeks. . . . His subject is his Gliding Experiments. Will was about to refuse but I nagged him into going. He will get acquainted with some scientific men and it may do him a lot of good. We don't hear anything but flying machine and engine from morning till night. I'll be glad when school begins so I can escape.

. . . .

Octave Chanute to Wilbur Wright

Chicago, Ill., September 5, 1901

The secretary of the Society, and the Publication committee are greatly pleased that you consent to giving the Western Society of Engineers a talk on the 18th. May they make it "Ladies night"?

. . . .

Wilbur Wright to Octave Chanute

Dayton, Ohio, September 6, 1901

I must caution you not to make my address a prominent feature of the program as you will understand that I make no pretense of being a public speaker. For a title, "Late Gliding Experiments" will do. As to the presence of ladies, it is not my province to dictate, moreover I will already be as badly scared as it is possible for man to be, so that the presence of ladies will make little difference to me, provided I am not expected to appear in full dress.

.   .   .   .

Katharine Wright to her father

September 11, 1901

The boys are still working in the machine shop. A week from today is "Ullam's" [Wilbur's] speech at Chicago. We asked him whether it was to be witty or scientific and he said he thought it would be pathetic . . . !

.   .   .   .

Wilbur Wright to George A. Spratt

Dayton, Ohio, September 21, 1901

Yours of recent date not yet received. Has it been written? . . .

Well, after you left camp, conditions which you know were none too pleasant in some respects became even worse, as they were no longer relieved by your funny stories and pleasant company, so four days after you left we also broke camp and returned home. . . .

I enclose a few prints. That of the Huffaker machine you will please not show too promiscuously. I took it as a joke on Huffaker but afterward it struck me that the joke was rather on Mr. Chanute, as the whole loss was his. If you ever feel that you have not got much to show for your work and money expended, get out this picture and you will feel encouraged.

We have been quite busy since returning home, putting in some new machinery and finishing a new gas engine on which we have been working for some time.

By Mr. Chanute's invitation I was up to Chicago a few days ago to address the Western Society of Engineers on our experiments. His faith in Lilienthal's tables is beginning to waver, though it dies hard.

. . . .

Katharine Wright to her father

High School, Dayton, Ohio, September 25, 1901

We had a picnic getting Will off to Chicago. Orville offered all his clothes so off went "Ullam," arrayed in Orv's shirt, collars, cuffs, cuff-links, and overcoat. We discovered that to some extent "clothes do make the man" for you never saw Will look so "swell."

. . . .

Orville was the more particular of the two about personal appearance. Wilbur was inclined to let his clothes alone. Carrie Grumbach recalled that Katharine would say, "Will, aren't the knees of your trousers getting a little baggy?" He would look thoughtful and pretty soon would come to the kitchen to heat up the flat iron.

But Orville in his younger days seems to have been a bit of a dandy. Sun tan was not so fashionable at the turn of the century as it became later, and whenever the brothers returned from Kitty Hawk, bronzed as Indians, Carrie would notice a lemon in the soap dish on Orville's washstand. Mr. Orville's face, she said, would be pale weeks sooner than Mr. Will's.

In his Chicago speech Wilbur boldly declared that the best sets of figures obtainable regarding air pressure against airplane surfaces appeared to contain many serious errors. Orville, at the shop in Dayton, was a little alarmed about that part of the speech. What if something about their own work had somehow been wrong and the figures compiled by various scientists should finally be proved correct? It would be both presumptuous and risky to brand supposedly established facts as untrue unless the person doing so could be unassailably sure of his ground. In this cautious state of mind Orville picked up an old starch box and contrived a little wind tunnel for the purpose of making a series of tests.

The experiments with this crude apparatus did not go beyond one day. They were conclusive enough so far as they went, indicating that Wilbur was on solid ground in his criticism of scientific works; but as Orville was later to learn, the published errors were greatest in regard to small angles, such as would be used in flying, and he had tested in the

starch box only larger angles. He and Wilbur decided to
stay on the safe side and omit from the published record of
Wilbur's speech the more severe part of his attack on available figures. They would wait until further wind-tunnel
experiments could give them more detailed knowledge.
Consequently, when the speech was printed in the December, 1901, issue of the *Journal of the Western Society of
Engineers,* it was less shocking than the one delivered—
though there still remained strong hints that accepted tables
of figures might be wrong. Even as published, however, the
speech was treated as of great importance. It has been reprinted and quoted as often as any article ever written on the
subject of flying.

III

SECRETS FROM A WIND TUNNEL

Wilbur Wright to Octave Chanute

Dayton, Ohio, October 6, 1901

We have made the experiment of balancing a curved surface against a plane surface 66 per cent as large, placed
normal to the wind, and find that instead of 5° as called for
in Lilienthal's table an angle of 18° was required. The test
was made by mounting the surfaces on a bicycle wheel
turned over so that its axis was vertical. . . .

We found it impossible to get satisfactory results with a
natural wind, so we mounted the wheel on a spar projecting in front of a bicycle and made tests in an almost perfect calm. We rode at right angles to the wind so that the
natural wind was first on one side and then on the other as
the direction of the course was reversed.

.   .   .   .

That experiment with the bicycle was tried only once.
Soon the Wrights rigged up a much better wind tunnel
about 6 feet long and 16 inches square (interior measurement), and for two months, toward the end of 1901, tested

more than two hundred types of miniature wing surfaces. Among other things, they proved the fallacy of the sharp edge at the front of an airplane wing and the inefficiency of deeply cambered wings, then generally advocated by others. As the experiments continued, they marked a turning point in the efforts of man to fly for they gave knowledge no one had ever had before of how to design wings efficient enough to make possible a flying machine. It is the design of the wings rather than the engine or propellers that enables a plane to lift itself in the air. If this were not so, a glider, with neither an engine nor propellers, could not fly.

Octave Chanute to Wilbur Wright

Chicago, Ill., October 12, 1901

I have read with very great interest your letter of Oct. 6th, and I esteem greatly the experiments which you have lately made. I hope that you will continue them as proposed and advise me of the result.

I have been endeavoring to account for the discrepancy of your results with those of Lilienthal.

.   .   .   .

Wilbur Wright to his father

Dayton, Ohio, October 24, 1901

Since returning we have been experimenting somewhat with an apparatus for measuring the pressure of air on variously curved surfaces at different angles, and have decided to prepare a table which we are certain will be much more accurate than that of Lilienthal. Mr. Chanute has several times kindly offered to help bear the expense of these experiments but we have refused to accept money because we would be led to neglect our regular business too much if the expense of experimenting did not exercise a salutary effect on the time devoted to them.

. . . .

Wilbur Wright to Octave Chanute

Dayton, Ohio, November 22, 1901

After almost numberless small changes we think our machine will now give results within 2 or 3 per cent of the real truth, and will give the same result at every test at any given angle. We are now engaged in making a large number of models of typical shapes and will measure them with the greatest care. The comparative lifts of different surfaces will be obtained with almost absolute correctness.

. . . .

Wilbur Wright to George A. Spratt

Dayton, Ohio, December 15, 1901

We were pleased to receive your letter and the photograph of your new testing machine. It seems quite ingeniously designed and I think should give good results. As you say, the greatest trouble will probably be with the change-ableness of the wind. If I understand you properly, the machine is intended for locating the center of pressure at any angle (or rather locating the angle for any center of pressure) and for finding the direction of the resultant pressure as measured in degrees from the wind direction.

I think I told you in my last that we had been experiment-ing with a "lift" measuring machine. We have carried our experiments further and have made a measurement of the lifts of about thirty surfaces. The results have rather sur-prised us as we find at angles of 7° to 15° *with some surfaces* a greater lift than Lilienthal gives in his table.

.   .   .   .

A few years later, after the Wrights were famous, Spratt wrote to Wilbur expressing a wish that he could have credit for suggestions regarding the testing of miniature wings. Wilbur discussed this in a letter written much later—Octo-ber 16, 1909.

Wilbur Wright to Octave Chanute

Dayton, Ohio, December 15, 1901

I regret that we did not have time to carry some of these experiments further, but having set a time for the experi-ments to cease, we stopped when the time was up. At least two thirds of my time in the past six months has been de-voted to aeronautical matters. Unless I decide to devote myself to something other than a business career, I must give closer attention to my regular work for a while. I hope at some later time to resume these investigations.

. . . .

Octave Chanute to Wilbur Wright

Chicago, Ill., December 19, 1901

I have read your letter . . . with absorbing interest. If your method and machine are reliable you have done a great work, and have advanced knowledge greatly. Your charts carry conviction to my mind and your descriptions and comments are very clear. I must especially commend the system by which you went about to ascertain the best form of surface, instead of trying haphazard experiments.

I very much regret, in the interest of Science, that you have reached a stopping place, for further experimenting on your part promises important results, yet my judgment cannot but approve of your decision, for I see as yet no money return for the pursuit, save from possible exhibition. If, however, some rich man should give you $10,000 a year to go on, to connect his name with progress, would you do so? I happen to know Carnegie; would you like for me to write to him?

. . . .

Wilbur Wright to Octave Chanute

December 23, 1901

As to your suggestion in regard to Mr. Carnegie, of course nothing would give me greater pleasure than to devote my entire time to scientific investigations; and a salary of ten or twenty thousand a year would be no insuperable objection, but I think it possible that Andrew is too hard-headed a Scotchman to become interested in such a visionary pursuit as flying. But to discuss the matter more seriously, I will say that several times in the years that are past I have had thoughts of a scientific career, but the lack of a suitable opening, and the knowledge that I had no special preparation in any particular line, kept me from entertaining the idea very seriously. I do not think it would be wise for me to accept help in carrying our present investigations further, unless it was with the intention of cutting loose from business entirely and taking up a different line of life work. There are limits to the neglect that business will endure, and a little pay for the time spent in neglecting it would only increase the neglect, without bringing in enough to offset the damage resulting from a wrecked business. So while I would give serious consideration to a chance to enter upon a new line of work, I would not think it wise to make outside work too pronounced a feature of a business life.

. . . .

Wilbur Wright to Octave Chanute

January 5, 1902

The relation of men of wealth to the flying problem presents many points of similarity to that of North Pole hunting. It would be folly to back such attempts as business propositions, or at least it could be considered nothing better than the very rashest speculation. Although I personally believe that constant systematic effort would bring about a successful machine in the course of a very few years, yet in view of the universal failures of the past no man could honestly make such a belief the basis of an appeal to some rich man for help on a business basis. If wealth is to be interested it would more properly be in the line of instituting a fund to be known as "The Croesus Fund for the promotion of Aeronautical Science," with the condition that all experiments should be published as "Croesus Fund" experiments and that the successful machine should in some way have this name linked with it. Another plan would be to offer a permanent prize of a considerable amount to be awarded only for a machine which was capable of meeting rigid tests, but the interest each year to be awarded to the most valuable improvement or contribution to aeronautical science made during the year.

The first plan would be somewhat on the plan of the Smithsonian Institution, or the recent Carnegie Institute, only on a much smaller scale of course and with no permanent buildings, etc. The other would be similar to that of the Nobel Fund except that the endowment would become the grand prize in case of absolute success.

Since donations of ten to thirty millions have become the style, little fame is to be obtained by comparatively small gifts to colleges. For the money expended, an aeronautical fund would probably give a man as much fame as any that could be named, as the newspapers keep a closer watch on such matters than on colleges.

If wealth is to be interested on a mixed basis of benevolence and hope of pecuniary return, it ought to be made sufficiently clear that the latter could hardly be considered a satisfactory insurance against finally resting in a pauper's grave.

Your news in regard to the St. Louis Exposition [prizes for different kinds of aerial apparatus] is interesting certainly. If the plan is carried through, it will undoubtedly have the effect of greatly stimulating public interest at least, and may bring some new workers into the field. Whether it will have much immediate effect so far as a complete flying machine is concerned, I much doubt, because where all is attempted at once in haste, no one point receives sufficient attention to lead to a real advance. The probability is that the department of aviation would be a competition between *engine* builders rather than *flying machine* builders.

.   .   .   .

Wilbur Wright to Octave Chanute

Dayton, Ohio, January 19, 1902

I am sending you herewith photo and description of our pressure testing machine. It is our belief that the method and construction employed entirely avoid errors from the following sources: (1) Variation in wind velocity; (2) Variations in temperature and density of the atmosphere;

(3) Travel of center of pressure; (4) Variation in angle of incidence owing to movements of the mounting arms. The first two causes gave Mr. Langley trouble; while the third and fourth vitiate somewhat the *natural wind* experiments of Lilienthal. Gravity and centrifugal force are also rendered nugatory.

Our greatest trouble was in obtaining a perfectly straight current of wind, but finally by using a wind straightener, and changing the resistance plane to a position where its ill influence was much reduced and also by breaking it up into a number of narrow vertical surfaces instead of a single square, we obtained a current very nearly constant in direction. The instrument itself was mounted in a long square tube or trough having a glass cover. After we began to make our record measurements we allowed no large object in the room to be moved, and no one except the observer was allowed to come near the apparatus, and he occupied exactly the same position beside the trough at each observation. We had found by previous experience that these precautions were necessary, as very little is required to deflect a current a tenth of a degree, which is enough to very seriously affect the results. I will send another batch of data in a few days.

Your letter from St. Louis of course interested us very much. The newspapers of yesterday announce that the fair will be held in 1903 as originally planned. If this be final there will be little time for designing and building a power machine, which is, I suppose, the only kind that could hope to be awarded a prize of any size. Whether we shall compete will depend much on the conditions under which the prizes are offered. I have little of the gambling instinct, and unless there is reasonable hope of getting at least the amount expended in competing, I would enter only after very careful

consideration. Mathematically it would be foolish to spend
two or three thousand dollars competing for a hundred thousand dollar prize if the chance of winning be only *one* in a
hundred.

. . . .

Wilbur Wright to George A. Spratt

Dayton, January 23, 1902

I see from your remark about the "blues" that you still retain the habit of letting the opinions or doings of others
influence you too much. We thought we had partly cured you
of this at Kitty Hawk. It is well for a man to be able to see
the merits of others and the weaknesses of himself, but if
carried too far it is as bad or even worse than seeing only his
own merits and *others'* weaknesses. . . .

You seem to be having trouble to obtain satisfactory surfaces. Possibly our experience will be of assistance in deciding on proper material. But first you ought to decide on
the length, breadth, and thickness of your surface. It ought
to be as near as possible proportionate in every dimension to
the surfaces to be used in large machines. Now, the experiments of Lilienthal, Langley, Dines, Maxim, Wenham, and
others, as well as our own recent experiments, show that the
efficiency at small angles is greatest in surfaces having the
latitude much greater than the fore and aft dimension. And
this agrees with what we find in birds, as the tip to tip measurement is never less than five times the longitude of wing
from front to rear, and in the sea birds, which live on the

wing, the tip to tip spread is sometimes twenty times the fore and aft dimension. If you would copy nature your surfaces should have a lateral breadth not less than six times the length fore and aft, nor more than twenty times.

. . . .

Wilbur Wright to Octave Chanute

Dayton, February 7, 1902

The newspapers are full of accounts of flying machines which have been building in cellars, garrets, stables, and other secret places, each one of which will undoubtedly carry off the $200,000 at St. Louis. They all have the problem "completely solved," but usually there is some insignificant detail yet to be decided, such as whether to use steam, electricity, or a water motor to drive it. Mule power might give greater *ascensional force if properly applied,* but I fear would be too dangerous unless the mule wore pneumatic shoes. Some of these reports would disgust one, if they were not so irresistibly ludicrous.

. . . .

Octave Chanute to Wilbur Wright

Pasadena, Cal., February 13, 1902

I have a letter from Capt. [Louis F.] Ferber, of Nice France, who has made some glides himself on a Lilienthal machine. He says that he is in a state of *admiration* of your performances and wishes me to convey his felicitations.

.   .   .   .

Letters began to come to the Wrights, also, from Captain Ferber. He was in the French Army and had made his gliding experiments as a hobby while serving in an Alpine artillery corps. As early as 1901, he had written to Chanute about the Wrights after reading of their experiments. He called himself a disciple of the Wrights.*

Wilbur Wright to George A. Spratt

Dayton, February 14, 1902

Your letter and the surfaces received. Sorry you do not find sheet steel applicable to your needs. I recommended it because it is so stiff, so easily formed into any desired shape, and so cheap. In fifteen minutes any curvature desired can be obtained with no other tools than a hammer and anvil, either a plain curve, or spoon shaped, or bowl shaped. Carving surfaces out of wood is all right, but it is awfully tedious work.

Your reasoning in regard to two 6″ x 12″ being equal to one 6″ x 24″ in lift is hardly sound. The two halves of a broken pitcher are equal in *weight* to the unbroken pitcher but they will not hold as much water. Your two surfaces will equal the larger one in *area* but it does not necessarily follow that they

---

* See letter from Orville Wright to Henri Hegener, September 5, 1945.

will be equal in any other respect. As a matter of fact the conditions are materially different owing to the fact that in the 6″ x 24″ surface there are only two ends (tips) for the wind to escape around, while in the two 6″ x 12″ surfaces there are *four* such ends. Thus there is less *loss* in the 6″ x 24″ surface, and its lift is relatively greater.

You are quite right in saying that a gas engine and tools are an advantage in experimenting. It is possible that in the long run you could do more experimenting in a given time by spending part of your time earning money by running a bicycle repair shop, or something of the kind, and incidentally fitting up with an engine which would come in handy in aeronautical work. In the present stage of the game aeronautical experimenting alone is not a very sure way of earning bread and butter.

.   .   .   .

The Wrights were the first to know that there was a loss of lifting power from placing one wing above another, and how much loss.

Wilbur Wright to Octave Chanute

Dayton, March 11, 1902

Your inquiry as to my opinion of the best surfaces to use and how many to superpose, I am unable to answer definitely. There are a number of points which need to be investigated first. Our experiments showed that with surfaces of a given thickness and longitude, the lift and dynamic efficiency increased as the latitude became greater. But as structural reasons demand that the thickness of the lateral spars must increase as the latitude becomes greater, a point is finally reached where a further increase of the relative latitude is harmful in dynamic efficiency—the drift increases faster than the lift. Just what the proper proportions are I do not know, but I think that with a surface 1 foot thick and 3 feet from front to rear, the spread should be from 15 to 25 feet.

As to superposing, our tables give all that I know. A machine with several surfaces will be stronger and possibly more manageable but not quite so efficient as a single surface. It is probable that trial alone will show just how far superposing can be carried with advantage.

.   .   .   .

Wilbur Wright to Octave Chanute

Dayton, March 23, 1902

My idea of the correct use of the terms drift and head resistance is well exemplified by . . . a man rowing across a rapid stream. If he points the boat directly across the current, it will take just as much work to reach the opposite shore as if the water were still; but he will land much lower down than his starting point. The power required to drive the boat is the "head resistance," while the distance he drifts down stream is the "drift." In both nautics and aeronautics drift is a loss of position rather than a resistance. It is important therefore to carefully distinguish in calculations between the power consumed in overcoming *resistance* and the power consumed in *recovering position.* The man, in order to avoid loss of position, must point his boat somewhat up stream while crossing, and his *relative distance rowed* will be the actual distance across the river divided by the cosine of his "angle of incidence.". . .

I think that the St. Louis Exposition authorities will have to increase the amount of their prizes, as I have already been offered so many shares of the prize by various persons who have a cinch on it, that the sum of my shares would amount to more than the total prize. Consequently the St. Louis men must put up more money or take advantage of the bankruptcy laws.

. . . .

The Wrights had faith in the tables of air pressures they had compiled from their wind-tunnel experiments and wanted to see them verified in actual gliding; yet so much remained to be discovered, and the whole job seemed so formidable, that Wilbur hesitated about making another trip to Kitty Hawk. Then something else came up, unrelated to aviation, which might have prevented their going. Wilbur felt duty bound to give some help to his father in an important church problem. It had become known in the inner councils of the United Brethren Church that a layman connected with the church publishing business had mishandled some funds. Bishop Wright, tolerant as he was, could not condone dishonesty and wanted to see the man removed, if not prosecuted. But one faction sought to whitewash the case, to hush up any possible scandal, and started a fight to oust the Bishop from office. Wilbur went to work on the account books and found proof of dishonesty. Then he wrote a

blistering tract, setting forth the facts and the Bishop's
determined view of them. He made a study of the legal
aspects of the case. The whole Wright family became as
much concerned over the church issue as they were about
flying experiments. Bishop Wright was never deposed, but
the fight went on for a long time.

The brothers finally decided to go on with their plans to
build and test a new glider, but not until a week or two before they planned to go to Kitty Hawk was Orville sure that
Wilbur would go, and he would not have gone alone.

Chanute, not intending to attempt any new experiments
himself, wanted to have rebuilt some of the gliders he had
designed, "to test the comparative merits" of what he had
done. He was still hoping they might contain something
of scientific value.

Wilbur Wright to Octave Chanute

Dayton, May 29, 1902

We consented to undertake the building of machines for
you for the good of the cause. If you make other arrangements, it will be all right with us. To tell the truth, the building of machines for other men to risk their necks on is not a
task I particularly relish, and if Mr. Herring* is at leisure to
take charge of the matter for you it will relieve us.

Our busy season is about over, and if we could depend
on proper winds, we would probably spend July and August

---

* Augustus M. Herring had made aeronautical experiments of his own.
As will appear, his acquaintance soon became a great annoyance to
the Wrights.

at Kitty Hawk. These are the months that we would prefer to spend in camp but we are dubious about the winds and weather after our experience of last year. If we go to Kitty Hawk it will probably be some time between August 15th and September 15th. It is a pity that the hills near Chicago are not smooth bare slopes.

Will try to furnish drawings as soon as convenient to do so. I do not think that drawings will reveal very much of the principles of operation of our machines, unless accompanied with somewhat extended explanations, so our secrets are safe enough.

.   .   .   .

The Wrights did not want to take time for testing or experimenting with gliders designed or built by others, on principles which they questioned, when they had so limited a season for testing their own. But in dealing with a friend they were polite!

Wilbur Wright to Octave Chanute

Dayton, June 2, 1902

If I understand you properly, you propose to build the multiple-wing and double-deck machines and give them to us as presents. You hinted something of this kind in a former letter, but it surpasses our capacity for belief that you were intending to exercise the virtue of benevolence on so magnificent a scale as your words seemed to imply. The kindness and enthusiasm in the cause which prompted such a generous offer strike a very deep chord in our hearts. We thank you most earnestly. Yet the question arises whether it would be wise to spend so much for such a purpose. It is not certain that we would be able to find opportunity for such extended use of the machines as would justify so great an expenditure on your part. Our use of the machines ought to be an incident rather than the primary purpose of their construction. We are yet in hopes that you may decide to resume experiment on your own account.

.   .   .   .

Wilbur Wright to Octave Chanute

Dayton, July 9, 1902

In our conversation you raised the point of the advisability of sending Mr. Avery* or Mr. Herring down to Kitty Hawk. I did not feel prepared to give a definite opinion without full consideration of the matter with my brother. We think that there are reasons that make it very desirable that an expert should be present during the trials of your machines. (1) The expense incurred in building the machines is such as to make it very desirable that the tests should be as *perfect as possible*. (2) An expert would know just how the machines ought to act, and would at once detect radical imperfections in their actions, and thus materially reduce the time required to "tune up" the machines. (3) We would be very loath to assume sole responsibility for the tests, for if from any cause whatsoever the results obtained should fail to equal those obtained by Messrs. Herring and Avery it might raise a

---

* William Avery was a mechanical and electrical engineer in Chicago who had done work for Chanute on gliders.

suspicion that we had not acted fairly. We would have no fears of your own personal opinion; but others hearing of the matter might with apparent justice form a very different opinion. We would be very unwilling to subject ourselves to the possibility of such a misapprehension of the facts.

. . . .

Katharine Wright to her father

Dayton, August 20, 1902

The flying machine is in process of making now. Will spins the sewing machine around by the hour while Orv. squats around marking the places to sew. There is no place in the house to live but I'll be lonesome enough by this time next week and wish that I could have some of this racket around.

Will and Orv. . . . . really ought to get away for a while. Will is thin and nervous and so is Orv. They will be all right when they get down in the sand where the salt breezes blow, etc. They insist that if you aren't well enough to stay out on your trip you must come down with them. They think that life at Kitty Hawk cures all ills you know.

. . . .

Through the early years of the experiments in gliding, the Wright family, and the brothers themselves, looked upon the trips to Kitty Hawk simply as vacations. Everyone in the family was glad to have them go because the sunshine, sea air and exercise seemed to be good for their health.

The new glider did not have a much greater lifting area than that of 1901, though the wing span had been increased from twenty-two to thirty-two feet. As the Wrights now understood the importance of "aspect ratio," they made the span about six times the fore and aft measurement instead of three. The most noticeable change was the addition of a tail, fixed twin vertical vanes with a total area of about twelve feet. Its purpose was to overcome certain difficulties encountered the previous year.

Wilbur Wright to his father

Kitty Hawk, August 31, 1902

We left Dayton at 9 A.M. last Monday and reached Elizabeth City at 5.45 P.M. Tuesday after a very nice trip. We found the schooner *Lou Willis,* Captain Midgett, lying at the wharf intending to start for Kitty Hawk at 4 A.M. Wednesday morning. To rush back to the station and get our trunks out of the baggage room and our freight out of the freight depot before 6 P.M., the shutting up time, required fast work, but we succeeded. By extraordinary luck we also succeeded in buying a barrel of gasoline just as the men were leaving the Standard Oil Company warehouse, and Orville succeeded in getting an oven by rushing from store to store till he found one where the man was locking up, but reopened long enough to sell an oven. The groceries were mostly closed but we finally found one open and got a few cans of baking powder. It was long after dark before we got our things aboard the boat.

The boat set sail at 3.45 A.M. next morning, or rather we

poled out, for the wind was too light to sail. At 6 o'clock we had made nearly a mile. At noon we had gone about 6 miles. Then the wind came up a little stronger, but changed its direction so that it came dead ahead, so that while the boat moved through the water with fair speed it was mostly back and forth across the river and very little onward in the direction we wanted to go. By 3 o'clock we had made about 15 miles, about 1⅖ miles an hour for eleven hours' sailing. As the captain saw that there was no hope of getting to Kitty Hawk till long after midnight he decided to cast anchor till daylight next morning. . . .

On reaching shore we hurried about and soon got Dan Tate and his boat and Captain Hobbs' horse and cart and, putting our trunks, gasoline stove, and a few necessary articles of food in boat and cart, we set out for camp 4 miles south of the wharf, and reached there about 6 o'clock. We found that the wind had blown the sand out from under the ends of our building and let them down about 18 inches so that the floor inside sloped very much like a mountain side each way from the center. However, we got our stove to work and made some beef-extract soup, and this with crackers made us a little supper, and we went to bed happy.

. . . .

Wilbur Wright to his sister

Kitty Hawk, August 31, 1902

We drove our well a few days ago by a method we shall probably patent immediately after returning home, and obtained water suitable for all purposes. It is the best in Kitty

Hawk. We also set up our table and covered the top with
white oilcloth over two thicknesses of burlap, so you see we
have an up-to-date soft-top dining table. Strict orders have
been given to set nothing hot on it or anything that can dis-
color it. We also upholstered our dining-room chairs with
excelsior and burlap, and have put in other royal luxuries.
So far, in addition to cookery, etc., we have exercised ourselves in the trades of carpentering, furniture making, up-
holstering, well driving, and will add house moving next
week.

.   .   .   .

From Orville Wright's Diary

Monday, September 1, 1902

Spent day raising building. . . . Sawed lumber for addition. Made up bed for 6 months.

.   .   .   .

Wilbur Wright to Octave Chanute

Kitty Hawk, September 5, 1902

As to the choice of a man to experiment your machines, we
wish you to get the one whom you think most available. In a
former letter I expressed a preference for Mr. Avery because
several things I had heard about Mr. Herring's relations
with Mr. Langley and yourself seemed to me to indicate that
he might be of a somewhat jealous disposition, and possibly

inclined to claim for himself rather more credit than those with whom he might be working would be willing to allow. While I do not anticipate trouble for ourselves on this score, yet I thought that with Mr. Avery there would not be the same risk. If you should find it most convenient to send Mr. Herring it will be entirely satisfactory to us. If you also are in camp during the time that he is here I do not see how any misunderstanding could arise.

. . . .

Wilbur Wright to Octave Chanute

Kitty Hawk, September 12, 1902

We thank you for your caution against rashness. We will be very careful as we have special reasons for not wishing to be injured just at this time.

. . . .

Wilbur Wright to George A. Spratt

Kitty Hawk, September 16, 1902

Yours of the 9th received. We learned with much regret that there is a possibility that you may not get down here this year, as we had looked forward to your visit with pleasure. Everything is so much more favorable this year than last that it would be a pity to have your ideas of camp life here based on your experience of one year ago. First, we have not seen a dozen mosquitoes in the two weeks and a half we have been here. I have not seen a half dozen myself. Second, we fitted up our living arrangements much more comfortably than last year. Our kitchen is immensely improved, and then we have made beds on the second floor and now sleep aloft. It is an improvement over cots. We have put battens on the cracks of the whole building, including the addition, so it is much tighter and more waterproof than before, as well as more sandproof. Our new well goes down 6 or 8 feet below water mark on the ocean . . . and we now have good water. We also have a bicycle which runs much better over the sand than we hoped, so that it takes only about an hour to make the round trip to Kitty Hawk instead of three hours as before. There are other improvements too numerous to mention . . . so we are having a splendid time.

Mr. Chanute is sending down two machines. One built for him by Mr. Herring, and one built by Mr. Lamson (of kite fame). He is expecting to come down himself about October 1st. Mr. Herring will come down to manipulate the Chanute machines.

At present Orville and I are alone in camp. We made arrangements, before coming down, to have Dan Tate with us as soon as we were ready to begin experimenting. This is all the force we absolutely need, as we will do little measuring and photographing till later when we have more men. We do not absolutely need a fourth man, yet he would not be an incumbrance by any means, especially if he was as good a companion as I know you to be.

. . . .

Wilbur Wright to Octave Chanute

Kitty Hawk, September 21, 1902

You should bring warm clothing and not less than the equivalent of two heavy double blankets for bedding, as we may have cool nights in October. We will arrange to have the necessaries of life in the way of food, but as our food was selected according to our own tastes, it may be that it may lack some things you would prefer. If there is anything for which you have a particular fondness you can bring it down, though I much doubt whether you will have much opportunity. My brother and I are sleeping on special cots in the second story of our building. We therefore have the two cots which we used last year in reserve for visitors. If you would prefer to sleep aloft as we do, suitable cots can quickly be improvised if you will bring down two yards of heavy canvas or sail cloth (about 16 oz. would be best) for each cot. We prefer the upper story ourselves.

. . . .

From Orville Wright's Diary

Monday, September 22, 1902

After altering truss wires so as to give an arch to the surfaces making the ends 4 inches lower than the center, and the angle at the tips greater than that at the center, we took the machine out, ready for experiments. We had a steady wind of 11 to 12 meters. After waiting a while for Dan Tate to show up, which he failed to do at all during the day, we took the machine to the small hill, where we flew it as a kite, with very satisfactory results. We found that the trouble experienced heretofore with a cross wind turning up the wing it first struck had been overcome.

Tuesday, September 23

On my third or fourth glide with the end control loose so that it could be used, I was sailing along smoothly without any trouble at all from the fore and aft control, when I noticed that one wing was gradually getting a little too high and that the machine was slowly sliding off in the opposite direction. I thought that by moving the end control mechanism an inch or so I would bring the wing back again to its proper position, and as I was going along so smoothly with no need of changing the front rudder, I attempted to make the change. The next thing I knew was that the wing was very high in the air, a great deal higher than before, and I thought I must have worked the twisting apparatus the wrong way. Thinking of nothing else than the end control, after reassuring myself as to what was the proper motion, I threw the wing tips to their greatest angle. By this time I found suddenly that I was making a descent backwards toward the low wing from a height of 25 or 30 feet, as a result of the machine having turned up at an angle of nearly 45° in front, which fact I had not noticed at all while occupied in the manipulation of the ends, but which had been witnessed by Will and Dan with alarm, for several seconds before. The result was a heap of flying machine cloth and sticks, with me in the center without a bruise or a scratch. The experiments thereupon suddenly came to a close till the repairs can be made. In spite of this sad catastrophe we are tonight in a hilarious mood as a result of the encouraging performances of the machine, both in control and in angles of flight, which we are convinced will be at least 3° better than any machine ever tried before.

. . . .

Katharine Wright to her father

Dayton, Ohio, September 25, 1902

Lorin has decided to go to Kitty Hawk if he can get away now. . . .

I feel virtuous because I took no trip this summer. I'd lots rather have Lorin take it for me. He can come back with the boys. They will all enjoy it so much.

. . . .

From Orville Wright's Diary

Wednesday, September 24, 1902

Spent the day in making repairs on the machine. We took the cloth off of last section of both upper and lower surfaces, spliced the broken spars and ribs, and are ready for tacking on cloth again. The *Lou Willis* came in today with provisions and Mr. Chanute's multiple-wing machine, which Will and Dan Tate carried from the Sound to Camp.

Friday, September 26

Will continued repairs on machine, completing them this evening. The machine is now ready for use at first favorable weather. I put in a part of the day in constructing a "death trap" for a poor mouse that has been annoying us by prowling about our kitchen shelves at night. We are now anxiously awaiting the arrival of the "victim."

Saturday, September 27

At 11 o'clock I was awakened by the mouse crawling over my face. Will had advised me that I had better get something to cover my head, or I would have it "chawed" off. I found on getting up that the little fellow had only come to tell me to put another piece of corn bread in the trap. He had disposed of the first piece.

Wednesday, October 8

We took both our own and the multiple-wing machines to the north slope of the large hill, where Mr. Herring attempted to glide on a slope of 13° but could not get sufficient speed to sustain and glide on that angle.

Saturday, October 11

Mr. Herring has decided that it is useless to make further experiments with the Mult. Wing. I think that a great deal of the trouble with it came from its structural weakness, as I noticed that in winds which were not even enough for support, the surfaces were badly distorted, twisting so that, while the wind at one end was on the under side, often at the other extreme it was on top. Mr. Chanute seems much disappointed in the way it works.

. . . .

When Herring left Kitty Hawk, he made a beeline to Washington, where he sought an interview with Professor Langley, perhaps to offer to reveal to him construction details of the Wrights' 1902 glider and its performance. Langley declined to see him. The Wrights appreciated Langley's ethical attitude. Further annoyances from Herring, however, were to come.

Wilbur Wright to his father

Kitty Hawk, October 2, 1902

Our new machine is a very great improvement over anything we had built before and over anything any one has built. We have far beaten all records for flatness of glides as we in some cases have descended only 5⅓ degrees from the horizontal while other machines descended from 7½° to 11°.

This means that in soaring we can descend much slower, and in a power machine can fly with much less power. The new machine is also much more controlable than any heretofore built so the danger is correspondingly reduced. We are being very careful and will avoid accident of serious nature if possible. Yesterday I tried three glides from the top of the hill and made 506 ft., 504½ ft. and 550 ft. respectively in distance passed over. Everything is so much more satisfactory that we now believe that the flying problem is really nearing its solution.

. . . .

They found that they could glide at a smaller angle than could any of the hawks they had observed.

Katharine Wright to her father

Dayton, Ohio, October 20, 1902

Lorin came home last Wednesday afternoon. . . . The boys are having splendid success and will stay to the limit of their ticket which is October 31. Mr. Chanute and Mr. Herring were still there when Lorin left. They were all busy setting up Mr. Chanute's machine that was made in California.* Herring's machine, made for Mr. Chanute, was a total failure. It would not fly at all.

. . . .

Orville Wright to his sister

Kitty Hawk, October 23, 1902

Everybody is out of camp today but Will and myself. Spratt left Monday. We had a good time last week after

---

* It was built by Charles Lamson, originally of Portland, Maine, then living in California.

Chanute and Herring left. The work . . . was so much easier, besides the fact that the fewer in camp the more there is for each one to eat, that we had lots of time to go over to the woods botanizing and looking after birds. We went to the beach a number of times and have collected a whole bucketful of starfish besides a lot of shells and a couple of king crabs which we will bring home. Spratt is a fine fellow to be with in the woods, for he knows every bird, or bug, or plant that you are likely to run across.

Day before yesterday we had a wind of 16 meters per second or about 30 miles per hour, and glided in it without any trouble. That was the highest wind a gliding machine was ever in, so that we now hold all the records! The largest machine, the longest time in the air, the smallest angle of descent, and the highest wind!!! Well, I'll leave the rest of this "blow" till we get home.

. . . .

About one time in fifty the machine behaved in a mysterious manner. It would turn up sidewise and come sliding to the ground in spite of all the warp the operator could give to the wing tips. At one trial the lateral control would work perfectly and then the next time, under conditions that seemed to be about the same, it was impossible to prevent one wing end from striking the sand with a kind of spinning movement that the brothers called "well-digging."

This new problem that had not occurred in their previous gliders came from the fact that the machine had a tail. Those "well-digging" accidents were tail-spins—though that term did not come into use until several years afterward. But even after it was evident that the tail had something to do with the machine's peculiar behavior, neither brother was prepared to explain *why*. Then one night Orville drank more than his customary amount of coffee. Instead of going to sleep as usual the moment he got into bed, he lay awake for several hours. Those extra cups of coffee may have been important for the future of practical flight for, as he tossed about, he figured out the explanation of the phenomenon caused by the tail.

He was so sure he was right and that it was a basic discovery, as indeed it was, that he wanted credit for it. Sometimes when he told Wilbur something, Wilbur would act as if he already knew it. So at breakfast the next morning he winked at his brother Lorin, who was visiting them, to get his attention as a witness, and then asked Wilbur if he could explain the machine's peculiar behavior that had puzzled them. Wilbur shook his head.

Orville then gave this explanation:

When the machine became tilted laterally it began to slide sidewise while advancing, just as a sled slides downhill or a ball rolls down an inclined plane, the speed increasing in an accelerated ratio. If the tilt happened to be a little worse than usual, or if the operator were a little slow in getting the balance corrected, the machine slid sidewise so fast that this movement caused the vertical vanes to strike the wind on the side toward the low wing instead of on the side toward the high wing, as it was expected to do. In this state of affairs the vertical vanes did not counteract the turning of the machine about a vertical axis, caused by the difference of resistance of the warped wings on the right and left sides; on the contrary, the vanes assisted in the turning movement, and the result was worse than if there were no fixed vertical tail.

If his explanation was sound, as Orville felt sure it was, then, he said, it would be necessary to make the vertical tail movable to permit the operator to bring pressure to bear on the side toward the higher wing—(the form of the Wright system of control that came into general use).

Wilbur promptly saw that the explanation was probably correct and nodded approvingly. And he immediately made a suggestion. A particular relation existed, he said, in the desired pressures on the tail, no matter whether the trouble was due to difference of resistance of the wing tips oɪ on account of sliding. Whatever the reason, it was desirable to get rid of the pressure on the side toward the low wing, to which a greater angle of incidence must be imparted in restoring lateral balance, and bring pressure on the side of the tail toward the high wing where there must be a reduced angle. So why not have the mechanism that controlled the wing warping and that which moved the tail operated in conjunction? Then the pilot, instead of having to control three things at once, would need to attend only to the front elevator and the wing-warping device. The brothers at once attached the wires controlling the tail to those that warped the wings—and they also changed the tail from two vertical fins to a single vertical rudder.

The experiments with the 1902 glider were almost as important as those the next year with the powered machine, for in 1902 the Wrights had solved most of the problems of stability and control. Their basic patent was on the mechanism of this glider.

Wilbur Wright to Octave Chanute

Dayton, November 2, 1902

We left Kitty Hawk at daybreak on last Tuesday and reached home at 3 P.M. on Friday after a very exciting but tiresome trip.

Into the last ten days of practice we crowded more glides than in all the weeks preceding. In two days we made about two hundred and fifty, all of which were made in winds ranging from 9 to 16¾ meters per second. The duration of these glides ranged from seven to sixteen seconds. This practice enabled us to very greatly increase our skill in the management of the machine. We increased our record for distance to 622½ feet, for time to 26 seconds, and for angle to 5° for a glide of 156 feet.

. . . .

Wilbur Wright to Octave Chanute

Dayton, November 12, 1902

We received from Mr. Langley, a few days before we finished our experiments at Kitty Hawk, a telegram and afterwards a letter, inquiring whether there would be time for him to reach us and witness some of our trials before we left. We replied that it would be scarcely possible as we were intending to break camp in a few days. He made no mention of his experiments on the Potomac. . . .

Orville is at work on a new testing machine and it is possible that we may decide to make an entirely new series of measurements covering in part the same ground as before.

. . . .

Octave Chanute to Wilbur Wright

Chicago, Ill., December 9, 1902

I met last week Mr. Manly,* Prof. Langley's assistant, while on a visit to his brother. . . . This brings me the enclosed letter which seems to me cheeky. Kindly advise me what to reply.

. . . .

The letter Chanute referred to them was from Professor Langley.

December 7, 1902

I should be glad to hear more of what the Wright Brothers have done, and especially of their means of control, which you think better than the Pénaud. I should be very glad to have either of them visit Washington at my expense, to get some of their ideas on this subject, if they are willing to communicate them.

Wilbur Wright to Octave Chanute

Dayton, December 11, 1902

I thank you for the copy of the Mouillard patent and for your words of advice. We have our patent specifications about complete and hope to have them filed soon.

---

* Charles M. Manly, besides being Langley's chief assistant, was later the pilot in the two unsuccessful attempts to fly the full-size Langley machine.

It is not at all probable that either Orville or myself will find opportunity to visit Prof. Langley in response to his suggestion. We have a number of matters demanding our attention just now. . . .

It is our intention next year to build a machine much larger and about twice as heavy as our present machine. With it we will work out problems relating to starting and handling heavy-weight machines, and if we find it under satisfactory control in flight, we will proceed to mount a motor.

. . . .

Wilbur Wright to George A. Spratt

Dayton, December 29, 1902

We have recently done a little experimenting with screws [propellers] and are trying to get a clear understanding of just how they work and why. It is a very perplexing problem indeed.

We are thinking of building a machine next year with 500 sq. ft. surface, about 40 ft. x 6 ft. 6 in. This will give us opportunity to work out problems connected with the management of large machines both in the air and on the ground, such as starting, etc. If all goes well the next step will be to apply a motor.

. . . .

After the successful experiments with the 1902 glider, Wilbur considered becoming a lecturer. He wrote to the Redpath Lyceum Bureau suggesting that he be booked to lecture on man's attempts to fly, and the nature of the problem. The bureau replied that such a lecture might be successful if it included enough humor. If he would furnish a lantern operator and pay all his expenses, he might receive from fifty to seventy-five dollars for each lecture, less the bureau's twenty per cent commission. Possibly, a little later, when Wilbur was world famous, the bureau would have offered more!

Entry from Bishop Milton Wright's Diary of 1903

February 18, 1903

The boys increased the flow of gas by putting a "snorter" in the radiator in my room. Our gas radiators are of their invention and their making.

. . . .

Captain Ferber, in France, now wanted to buy a glider from the Wrights.

Wilbur Wright to Octave Chanute

Dayton, Ohio, March 29, 1903

A machine could undoubtedly be so constructed that it could be readily taken apart and packed for shipment, but we would scarcely be able to enter upon the construction of one before next Winter. We are planning rather more work than usual for ourselves this year and would be very loath to permit anything to obstruct it. Next Winter we could, if desired, construct a machine for Capt. Ferber, and early in the spring give him practical instructions in the use of it, should he think it advisable to come to America.

. . . .

Octave Chanute to Wilbur Wright

London, April 11, 1903

I read between the lines that you contemplate some further improvement upon your 1902 machine, and do not wish to dispose of it to Capt. Ferber until you are certain of the result. If my imagining is correct, I think that you are right.

. . . .

Chanute was in London en route to France to try to arrange with Santos-Dumont to fly his dirigible airship at the St. Louis Exposition. While in Paris Chanute gave a talk before the Aéro Club of France about the Wrights' experiments, and described their system of control. This appeared in a Paris paper. A little later, *L'Aérophile* published an article by Chanute giving a description, photographs and drawings of the 1902 Wright glider. The French promptly made use of that information and began to experiment with gliders of the "type Wright." These experiments marked the real beginning of European aviation.

Wilbur Wright to George A. Spratt

Dayton, Ohio, April 20, 1903

You make a great mistake in envying me any of my qualities. Very often what you take for some special quality of mind is merely facility arising from constant practice. It is a characteristic of all our family to be able to see the weak points of anything, but this is not always a desirable quality as it makes us too conservative for successful business men, and limits our friendships to a very limited circle.

. . . .

Wilbur Wright to George A. Spratt

Dayton, Ohio, April 27, 1903

If a man is in too big a hurry to give up an error he is liable to give up some truth with it, and in accepting the arguments of the other man he is sure to get some error with it. Honest argument is merely a process of mutually picking the beams and motes out of each others' eyes so both can see clearly. Men become wise just as they become rich, more by what they *save* than by what they receive. After I get hold of a truth I hate to lose it again, and I like to sift all the truth out before I give up an error.

. . . .

Orville Wright to George A. Spratt

Dayton, Ohio, June 7, 1903

While I am aware that the shock of receiving a letter from me is apt to bring on a fit, yet I assure you that my writing is with no "design" on your life, which you mention in your letter to Wilbur. We both take great interest in your letters, and my not writing to you is not from a lack of interest in what you are doing, but rather from a lack of ability as a letter writer. Will seems to enjoy writing, so I leave all the literary part of our work to him. But I see that he has failed to make you understand exactly what our ideas are on some of the points that have been under discussion.

[The next part of the letter was devoted to a highly technical discussion of air pressures.]

I will drop the argumentative a while to tell you of what has been going on since we last met in Kitty Hawk. Immediately after our return we began the construction of a new testing apparatus for measuring the effects of wind at various angles on surfaces. After almost completing the machine, we discovered that we would have to have a very large room in which to operate it, as the current in our tunnel would be stronger on one side and then on the other, according to the course taken by the air in returning to our fan. Consequently we were compelled to lay the whole matter aside until we are able to find a more favorable place for operating. We may take it to Kitty Hawk.

We next began the designing of ribs, spars, etc., for our next machine, on which we had decided to put a motor with propellers. We had already before leaving Kitty Hawk about decided on many of the points of construction, but it takes considerable figuring to determine the proper sizes of the different parts so as to maintain a high enough factor of safety in so large a machine.

We are going to make the surfaces 40 x 6 feet, about 6 feet apart. . . .

Our curvature of surface will be about one in twenty, probably not as easy in control as the shape used last year, but of better lifting capacity. We are greatly increasing the size of the front rudder so as to have an abundance of control anyway. About Christmas time we began the construction of the motor, which is of four cylinders, 4-inch bore and 4-inch stroke. We had estimated that we would require a little over 8 horsepower to carry our weight of 625 pounds of machine and man. Our motor on completion turned out a very pleasant surprise. Instead of the 8 horsepower, for which we hoped but hardly expected, it has given us 13 horsepower on the brake, with a weight of only 150 pounds in the motor. During the time the engine was building we were engaged in some very heated discussions on the principles of screw propellers. We had been unable to find anything of value in any of the works to which we had access, so that we worked out a theory of our own on the subject, and soon discovered, as we usually do, that all the propellers built heretofore are *all wrong*, and then built a pair of propellers 8⅓ feet in diameter, based on our theory, which are *all right!* (till we have a chance to test them down at Kitty Hawk and find out differently). Isn't it astonishing that all these secrets have been preserved for so many years just so that we could discover them! Well, our propellers are so different from any that have been used before that they will have to either be a good deal better or a good deal worse.

We have also made some experiments on the best shapes

for the uprights of our machine, and again found out that everybody but ourselves is very badly mistaken!!! We simply tested the shapes here illustrated for the purpose of finding which was the best; exact measurements or ratios of resistance in the various shapes were not made, and the figures I give are only approximations. The "fair" or fish shape, like that recommended by Mr. Chanute, did not give as good results as that of the piece with the corners simply rounded. Mr. Chanute seems to very seriously doubt the accuracy of our measurements, as do some others who have made measurements along the same line. We are building our new uprights with simply rounded corners, nevertheless. We are going to have the chance to learn a whole lot of things when we get to Kitty Hawk this year, maybe very much to our sorrow. By the way, I will state that you will receive an invitation as soon as we determine our time of going, to visit us again at camp. . . .

The theories you advance on the effects of straight winds on curved surfaces, and of curved winds on straight surfaces or planes, seem very original and interesting. I hope that you will have more time to carry on your experiments, and to develop these ideas to their fullest extent. You doubtless will make some mistakes, just as we do, and just as everybody else does, but if we all worked on the assumption that what is accepted as true is really true, there would be little hope of advance. . . .

P.S. Please do not mention the fact of our building a power machine to anybody. The newspapers would take great delight in following us in order to record our *troubles*.

. . . .

Almost as important as their research on wing curvatures and their method of control was the Wrights' work on propellers. They were the first to be able to calculate accurately in advance a screw propeller's performance. They had assumed that they could learn all they needed about the theory of propellers from books on marine engineering, and then substitute air pressures for water pressures. But when they began to read such books, they discovered that, though screw propellers had been in use for a century, surprisingly little was known about them.

Wilbur Wright to Octave Chanute

Dayton, June 18, 1903

The papers on screws [propellers], by various writers, do not seem to me of very much value. The chapter in the French book of André which is devoted to screws seems about as good as anything, but the final conclusion is that very little is known of the action of screws in motion forward. The action of screws not moving forward presents a very different case, and experiments based on such conditions are not applicable to the conditions met in practical flying. . . . Some of the writers see that running forward introduces new conditions but they do not seem to have any very definite ideas as to the amount and nature of the differences. We think we have a method of figuring a screw in action but of course it is all mere theory as yet. We will know more about its correctness when we have had a chance to try it.

. . . .

At Kitty Hawk, when Spratt was the Wrights' guest, they had many arguments and discussions about technical questions, and some of these arguments were continued in letters.

Orville Wright to George A. Spratt

Dayton, June 28, 1903

Your letter of the 12th was received some days ago, and has been read over a number of times by Wilbur and myself. Your speaking of knocking the props out from under us and allowing us to come up to your way of thinking reminds me of a new flying machine which Mr. Chanute saw in Europe. It was built to run along on some long legs or stilts until it has attained a pretty good speed, when it kicks its own legs out from under itself and allows itself to rise. However, I guess our props are stuck pretty well down into the mud, for we do not feel them giving under us much.

We made up several styles of ribs before adopting our present method of making them, but found nothing more satisfactory than the one I described to you. Those with holes bored in them, like you mentioned, we found to be heavier for the same strength. We wrap the ribs at all places where blocks are put in with glued paper, which adds greatly to the strength. Since putting in heavier springs to actuate the valves on our engine we have increased its power to nearly 16 horsepower, and at the same time reduced the amount of gasoline consumed per hour to about one half of what it was before.

You were inquiring, some time ago, about Langley's *Experiments in Aerodynamics*. We do not think it would pay you to buy this. In fact, we place very little confidence in the work. Lilienthal's *Der Vogelflug*, Chanute's *Progress in Flying Machines*, and the *Aeronautical Annuals* of 1896 and 1897 contain most of what has been published that is of much value. . . .

We cannot tell with any certainty yet as to when we will be ready to go to Kitty Hawk, but we are hoping to be off about the middle of August. The motor greatly complicates the difficulties of building. We find it no easy matter to convey 16 horsepower from the motor to the two propellers. A French army officer [Captain Ferber] has been very anxious to visit us at Kitty Hawk this year, but knowing that we will have much more work this year than heretofore, we do not feel that we ought to try any new visitors. We are collecting a whole lot of material for argument in camp, and hope to give you a good time when you meet us there.

. . . .

Wilbur Wright to Octave Chanute

Dayton, July 2, 1903

What you have written to Captain Ferber will probably be a sufficient hint that for the present we would prefer to carry on our experiments undisturbed.

The method we employ in securing lateral equilibrium is of a somewhat complex nature, and unless a very minute description of the structure and theory of operation is given, there is danger to novices in attempting to use it. Both Orville and myself had trouble in our early experiments last year and it is our belief that beginners will be much safer

on a machine without tail, and with the lateral balance secured by slightly shifting weight just as in our 1900 and 1901
machines. It is not our wish that any description of this feature of our machine be given at present.* Beginners should
be cautioned to use machines of less than 20-foot spread
from tip to tip, and to learn the longitudinal control thoroughly before attempting to use large machines and complex
methods of operation. One thing at a time is the safe
rule. . . .

Professor Langley seems to be having rather more than
his fair share of trouble just now with pestiferous reporters
and wind storms. But as the mosquitoes are reported to be
very bad along the banks where the reporters are encamped
he has some consolation. It would be interesting to attempt
a computation of the possible performance of his machine
in advance of its trial, but the data of the machine as given
in the newspapers are so evidently erroneous that it seems
hopeless to attempt it. It is a sure thing that the speed will
not be from 60 to 90 miles an hour with an expenditure of
25 horsepower as the papers have reported its prospective
flight. I presume that you are to be one of the guests of honor
at the launching festivities. Our invitation has not yet
arrived.

.   .   .   .

---

* Chanute had submitted for comment something he had written.

Wilbur Wright to Octave Chanute

Dayton, July 24, 1903

Your special delivery letter of 23rd inst. is at hand and I hasten to reply.

The vertical tail is operated by wires leading to the wires which connect with the wing tips. Thus the movement of the wing tips operates the rudder. This statement is not for publication, but merely to correct the misapprehension in your own mind. As the laws of France and Germany provide that patents will be held invalid if the matter claimed has been publicly printed we prefer to exercise reasonable caution about the details of our machine until the question of patents is settled. I only see three methods of dealing with this matter: (1) Tell the truth. (2) Tell nothing specific. (3) Tell something not true. I really cannot advise either the first or the third course.

. . . .

Wilbur Wright to Octave Chanute

Dayton, August 2, 1903

Your letters of 27th, 28th ult. are at hand. We thank you for striking out of your "Revue" article the sentence relating to steering. You have, however, entirely mistaken the ground of our objection to it. The trouble was not that it gave away our secrets, but that it attributed to us ancient methods which we do not use. We could not propose a substitute without going into matters we think it safest to keep out of print

for the present. But for the fact that the article was submitted to us in advance of publication and might therefore
be considered as approved by us, I should not have considered it necessary to mention any of the matters which I
called attention to.

Captain Ferber need have no fears that we are offended
at his patriotism. If we had facilities for entertaining him,
and nothing but gliding on the program, and four months
instead of less than two in our season, he would have been
very welcome.

.   .   .   .

Wilbur Wright to Octave Chanute

Dayton, Ohio, September 19, 1903

I had a very nice letter from Captain Ferber a few weeks
ago, just as he was about to start for the sand hills I presume.
The troubles described with vivid illustrations in his letter
to you are evidently due chiefly to *too great depth of curvature* and the fact that the surfaces are not sufficiently held
to shape by ribs. There is also a possibility that his front
rudder may not be arranged to act with sufficient quickness
and exactness. We never had such extreme instability as he
describes, but my first address gave some account of our
troubles with a surface of too great curvature and the means
we used to correct it.

We were glad to learn that Mr. Alexander* is thinking

---

* Patrick Y. Alexander was a member of the Aeronautical Society of
Great Britain. He was one of the first in England to become interested
in what the Wrights were doing.

of visiting this country again. Orville and I had made a firm resolve that Dr. Spratt and yourself should be the only visitors in camp this year up to the moment of actual trial. We have so much to do, and so little time to do it in. However, if Mr. Alexander's trip should occur at a time that would make it at all practicable to invite him to camp we shall certainly do so, as we were much pleased with him so far as his brief visit last year enabled us to make his acquaintance. We both liked him very much. We will consider the matter further when we see how things progress in camp.

We thank you for your offer of the loan of your camp tableware but think that with the additions we are ourselves sending this year we will have all we need.

. . . .

Not until September 23 were the Wrights ready to set out for Kitty Hawk. They made good connections with a boat and arrived at camp two days later. A storm had blown their shed from its foundation posts. They repaired it and also built a new one. With two sheds they had room for housing both the 1902 glider and the power machine.

It took three weeks to assemble the new machine. From time to time they also took out the 1902 glider for practice. After a few trials each brother was able to make a new world's record by gliding for more than a minute.

IV

POWER FLIGHT

Orville Wright to his sister

Kitty Hawk, N. C., October 4, 1903

These two days of gliding have made us much more expert in handling the machine, and on the next day we have 18 to 20 miles of wind we expect to go up and stay up for at least several minutes. . . .

We haven't had but one newspaper since we came down here, so you see we are living in blissful ignorance. . . .

I bought this paper and envelopes in Norfolk as we came down. The young lady in the store recognized me at once as of the aristocracy, and so palmed off these envelopes without gum. As I will have to spend the next half hour heating up some tire cement to seal it I will have to close now.

. . . .

Wilbur Wright to his father

Kitty Hawk, October 4, 1903

We have increased our time for length of flight [with glider] to 43 seconds, which is 1% over last year's record

103

and about three times the best of any one else. We will soon have it up to more than a minute as we are now able to remain practically stationary when a suitable wind blows up a good slope. This is something former experimenters were entirely unable to accomplish. . . .

. . . .

Wilbur Wright to Octave Chanute

Kitty Hawk, October 16, 1903

We regret to learn that there is danger of your being unable to visit our camp this year. We are expecting the most interesting results of any of our seasons of experiments, and are sure that, barring exasperating little accidents or some mishap, we will have done something before we break camp. . . .

I see that Langley has had his fling,* and failed. It seems to be our turn to throw now, and I wonder what our luck will be.

. . . .

No one was more keenly interested in what the Wrights were doing than their chief mechanic, Charles Taylor, at their bicycle shop in Dayton. He had given them enthusiastic help in building their engine.

---

* October 8, 1903.

Orville Wright to Charles Taylor

Kitty Hawk, N. C., October 20, 1903

Flying machine market has been very unsteady the past two days. Opened yesterday morning at about 208 (100% means even chances of success) but by noon had dropped to 110. These fluctuations would have produced a panic, I think in Wall Street, but in this quiet place it only put us to thinking and figuring a little. It gradually improved during rest of yesterday and today and is now almost back to its old mark.

.   .   .   .

Orville Wright to his sister

Kitty Hawk, November 1, 1903

About a week ago the weather turned very cold (about zero according to my backbone) and another rain set in which continued for several days without intermittence. We found that a fire was absolutely necessary, especially on account of Spratt, who suffers much from cold. We took one of the carbide cans and, after punching some holes in the bottom for air, built a fire in it inside the building. Of course the smoke was so intense that there was no standing up in the room, so we sat down on the floor about the can with tears streaming down our cheeks enjoying its kindly rays of heat. Everything about the building was sooted up so thoroughly that for several days we couldn't sit down to eat without a whole lot of black soot dropping down in our plates. We decided a change was necessary, so we got a little stove pipe and built a stove out of the can, adding strap iron legs to it, and a number of patent dampers, so that now we have about as good control in our stove as we have on our machine. We are now living in luxurious ease.

Your asking that we telegraph after every storm would soon have us "busted" if complied with. We have been having an almost continuous succession of storms the past few weeks. . . .

I suppose you have read in the papers the account of the failure of Langley's big machine. He started from a point 60 feet in the air and landed 300 feet away, which is a drop of 1 foot for every 5 forward. We are able, from this same height, to make from 400 to 600 feet without any motor at all, so that I think his surfaces must be very inefficient. They found they had no control of the machine whatever, though the wind blew but 5 miles an hour at the time of the test. That is the point where we have a great advantage. We have been in the air hundreds and hundreds of times, and have pretty well worked out the problem of control. We find it much more difficult to manage the machine when trying to soar in one spot than when traveling rapidly forward. We expect no trouble from our big machine at all in this respect. Of course we are going to thoroughly test the control of it on the hills before attaching the motor. We are highly pleased with our progress so far this year. . . .

I have been putting in about an hour every night down here in studying German and am getting along pretty well.

.   .   .   .

It was hoped to have the power machine ready for its first trial early in November. But at the first run of the motor on the completed machine, an unexpected strain from backfiring twisted one of the propeller shafts and tore loose the cross-arm to which the propeller was fastened. Both shafts were then sent back to the bicycle shop in Dayton to be made stronger. Dr. Spratt started home on November 5, taking with him as far as Norfolk the shafts for shipment to Dayton.

Orville Wright to his father and sister

Kitty Hawk, November 15, 1903

We are now alone again. The first time for about a month. . . .

Mr. Chanute says that no one before has ever tried to build a machine on such close margins as we have done to our calculations. He said that he nevertheless had more hope of our machine going than any of the others. He seems to think we are pursued by a blind fate from which we are unable to escape. He has been trying to purchase the Ader machine built by the French government at an expense of $100,000, which he was intending to have us fix up and *run* for him. He thinks we could do it! He doesn't seem to think our machines are so much superior as the manner in which we handle them. We are of just the reverse opinion.

.   .   .   .

Orville Wright to his sister

Kitty Hawk, N. C., November 16, 1903

Please get the check enclosed cashed in $5 bills and regis-
ter to us at once.* We will have to have it before we can get
home. . . . It will be next week before we are ready for
a trial. Stock in Flying Machine sells one day at 175 and the
next at about 17. Last night it got down to 3 but before bed
time had gone up again to about par, where it now stands.

.   .   .   .

Orville Wright to his father and sister

Kitty Hawk, November 19, 1903

Mr. Chanute brought several pictures of the Langley machine which have furnished us matter for a good deal of
speculation. It would appear from what Mr. Chanute learned
in Washington that the machine weighed 750 pounds and
had a 50-horsepower engine. The weight is about the same
as ours but the power—four times as much. . . .

Judging from present prospects, it is probable that we will
not be home before the first of next month. Of course we can
not tell what is going to happen when we try the engine and
screws again, but if the propeller shafts stand up, I think the
rest will. If we should succeed in making a flight, and telegraph, we will expect Lorin as our press agent(!) to notify
the papers and the Associated Press. Chanute was much

---

* No one at Kitty Hawk kept enough money on hand to cash checks
of any sizable amount.

surprised that none of the reporters had learned of our experiments. Langley told him that they nearly worried him to death. Will thought that our best chance of doing the bird act would be to get home before Thanksgiving, but that now seems hopeless, so we will try it here.

. . . .

Wilbur Wright to his family

Kitty Hawk, November 23, 1903

Our track for starting the machine (total cost about $4) amused Mr. Chanute considerably, as Langley is said to have spent nearly $50,000 on his starting device, which failed in the end to give a proper start he claims. At least this is the reason he gives for the failure last month. We have only tried ours with the little machine, so far, but it seems to work well.

. . . .

The shafts, made of larger and heavier tubing, arrived from Dayton on November 20. Then a new difficulty appeared. The sprockets kept coming loose.

Orville Wright to Charles Taylor

Kitty Hawk, November 23, 1903

We thought that when we could get both propellers on, the shock would be divided between the two, but on the con-

trary we found the shock greatly increased on each. The jerk-
ing of the propellers back and forth would loosen up the
sprockets in spite of all the tightening we could do. . . .

We used a chain and a 6-foot 2 x 4 to tighten them and
the nuts, but 10 seconds more run and they were loose again.
We kept that up all Friday afternoon. . . . The next morning, thanks to Arnstein's hard cement, which will fix anything from a stop watch to a thrashing machine, we stuck
those sprockets so tight I doubt whether they will ever come
loose again. . . . When Mr. Chanute was here* he said that
from 25 to 30 per cent should be allowed for loss from transmission. As we had allowed but 10 to 15 per cent, we saw
that the gears we have would not allow us to speed the
engine up enough to get the thrust. However, the loss of
transmission is not as much as we had calculated, or the
power of the engine is more, for the propellers speeded up
more than we had ever hoped for (standing still) but gave
exactly the thrust we had calculated that it should give at
this speed. We will not be ready for trial for several days yet
on account of having decided on some changes in the machine. Unless something breaks in the meantime we feel
confident of success.

.   .   .   .

Wilbur Wright to George A. Spratt

Kill Devil Hills, December 2, 1903

Your letter received some days ago but answer was delayed in hope that we could report the result of our experi-
_____
* Because of the cold weather Chanute stayed less than a week.

ment. The result so far is that one of the shafts twisted off in the middle, and Orville has gone home to make new ones, leaving me to keep house alone. However, before it gave way we succeeded in getting a measurement of the thrust and found it 132 lbs. This indicated that we will have ample propulsion, as we expect the resistance of the machine to be only about 95 lbs.

Mr. Chanute had been gone nearly two weeks before your letter reached us, so of course, we could not communicate your message. He was with us just a week but the weather was so bad that we did little but sit round the stove and talk. We have not tried to glide the big machine yet, and probably shall not this year, as favorable days are very scarce now. We hung it on its wing tips some days ago and loaded the front set of trussing to more than six times its regular strain in the air. We also hung it by the tips and run the engine and screws, with the man also on board. The strength of the machine seems "o.k."

We have mounted the anemometer and stop watch on the machine and put a counter on the engine, all operating together. So we expect to get the distance through the air, the speed, the power consumed, and the number of turns of the screws.

Your experience with the little piece of pine from the scrap heap is not at all strange, as that "sappy cheap pine" is the very best there is. Pine is as strong as spruce but not so resilient, it will not bend as far without breaking, consequently will not absorb shocks as well.

. . . .

During a test of the engine on November 28 they discovered that one of the recently strengthened tubular shafts had developed a flaw and cracked.

With winter almost upon them, there was no time to trust to express service in getting the shafts to Dayton. Orville decided he would go there at once. Instead of tubular shafts, they would use solid tool steel, necessary, it seemed, to take up the shock of premature or missed explosions of the engine.

Soon after he reached home, Orville, standing on the front porch, saw Carrie come into the yard with a bag of groceries. "Carrie," he said, as she recalled, "you feed me too much. I'll get too heavy to fly."

He was joking. There was plenty of margin for extra weight in the calculations for the untried machine.

Not until Friday, December 11, did Orville get back to camp. (En route he had read in a newspaper of the last unsuccessful attempt to fly the Langley machine over the Potomac at Washington on December 8.)

On his return to camp Orville added the expense of his railroad journey to other items of cost of the power plane. The total was still under $1,000.

Wilbur Wright to his family

Kitty Hawk, December 14, 1903

We gave machine first trial today with only partial success. The wind was only about 5 miles an hour, so we anticipated difficulty in getting speed enough on our short track (60 ft.)

to lift. We took to the hill and after tossing for first whack, which I won, got ready for the start. The wind was a little to one side and the track was not exactly straight down hill, which caused the start to be more difficult than it would otherwise have been. However, the real trouble was an error in judgment in turning up too suddenly after leaving the track, and as the machine had barely speed enough for support already, this slowed it down so much that before I could correct the error, the machine began to come down, though turned up at a big angle.

Toward the end it began to speed up again but it was too late, and it struck the ground while moving a little to one side, due to wind and a rather bad start. A few sticks in the front rudder were broken, which will take a day or two to repair probably. It was a nice easy landing for the operator. The machinery all worked in entirely satisfactory manner, and seems reliable. The power is ample, and but for a trifling error due to lack of experience with this machine and this method of starting, the machine would undoubtedly have flown beautifully.

There is now no question of final success. The strength of the machine is all right, the trouble in the front rudder being easily remedied. We anticipate no further trouble in landings. Will probably have made another trial before you receive this unless weather is unfavorable.

. . . .

On December 15, the day after the first try of the power machine, a little short of success, Orville Wright sent a telegram to his father:

"Misjudgment at start reduced flight to hundred and twelve. Power and control ample. Rudder only injured. Success assured. Keep quiet."

From Orville Wright's Diary

Thursday, December 17, 1903

When we got up, a wind of between 20 and 25 miles was blowing from the north. We got the machine out early and put out the signal for the men at the station. Before we were quite ready, John T. Daniels, W. S. Dough, A. D. Etheridge, W. C. Brinkley of Manteo, and Johnny Moore of Nag's Head arrived. After running the engine and propellers a few minutes to get them in working order, I got on the machine at 10.35 for the first trial. The wind according to our anemometer at this time was blowing a little over 20 miles (corrected) 27 miles according to the Government anemometer at Kitty Hawk. On slipping the rope the machine started off increasing in speed to probably 7 or 8 miles. The machine lifted from the truck just as it was entering on the fourth rail. Mr. Daniels took a picture just as it left the trucks.*

I found the control of the front rudder quite difficult on account of its being balanced too near the center and thus had a tendency to turn itself when started so that the rudder was turned too far on one side and then too far on the other.

---

* The "trucks," or truck, on which the sledlike skids of the machine rested, consisted of a plank about six feet long laid across a smaller piece of wood to which were attached two small wheels, one in front of the other. These were modified hubs from the wheels of a bicycle. The rail itself was two by four inches, set on edge, the upper surface covered by a thin strip of metal.

As a result the machine would rise suddenly to about 10 feet and then as suddenly, on turning the rudder, dart for the ground. A sudden dart when out about 100 feet from the end of the track ended the flight. Time about 12 seconds (not known exactly as watch was not promptly stopped). The flight lever for throwing off the engine was broken, and the skid under the rudder cracked.

After repairs, at 20 minutes after 11 o'clock Will made the second trial. The course was about like mine, up and down but a little longer . . . over the ground though about the same in time. Distance not measured but about 175 feet. Wind speed not quite so strong.

With the aid of the station men present, we picked the machine up and carried it back to the starting ways. At about 20 minutes till 12 o'clock I made the third trial. When out about the same distance as Will's, I met with a strong gust from the left which raised the left wing and sidled the machine off to the right in a lively manner. I immediately turned the rudder to bring the machine down and then worked the end control. Much to our surprise, on reaching the ground the left wing struck first, showing the lateral control of this machine much more effective than on any of our former ones. At the time of its sidling it had raised to a height of probably 12 to 14 feet.

At just 12 o'clock Will started on the fourth and last trip. The machine started off with its ups and downs as it had before, but by the time he had gone three or four hundred feet he had it under much better control, and was traveling on a fairly even course. It proceeded in this manner till it reached a small hummock out about 800 feet from the starting ways, when it began its pitching again and suddenly darted into the ground. The front rudder frame was badly broken up, but the main frame suffered none at all. The distance over the ground was 852 feet in 59 seconds. The engine turns was 1071, but this included several seconds while on the starting ways and probably about a half second after landing. The jar of landing had set the watch on the machine back, so that we have no exact record for the 1071 turns. Will took a picture of my third flight just before the gust struck the machine. The machine left the ways successfully at every trial, and the track was never caught by the truck as we had feared.

After removing the front rudder, we carried the machine back to camp. We set the machine down a few feet west of the building, and while standing about discussing the last flight, a sudden gust of wind struck the machine and started to turn it over. All rushed to stop it. Will, who was near the end, ran to the front, but too late to do any good. Mr. Daniels and myself seized spars at the rear, but to no purpose. The machine gradually turned over on us.

Mr. Daniels, having had no experience in handling a machine of this kind, hung on to it from the inside, and as a result he was knocked down and turned over and over with it as it went. His escape was miraculous, as he was in with the engine and chains. The engine legs were all broken off, the chain guides badly bent, a number of uprights, and nearly all the rear ends of the ribs were broken. One spar only was broken.

.   .   .   .

When Orville put his camera on a tripod for Mr. Daniels to take a picture of the first flight, he had it aimed at a point short of the end of the sixty-foot starting rail. He said to

Daniels something like this: "When I turn the wings to a flying angle I'll leave the track and should be about two feet off the ground when directly in front of the camera. That's the time to press the button." The picture turned out perfectly balanced, exactly as Orville had hoped.

Except for the accident to the plane after the four flights were over, the brothers would have tried after lunch to fly to the Kitty Hawk weather station four miles way. Their gasoline tank, made by a tinner in Dayton, was only a foot long by three inches in diameter and contained about half a gallon. Since the machine with operator weighed only about 750 pounds, one filling of the tank would have lasted, they estimated, eighteen minutes and taken them at least nine or ten miles.

A surprising thing was that despite the historic importance of the demonstrations that man could fly, there was no trace of excitement at the scene of the flights, least of all by the Wrights themselves. They had done only what they had been fully expecting to do; and the others present did not then realize what an event they had witnessed.

Another astonishing thing about those first flights was that Wilbur and Orville each wore a stiff, white starched collar and a necktie! * Indeed, they *always* wore white starched

---

* A few years afterward when most air pilots wore Abercrombie & Fitch kind of costumes, with special goggled helmets, the Wrights continued to fly in ordinary business suits. Turning his cap around with the visor at the back of his neck, and sometimes on a cold day with his coat collar up, was as far as Orville departed from his usual dress. Pictures at the air field in France show Wilbur in a leather jacket, but that was only because the weather had turned cold. He still wore his stiff white collar. The Wrights dressed as most men did at the time. Special clothes would have been contrary to their habit of avoiding nonessentials.

collars, whether in their bicycle shop or at Kitty Hawk. The natives there used to say they must be men of means, they were so well dressed. Neither was ever known to wear a sweater or flannel shirt. Whenever they went to Kitty Hawk they took enough clean collars to last them all the time they were there.

The telegram to their father, written by Orville, said: "Success four flights Thursday morning all against twenty-one-mile wind started from level with engine power alone average speed through air thirty-one miles longest 59 seconds inform press home Christmas."

Carrie Grumbach remembered vividly, forty-five years after the event, what happened when the message was received at 7 Hawthorne Street. As it was late afternoon, already growing dark, she had lighted the gas in the kitchen and was starting to get supper. The doorbell rang and it was a messenger with a telegram for the Bishop. Carrie signed for it and took it upstairs to him. In a little while he came down and said to Carrie, "Well, they've made a flight." He was always calm and showed no excitement, but he looked pleased. Just then Miss Katharine came home, Carrie remembered, and when she saw the telegram she asked Carrie to delay supper while she took the telegram to her brother Lorin. (Soon afterward Lorin took the message to the office of the Dayton *Journal* and showed it to the city editor, Frank Tunison, who also represented the Associated Press, but he didn't think a flight of less than a minute worth a news item and seemed annoyed over being bothered about such nonsense. No reference to the flight appeared in the *Journal* the next morning. See letter of Orville Wright January 22, 1937.)

At the supper table, Carrie said, the Bishop and Miss Katharine were in high spirits, not because of the historic importance of the first official announcement that man could fly, but because now the boys would be home for Christmas. That meant that Mr. Wilbur would be on hand to stuff the Christmas turkey.

Stuffing the turkey had always been Wilbur's privilege, and the way he did it was something special. He made a ceremony of it, with all the ingredients arranged before him just so, and solemnly he'd rub his hands as if about to perform a piece of magic.

From Orville Wright's Diary

December 18, 1903

Commenced tearing down machine ready for packing.

December 19, 1903

Completed packing machine and tools. About noon Capt. Jesse Ward brought telegrams from Norfolk correspondent of N. Y. *World* asking price for exclusive rights to pictures and story, and one from Editor *Woman's Home Companion,* wanting pictures. Later in the day Mr. Daniels brought over another batch, N. Y. *World* wanted a 600 word account telegraphed to them. *Scientific American* wanted pictures, *Century Magazine* wants exclusive account and pictures, Chanute and A. A. Merrill, of Boston, sent congratulations.

.   .   .   .

Two days were needed at Kitty Hawk for crating the machine to ship home and the brothers arrived the evening of December 23. Carrie had taken pains to have a good meal ready, and she assured them as they sat down that there was "more of everything in the kitchen." But she had not accurately estimated what a craving Orville would have for fresh milk after weeks without any at Kitty Hawk. When she went to refill his glass for the sixth or seventh time there was not quite enough milk left, so she added just a little water, so little, she thought that surely no one could know. Instantly, though, Orville shouted a bitter protest. He felt grieved, he said, that Carrie would try to cheat him by "dairying" the milk supply. To the end of his life, he never let Carrie forget that episode of the milk at the first home meal after the first flight.

Wilbur Wright to Carl Dienstbach

December 28, 1903

Only those who have had actual experience in the air can appreciate the fact that the first trials of our successful machine were made in the midst of a gusty wintry gale.

.   .   .   .

Dienstbach, a musician living in New York and American correspondent for an aeronautical magazine in Berlin, had written on December 19, after seeing a brief report in the New York *Evening Telegram*, for particulars about the machine; his letter had been acknowledged the day before the brothers returned to Dayton by their father, who in a postscript commented: "About equal credit is due each."

Wilbur Wright to Octave Chanute

Kitty Hawk, December 28, 1903

Our next flights were on Thursday, December 17, on which occasion the flights were all made from a level spot about 200 feet west of our buildings. The conditions were very unfavorable as we had a cold gusty north wind blowing almost a gale. Nevertheless, as we had set our minds on being home by Christmas, we determined to go ahead. . . . The "Junction Railroad" worked perfectly and a good start was obtained every time. The machine would run along the track about 40 feet propelled by the screws alone, as we did not feel it safe to have strangers touch the machine. It would then rise and fly directly against the wind at a speed of about 10 miles an hour. The first flight was of about 12 second's duration and the last 59 seconds. The controlling mechanisms operated more powerfully than in our old machine, so that we nearly always turned the rudders more than was really necessary and thus kept up a somewhat undulating course, especially in the first flights. Under the prevailing conditions we did not feel it safe to rise far from the ground and this was the cause of our flights being no longer than they were, for we did not have sufficient room to maneuver in such a gusty gale. Consequently we were frequently on the point of touching the ground and once scratched it deeply but rose again and continued the flight. Those who understand the real significance of the conditions under which we worked will be surprised rather at the length than the short-

ness of the flights made with an unfamiliar machine after less
than one minute's practice. The machine possesses greater
capacity of being controlled than any of our former machines.

One of the most gratifying features of the trials was the
fact that all our calculations were shown to have worked out
with absolute exactness so far as we can see, though we have
not yet made our final computations on the performance
of the machine.

. . . .

Godfrey Cabot and his brother Samuel, businessmen in
Boston, were among the first to sense the importance of
what the Wrights had done. See Godfrey Cabot's letter,
footnote, on page 178.

Godfrey Lowell Cabot to Senator Henry Cabot Lodge

Boston, Mass., December 31, 1903

You will doubtless have noticed in the papers an account
of a successful trial of a flying machine made Dec. 17 in
North Carolina by Wilbur and Orville Wright of the Wright
Cycle Co., Dayton, Ohio.

In answer to an inquiry of mine, I have a letter from these
gentlemen to the effect that they made four successful trials
on that date, starting their machine with its own power and
that it showed a sustaining capacity of over 100 lbs., in excess
of the weight of the operator and motor.

It seems to me that this may fairly be said to mark the
beginning of successful flight through the air by men un-

aided by balloons. It has occurred to me that it would be eminently desirable for the United States Government to interest itself in this invention. . . .

.   .   .   .

Senator Lodge sent the Cabot letter to the War Department, which paid no attention to the suggestion.

Entries in Bishop Wright's Diary for 1903

December 31—The past year was full of stirring events. I was serene and happy through it all, though grieved at the folly of many, and the wickedness of not a few. I believed that God would at last vindicate the right.

.   .   .   .   .   .

Many have wondered which of the brothers made the greater contribution to the invention of the airplane. Their work cannot be separated. Neither one could or would have solved the problem alone. Each enjoyed the tremendous advantage of having someone to combat his theories and detect flaws or snags, which accounts for the astonishing fact that they were able to fly a power machine within a little more than three years from the time they started their gliding experiments.

Orville seems to have had a little the edge on Wilbur in the importance of suggestions offered: he was the first to think of the basic principle of presenting the right and left wings at different angles to the wind for lateral balance; and it was he who figured out the part of the rear rudder as a balancing device. But no matter what either one did, the other seemed sure to take the next needed step. It was almost as if they were deliberately taking turns. After Orville had conceived the idea of manipulating the right and left wings at different angles, Wilbur was the one who hit on a simple way to do it in the experimental stage, by warping the wings. When Orville explained the need for a movable instead of a fixed rear rudder, Wilbur saw that the rudder wings could be operated simultaneously. Orville made the original drawings for their engine, and Wilbur added improvements.

The record indicates that Wilbur at the beginning had more hope of flying than Orville did. It was Wilbur who first suggested that they go to a place with adequate winds to try out their theories. But Orville was the one with the stronger faith in what might be expected from their 1902 glider, built with knowledge gained from the wind-tunnel experiments. When Orville made the first successful flight, he doubtless profited from Wilbur's experience in the attempt three days earlier. In the other three flights that first day, in which the brothers took turns, each was a little longer, a little better, than the previous one.

It may be added that the brothers' habit of supplementing each other, of one making a move and the other taking the next step, showed up frequently in everyday affairs. One day when Orville returned from a trip east, he brought Carrie, their housekeeper, a handsome pocketbook. In a little while Wilbur went to the kitchen and asked Carrie to show her present to him. He examined it critically, finally opened it and then remarked, "That's no kind of a pocketbook to give anybody. It has no money in it." Then he put into it a five-dollar bill, closed it, handed it back to Carrie and quickly walked away.

V

WHAT NEXT WITH A FLYING MACHINE

Orville Wright to George A. Spratt

Dayton, January 7, 1904

Your letter congratulating us on our success was awaiting us on our return from Kitty Hawk, and we had expected to write thanking you long before this, but have delayed writing till we could write more fully the particulars of our trials. We are receiving letters of congratulation from people, many of whom we do not know personally, but none please us so much as those from friends who are acquainted with our work and take a personal interest in it. . . .

That we had quite a surplus of power was shown by the fact that on leaving the rail we could rise 8 or 10 feet in going forward about 50 feet. Of course this really amounted to about 150 feet through the air. Our engine ran at 1030 revolutions to the minute, which is not much, if any, more than three fourths of its maximum power. Our machine complete weighed a few pounds over 600 pounds, which with the weight of the operator made the total weight a little over 745 pounds. The lengths of our flights were limited only by our lack of acquaintance with this particular machine. The front rudder was so much more effective than those on our

former machines that we always turned it too far. As a result
the first flights were composed of a series of undulations as
were our first flights on our gliders. We were greatly pleased
with the performance of the machine.

Since our return we have been receiving daily offers of
stocking our company for us from some of these professional
promoters, who would like to get the chance to swindle some
of the people who think there is an immense fortune in the
flying machine. Even our friend Herring has made us a very
generous offer, a copy of which I am making for your amusement.

.   .   .   .

A. M. Herring had discovered that he had invented an
airplane some time previously and wanted to join forces with
the Wrights, taking a one third interest!

Wilbur Wright to Octave Chanute

Dayton, January 8, 1904

A copy is also enclosed of a letter received a few days ago
from Mr. Herring. This time he surprised us. Before he left
camp in 1902 we foresaw and predicted the object of his visit
to Washington; we also felt certain that he was making a
frenzied attempt to mount a motor on a copy of our 1902
glider and thus anticipate us, even before you told us of it
last fall. But that he would have the effrontery to write us
such a letter, after his other schemes of rascality had failed,

was really a little more than we expected. We shall make no answer at all.

. . . .

Chanute replied that he was "amazed at the impudence of Mr. Herring."

Wilbur Wright to the Editor of the Independent

Dayton, February 5, 1904

My attention has this day been called to a case of most unmitigated impudence in the *Independent* of February 4. On page 242 an article was published under my name which I did not write and which I had never seen. The bulk of the article consisted of carelessly arranged or garbled extracts from two addresses, which I delivered before the Western Society of Engineers, and which were published in the *Journal* of that Society in the issues of December, 1901, and August, 1903. Following this came extracts from two press dispatches which appeared in the daily papers of December 19, 1903 and January 7, 1904. A few sentences from a strange source were interpolated, in which an attempt was made to describe the methods by which the power machine was sustained and propelled. This part was entirely fanciful and untrue. The pictures which accompanied the article were not obtained from us, nor were they from any of our photographs.

I have never given to any person permission or encouragement to palm off as an original article extracts from these copyrighted addresses and newspaper dispatches. Neither have I given to the *Independent*, nor to any one, the least permission or excuse for using my name in the furtherance of such attempted fraud. Nor have I given the faintest permission to attach my name to any article of any kind in any paper, excepting the statement which my brother and I gave to the papers on January 6, 1904. Our attention had previously been called to cases in which conscienceless but enterprising reporters had utilized these addresses as mines from which to draw material for pretended interviews, but it remained for the *Independent* to serve them in the form of a forged signed article.

. . . .

In 1904 the Wrights built a new machine and arranged for a practice field on the farm of Mr. Huffman, a Dayton bank president, at Simms station, eight miles from Dayton, on an electric car line. Toward the end of the 1904 experiments they made two five-minute flights. Their total flying time that year was only 45 minutes, but the added knowledge and experience gained were of great importance.

Wilbur Wright to Octave Chanute

Dayton, Ohio, June 21, 1904

You are quite right in thinking our Kitty Hawk grounds possess advantages not found at our present location, but we must learn to accommodate ourselves to circumstances.

At Kitty Hawk we had unlimited space and wind enough to make starting easy with a short track. If the wind was very light we could utilize the hills if necessary in getting the initial velocity. Here we must depend on a long track, and light winds or even dead calms. We are in a large meadow . . . skirted on the west and north by trees. This not only shuts off the wind somewhat but also probably gives a slight down trend. . . . The greater troubles are . . . that in addition to cattle there have been a dozen or more horses in the pasture and as it is surrounded by barb wire fencing we have been at much trouble to get them safely away before making trials. Also the ground is an old swamp and is filled with grassy hummocks some six inches high so that it resembles a prairie dog town. This makes the track laying slow work. While we are getting ready the favorable opportunities slip away, and we are usually up against a rain storm, a dead calm, or, a wind blowing at right angles to the track.

. . . .

Wilbur Wright to Octave Chanute

Dayton, Ohio, June 21, 1904

We have about concluded to enter the St. Louis contest but are reluctant to do this formally, until we are certain of being ready in time.

. . . .

Wilbur Wright to Octave Chanute

Dayton, Ohio, July 17, 1904

It is to be regretted that the prospect of a race at St. Louis is vanishing into thin air, yet it causes us no surprise. When I first studied the rules, I said they were not fair to the competitors. Orville said they were fair because the persons offering the prize had a right to set any conditions they pleased, and if they chose to put the expense on the competitors, while they themselves pocketed the gate receipts in any event, and probably never would have any prize money to pay, the competitors had no right to complain because they were under no obligation to compete unless they wished.

.   .   .   .

Wilbur Wright to Octave Chanute

Dayton, Ohio, October 5, 1904

I think I mentioned in a former letter that we had made two attempts to circumnavigate the field where our present experiments are being made, but that neither was successful. On the 20th of September we renewed the attempt and on the second trial succeeded. . . .

Up to the present we have been very fortunate in our relations with newspaper reporters, but intelligence of what we are doing is gradually spreading through the neighborhood and we are fearful that we will soon have to discontinue experiment. If your business will permit you to visit us this year it would be well to come within the next three weeks.

As we have decided to keep our experiments strictly secret for the present we are becoming uneasy about continuing them much longer at our present location. In fact it is a question whether we are not ready to begin considering what we will do with our baby now that we have it.

. . . .

I once asked Orville Wright what kind of offer for all rights to the airplane they might have accepted in 1904. After reflecting a moment he said he thought an offer of $10,000 might have been too tempting to refuse. The records indicate that total profits from their bicycle business had never exceeded $3,000 a year. From this they had managed to save a little. After paying for the costs of their experiments, Orville once said, they had between them about $5,000 deposited in Dayton building and loan associations, besides a small joint checking account. Twice as much as their life savings, if held before them, might indeed have looked interesting.

Octave Chanute to Wilbur Wright

December 28, 1904

I have now a curiosity to know what are your final conclusions as to the power actually required for artificial flight, and whether you hope to reduce it. I am under the impression that birds use less power than you have found necessary.

. . . .

Wilbur Wright to Octave Chanute

Dayton, Ohio, January 1, 1905

Your suggestion regarding the power expended by birds found us considering that very point, having been led to consider the subject by the very ingenious calculations of Sir George Cayley as published in the *Aeronautical Annual* for 1895. He attempts to compute the power expended by a crow in its flight, but the result obtained was too favorable in his opinion, and I am inclined to think the same though I have been unable to complete some calculations of a somewhat similar nature from lack of definite information regarding the tip to tip measurement of a crow. Do you possess any information on this point? It is my present impression that 75 lbs. to the horse power is about the limit of what a flying machine will be capable, at a speed of thirty miles an hour; 35 lbs. at seventy-five miles; and less than 20 lbs. at one hundred miles. I see no hope, based on any information at present accessible, for any considerable advance on what we have already done in the matter of dynamic efficiency. I think the great room for improvement will be found to be in mechanical details and methods, and especially in the skill of the operators. If it could be definitely proved that the birds do very much better, it would lead to a revision of our present views, and therefore we are intending to give bird flight careful study when opportunity can be found. If it can be proved that a crow raises and lowers the tip of its wings less than twenty-two or twenty-four inches, it evidently flies with less power than is yet possible with a gliding machine or flyer. For if it be estimated that the crow moves twelve feet with each wing stroke it would have to raise itself the equivalent of eighteen inches vertically in order to maintain horizontal flight, assuming the gliding angle to be one in eight.

. . . .

Believing that the time had come to reap whatever reward they could from their invention, the Wrights wanted to offer it first of all to their own government. Their first step in this direction was a letter to the representative in Congress from the Dayton district.

Wilbur and Orville Wright to Congressman Robert M. Nevin

January 18, 1905

The series of aeronautical experiments upon which we have been engaged for the past five years has ended in the production of a flying-machine of a type fitted for practical use. It not only flies through the air at high speed, but it also lands without being wrecked. During the year 1904 one hundred and five flights were made at our experimenting station, on the Huffman prairie, east of the city; and though our experience in handling the machine has been too short to give any high degree of skill, we nevertheless succeeded, toward the end of the season, in making two flights of five minutes each, in which we sailed round and round the field until a distance of about three miles had been covered, at a speed of thirty-five miles an hour. The first of these record flights was made on November 9th, in celebration of the

phenomenal political victory of the preceding day, and the
second, on December 1st, in honor of the one hundredth
flight of the season.

The numerous flights in straight lines, in circles, and over
"S"-shaped courses, in calms and in winds, have made it
quite certain that flying has been brought to a point where
it can be made of great practical use in various ways, one
of which is that of scouting and carrying messages in time
of war. If the latter features are of interest to our own government, we shall be pleased to take up the matter either on a
basis of providing machines of agreed specification, at a contract price, or of furnishing all the scientific and practical
information we have accumulated in these years of experimenting, together with a license to use our patents; thus
putting the government in a position to operate on its own
account.

If you can find it convenient to ascertain whether this is
a subject of interest to our own government, it would oblige
us greatly, as early information on this point will aid us in
making our plans for the future.

. . . .

*Reply to Congressman Nevin from the Board of Ordnance
and Fortification, signed by Major General G. L. Gillespie*

I have the honor to inform you that, as many requests have
been made for financial assistance in the development of
designs for flying-machines, *the Board has found it necessary
to decline to make allotments for the experimental development of devices for mechanical flight,* and has determined

that, before suggestions with that object in view will be considered, *the device must have been brought to the stage of practical operation* without expense to the United States.

It appears from the letter of Messrs. Wilbur and Orville Wright that their machine has not yet been brought to the stage of practical operation, but as soon as it shall have been perfected, this Board would be pleased to receive further representations from them in regard to it. [Italics supplied.]

. . . .

In seeking to interest the U. S. War Department, and later in their dealings with foreign governments, the Wrights sincerely believed that the airplane could play a major part in preventing war because it would enable each side to know what the other was doing and thus make it more difficult for either to gain an advantage.

Wilbur Wright to Octave Chanute

Dayton, Ohio, April 12, 1905

That the French experiments in gliding were not altogether satisfactory was inferred from a rather amusing letter which we received from Mr. Archdeacon a short time ago. I think they are inclined to doubt not only the reports concerning the power "Flyer" but also much that you told them concerning gliding experiments. They are evidently learning that the first steps in aviation are much more difficult than the beginnings of dirigible ballooning, and are skeptical of

what others are reported to have done in that line. It is not
surprising. They have much to learn.

.   .   .   .

Immediately after Chanute's talk before the Aéro Club
in Paris, on April 2, 1903, about the Wrights' gliding experiments, Ernest Archdeacon, prominent member of the Aéro
Club, led a movement to organize a special committee on
aviation. He made an appeal for glider contests to show that
the French did not intend to let anyone surpass them in that
branch of aeronautics; and he subscribed three thousand
francs for such contests and prizes.

Archdeacon was skeptical for a long time about reports
of the Wrights' power flights. One reason that he and others
in France did not believe the reports was that it was impossible to learn who was financing the Wrights. Surely, they
thought, these brothers could not have conquered the air
unless they had spent vast sums of money.

At first the French copyists were not content to follow
Chanute's revelations and build gliders just like that of the
Wrights. Instead they tried to add improvements. The "improvements" were not successful because the builders did
not have the Wrights' knowledge and wind-tunnel data,
except that used in the 1902 glider, to guide them.

Before long Archdeacon was joined by another member
of the Aéro Club, Henri Deutsch de la Meurthe, a wealthy
oil man, in offering aviation prizes and in trying to get someone to try to build a successful power plane. As the tempo
of interest increased the Wrights were kept fairly busy writing letters to France in reply to requests for information.

Wilbur Wright to George A. Spratt

Dayton, Ohio, April 12, 1905

We are getting materials ready for a new machine and expect to be able to carry two men. We are thinking of adding a vertical front rudder but in other respects it will be almost like the 1903 machine which you saw at Kitty Hawk.

We have not decided where we will experiment this year. Our place near Dayton is too small and too public; Kitty Hawk is too sandy and too far from machine shops. We have thought some of hunting a prairie location in the West.

. . . .

Wilbur Wright to Octave Chanute

April 20, 1905

Mr. Archdeacon will find more compliments than information in our answer to his letter, as we are more ready to congratulate him upon the interest in aviation he has succeeded in arousing in France, than to show our machines and methods at this time. However we give some encouragement that we may go after the Deutsch-Archdeacon prize when our other arrangements will permit. We ourselves do not know when or where we will resume flying experiments.

I return the French clippings &c. with our thanks. They have given us much amusement.

. . . .

Wilbur Wright to Octave Chanute

May 6, 1905

One of the reasons which actuated us in keeping secret the construction of our power flyer was to give the French ample time to finish and test any discoveries of the secrets of flying which any Frenchman might possess, and thus shut them off afterward from setting up a claim that every thing in our machine was already known in France. Perhaps it is lucky for us that Goupil* has placed himself on record in his great work published in 1904. By waiting we have permitted the French to show both by their writings and by their experiments how little was known of the art of flying in that country in 1904-05. I suspect that it will come out later that Goupil is now at Chalais feverishly engaged in an attempt to forestall the Americans. If so, we prefer that his machine should be tried before he has opportunity to study our machine.

The last sentence of Capt. Ferber's letter is a pretty broad hint that in France the Americans are not believed upon their mere word. We regard all such intimations with great amusement and satisfaction. They present the best possible proof of the low state of the art in France at this time, since even the gliding stories are considered too wonderful to be true. Capt. Ferber himself seems to be a very honorable man and his conduct has been above criticism. No doubt his own acceptance of the truth of the stories has exposed him to the laughter of skeptical friends. If he finds himself hard pressed,

---

* Alexandre Goupil was a student of aeronautics and had published drawings of a proposed machine. See letter of Orville Wright, page 459.

he is at liberty to say for us that a prize sufficient in magnitude to compensate for the disclosure of the secrets of flying would be snatched up before Christmas.

. . . .

Wilbur Wright to Octave Chanute

May 28, 1905

We stand ready to furnish a practical machine for use in war at once, that is, a machine capable of carrying two men and fuel for a fifty-mile trip. We are only waiting to complete arrangements with some government. The American government has apparently decided to permit foreign governments to take the lead in utilizing our invention for war purposes. We greatly regret this attitude of our own country, but seeing no way to remedy it, we have made a formal proposition to the British Government and expect to have a conference with one of its representatives, at Dayton, very soon.

. . . .

Octave Chanute to Wilbur Wright

May 30, 1905

As an American I greatly regret that our government has apparently decided to allow foreign governments to take the lead in utilizing your invention. Please advise me, 1st,

Whether you have approached our war office? &c 2nd, Whether you would object to my putting a flea in its ear?

.   .   .   .

Wilbur Wright to Octave Chanute

June 1, 1905

We would be ashamed of ourselves if we had offered our machine to a foreign government, without giving our own country a chance at it, but our consciences are clear. At the Christmas holidays we talked with Mr. Nevin, congressman from this district, and he proposed that we write him a letter containing a general statement of our business, and that he take it to Mr. Taft [Secretary of War] and secure an appointment for us to meet with the War Department officials, thus saving us delay when we should visit Washington. But owing to sickness he was compelled to turn over our letter without personally seeing Mr. Taft and shortly afterward received the letter from the Ordnance Department which I enclose. As we had made no request for an appropriation, but on the contrary had offered to furnish machine of "agreed specifications at a contract price," (which offer was entirely ignored,) we were driven to the conclusion that the letter of the War Department was intended as a flat turn down. We still think so.

A note to Col. Capper informing him that we were ready to talk business with the British government soon brought a response from the English war office requesting us to make a definite proposition. We submitted our proposition, and now have an answer stating that an officer will be sent to see us.

It is no pleasant thought to us that any foreign country should take from America any share of the glory of having conquered the flying problem, but we feel that we have done our full share toward making this an American invention, and if it is sent abroad for further development the responsibility does not rest upon us. We have taken pains to see that "Opportunity" gave a good clear knock on the War Department door. It has for years been our business practice to sell to those who wished to buy, instead of trying to force goods upon people who did not want them. If the American government has decided to spend no more money on flying machines till their practical use has been demonstrated in actual service abroad, we are sorry, but we can not reasonably object. They are the judges.

. . . .

Col. J. E. Capper of the Royal Aircraft Factory, a British government experimental laboratory dealing with aeronautics, had called upon the Wrights in October, 1904, and frankly told them that he was seeing them at the request of his government. Before leaving, he asked them to make his government some kind of proposal.

Octave Chanute to Wilbur Wright

June 6, 1905

My first feelings were of mortification and regret that the United States war department should have extended to you "a flat turn down," as you express it. Now that I have cooled down I see some advantages in your being forced to consider the overtures made by Col. Capper for the British Government, because: First, your invention is worth far more to the British than to the United States government. Second, the British are less hampered than we in appropriating secret service funds, so that you can probably get a better price, and sooner. Third, your invention will make more for peace in the hands of the British than in our own, for its existence will soon become known in a general way and the knowledge will deter embroilments.

.   .   .   .

Wilbur Wright to Octave Chanute

June 18, 1905

We have no intention of forgetting that we are Americans, and do not expect to make arrangements which would probably result in harm to our native country. The exact date of meeting the British representative is not fixed but will probably be within a month. Meanwhile we have decided to complete the machine and take the risk of making a few private trials of the improvements we have added to the machine. The machine will probably be complete in a couple of days and we will be testing it the latter part of the week if the weather is suitable. Of course we would be glad to have you to visit us and see it go, if it should suit your convenience and pleasure.

The doubts of Capt. Ferber and other foreigners worry us not at all. In fact they are rather an advantage to us while we are wishing to secure privacy. We certainly shall not disarrange our own plans to satisfy either public or private curiosity at this time.

We find that we underestimated the weight of our last year's machine. We carried a total weight of about 915 lbs. This includes the 70 lbs. of steel bars, which we used as ballast. The new machine with water and fuel for an hour's run will weigh almost exactly 850 lbs., with one man.

We quite approve your decision to make only brief reference to our power machine in the Standard Encyclopaedia article. Until we are really ready to make the machine public there are many reasons why it is not best to say too much for publication.

. . . .

Wilbur Wright to Octave Chanute

August 6, 1905

The tragic death of poor Maloney* seemed the more terrible to me because I knew it was coming and had tried in vain to think of some way to save him. I knew a direct warning would tend to precipitate rather than prevent a catastrophe. The Montgomery pamphlet showed an entire misapprehension of the real facts regarding the distribution of pressures and the travel of the center of pressure with increasing speed, and it seemed to me something awful that poor Maloney should cut loose high in the air and lightly cause the machine to dart and describe circles without know-

---

* Pilot of a gliding machine, designed by John J. Montgomery, that was dropped from a balloon.

ing that there were critical points beyond which it would be absolutely impossible for him to right the machine.

. . . .

Wilbur Wright to Octave Chanute

August 16, 1905

The incredulity of Capt. Ferber is very natural under the circumstances but we can not do much to relieve it, without entering into explanations covering matters we wish to avoid at present. Consequently we can only say that we do not wish to make any statement until we are ready to explain everything. We ourselves had a letter from Capt. Ferber some two months ago which is not yet answered. He wished to buy a machine of us. There are several matters yet to be decided before we make reply.

. . . .

Wilbur Wright to Octave Chanute

Dayton, Ohio, September 17, 1905

Prof. Langley's account of the trials of the large machine seems to be almost as much of a hard luck story as that he published in the *Aeronautical Annual* in regard to his 1896 model. It is strange that the matters which gave him the chief trouble have bothered us scarcely at all. Possibly our troubles would seem equally ridiculous to him. . . .

We have had no word from the British war office since the letter informing us that an officer had been instructed to visit us at Dayton; nor have we written to them. We are waiting for them to move.

Our experiments have been progressing quite satisfactorily, and we are rapidly acquiring skill in the new methods of operating the machine. We may soon attempt trips beyond the confines of the field.

.   .   .   .

Wilbur Wright to George A. Spratt

Dayton, Ohio, September 17, 1905

We have been continuing the experiments with the power machine. In seven trials last week we covered almost fifteen miles altogether. The longest was a little over three miles. We have been specially studying the problems of circling, or rather the problem of stopping the circling under certain peculiar conditions. When turning a very small circle with the outside wing much elevated it is hard to bring the inside wing up again, or stop turning, unless the machine is high enough in the air to allow the whole machine to be turned downward for a short time. As we have heretofore been flying at heights of not over thirty feet, and usually only ten to twenty feet, we frequently touch the lower wing to the ground before we can bring it up to the level.

We are both in good health, and trust that you have gotten over your bad habit of lying awake all night studying.

.   .   .   .

Prodded by Chanute, the Wrights risked further rebuff by again writing to the War Department, this time to the Secretary of War himself:

Dayton, October 9, 1905

Some months ago we made an informal offer to furnish to the War Department practical flying-machines suitable for scouting purposes. The matter was referred to the Board of Ordnance and Fortification, which seems to have given it scant consideration. We do not wish to take this invention abroad, unless we find it necessary to do so, and therefore write again, renewing the offer.

We are prepared to furnish a machine on contract, to be accepted only after trial trips in which the conditions of the contract have been fulfilled; the machine to carry an operator and supplies of fuel, etc., sufficient for a flight of one hundred miles; the price of the machine to be regulated according to a sliding scale based on the performance of the machine in the trial trips, the minimum performance to be a flight of at least twenty-five miles at a speed of not less than thirty miles an hour.

We are also willing to take contracts to build machines carrying more than one man.

. . . .

The reply to the foregoing letter to the Secretary of War came from the Board of Ordnance and Fortification, signed by Major General J. C. Bates, member of the General

Staff, who had become president of the Board since the previous correspondence. Under date of October 16, he wrote:

I have the honor to inform you that, as many requests have been made for financial assistance in the development of designs for flying-machines, the Board has found it necessary to decline to make allotments for the experimental development of devices for mechanical flight, and has determined that, before suggestions with that object in view will be considered, the device must have been brought to the stage of practical operation without expense to the United States.

Before the question of making a contract with you for the furnishing of a flying-machine is considered it will be necessary for you to furnish this Board with the approximate cost of the completed machine, the date upon which it would be delivered, and with such drawings and descriptions thereof as are necessary to enable its construction to be understood and a definite conclusion as to its practicability to be arrived at. Upon receipt of this information, the matter will receive the careful consideration of the Board.

. . . .

Once more the War Department had failed to note that the Wrights were not seeking any financial aid for their experiments, and that the machine had already been brought to the stage of practical operation.

Wilbur Wright to Octave Chanute

October 19, 1905

Some friends whom we unwisely permitted to witness some of the flights could not keep silent, and on the evening of the 5th the daily *News* had an article reporting that we were making sensational flights every day. It was copied in the Cincinnati *Post* of the next day. Consequently we are doing nothing at present, but before the season closes we wish to go out some day and make an effort to put the record above one hour. If you wish we will try to give you notice in time for you to be present.

. . . .

When the Wrights were secretive it was because they had come to believe that patents covering the basic features of their invention would not be enough protection against infringers. Indeed, having the technical details on file in the Patent Office, where anyone who desired might see them, was to the advantage of those who would help themselves to an inventor's work and ideas. Only a decision in the courts could determine the justice of an inventor's claims.

In spite of their feeling of annoyance over receiving replies that bore almost no relation to what they had written, the Wrights sent another letter to the Ordnance Board.

October 19, 1905

We have no thought of asking financial assistance from the government. We propose to sell the results of experiments finished at our own expense.

In order that we may submit a proposition conforming as nearly as possible to the ideas of your board, it is desirable that we be informed what conditions you would wish to lay down as to the performance of the machine in the official trials, prior to the acceptance of the machine. We cannot well fix a price, nor a time for delivery, till we have your idea of the qualifications necessary to such a machine. We ought also to know whether you would wish to reserve a monopoly on the use of the invention, or whether you would permit us to accept orders for similar machines from other governments, and give public exhibitions, etc.

Proof of our ability to execute an undertaking of the nature proposed will be furnished whenever desired.

. . . .

It might have been expected that by that time the Ordnance Board could sense that the Wrights were claiming to have produced a machine that could fly. But that idea still did not sink in. The reply, signed by Captain T. C. Dickson, Recorder of the Board, said:

The Board of Ordnance and Fortification at its meeting October 24, 1905, recorded its action as follows:

The Board then considered a letter, dated October 19,

1905, from Wilbur and Orville Wright requesting the requirements prescribed by the Board that a flying-machine would have to fulfill before it would be accepted.

It is recommended that the Messrs. Wright be informed that the Board does not care to formulate any requirements for the performance of a flying-machine or take any further action on the subject *until a machine is produced which by actual operation is shown to be able to produce horizontal flight and to carry an operator.* [Italics supplied.]

．　．　．　．　．　．　．

On October 5, 1905, the Wrights had made their longest flight of the year, 24 1/5 miles in 38 minutes 3 seconds.

Octave Chanute to Wilbur Wright

October 22, 1905

It is a perfect marvel to me that you have kept your performances out of the newspapers so long. With so curious a public as our own, and such appetite for sensation as obtains in the press I felt convinced that some enterprising reporter would discover you some time and make you famous.

．　．　．　．　．　．　．

Inasmuch as the Huffman pasture where the Wrights were making their flights was bordered by two highways and an

interurban railway, no great degree of enterprise would have
been needed to discover them.

Orville Wright to Carl Dienstbach, New York

Dayton, Ohio, November 17, 1905

A good deal of doubt seems to exist in Europe as to
whether there is any truth in the reports that have been
made concerning our flights of 1903 and 1904; and it is not
at all surprising, under the circumstances, since there has
never been any account of any one having seen them, except the inventors themselves. There have been a number of
witnesses to every flight we have made in the last three
years. The flights near Kitty Hawk were seen by nearly all
the men at the U. S. Kill Devil Life Saving Station, who
were present, and by the Captain of the Kitty Hawk Station,
who viewed the flights through a glass. The flights in 1904
were witnessed by the farmers on the surrounding farms,
besides a number of citizens of Dayton, whom we had invited. Mr. A. I. Root, of Medina, Ohio, was also present a
number of times, and wrote an account of what he saw for
his journal, "Gleanings in Bee Culture," for January 1st, 1905.

The longer flights this year were witnessed by a number
of citizens of Dayton, among whom were Mr. Torrence Huffman, President, Fourth National Bank; Mr. C. S. Billman,
Secretary West Side Building & Loan Company; and Mr.
Edgar W. Ellis, Assistant Auditor of City of Dayton. If you
or the editor of your journal wish to make a personal investigation of the matter, we have no doubt any of these gentlemen would take pleasure corroborating the fact that they

were present when flights of fifteen to twenty-four miles were made. We would not want their names published, as they would no doubt be flooded with inquiries. None of these gentlemen has any financial interest in our machine, either directly or indirectly.

.   .   .   .

Their experiments of 1905 convinced the Wrights that the airplane would have practical use—but they did not foresee flying at night!

Wilbur Wright to Octave Chanute

Dayton, Ohio, November 20, 1905

After thinking the matter over we have decided that it will be best to absolve our friends from their obligation to keep secret the results of the seasons experiments now that the season is ended. The strict repression of authentic news may be harmful with widespread rumors in circulation.

.   .   .   .

Octave Chanute to Wilbur Wright

November 24, 1905

The fact that information concerning your doings emanates from Washington . . . suggests to me the surmise that the War Department, or perhaps Prof. Langley, has had a man to visit Dayton to pick up information, and has leaked as to the results.

I think that you are now at the mercy of any enterprising newspaper as to your performances, but that you can preserve your secrets of construction.

. . . .

VI

A MIRACLE HARD TO BELIEVE

Wilbur Wright to The French Ambassador,
French Embassy, Washington, D. C.

Dayton, Ohio, November 28, 1905

About two years ago we succeeded in making the first free flight through the air with a motor driven aeroplane. Since that time we have been busily engaged in developing the invention to the point of practicability. Though the difficulty of the task was increased not a little by the necessity of avoiding the eyes of the curious during the necessary preliminary flights, we have finally carried the machine through the experimental stage and are now ready to offer it for sale as a secret practical invention.

We are about to make a formal proposition to the French War Office, but we realize that it will seem incredible not only that long flights have really been made with motor aeroplanes, but also that they have been made so quietly as to escape the attention of the newspapers. We suggest, therefore, that you send an attaché to Dayton at once to make such careful preliminary investigation on the spot as will enable the War Office to judge whether the offer is worthy of serious consideration. The trial flights were made near Simm's Station on the electric road connecting Dayton and Springfield, and were witnessed by a dozen or more families liv-

ing in the neighborhood, as well as by a number of prominent citizens of Dayton who were present at our invitation.
We inclose a note from Mr. E. W. Ellis, assistant auditor
of the City of Dayton, who was present at one of the flights.
We will be glad to furnish the names of other witnesses to
your attaché in order that he may have personal conference
with them if he desires.

. . . .

Wilbur Wright to Octave Chanute

December 4, 1905

A few days ago Mr. F. S. Lahm, a member of the French
Aéro Club cabled his brother-in-law Mr. H. M. Weaver of
Mansfield, Ohio, as follows: "Verify what Wright Bros. claim,
necessary, go Dayton today, prompt answer cable." Mr.
Weaver, who is a manufacturer of cash carriers used in stores,
came down Sunday and after interviewing several farmers
at Simms and a few of our friends in Dayton, who had been
present at our long flights, cabled back "Claims fully verified, particulars by mail."

. . . .

Wilbur Wright to Octave Chanute

December 8, 1905

On further consideration we are inclined to think that the
best course regarding the correspondence with the American

war department is complete suppression. We do not think there would be any advantage in bringing the matter to the attention of the President, or Sec. of War, unless they were previously *fully convinced* of the practicability of the machine and the desirability of securing it for the government. No such condition exists at present. Neither can we see any advantage in letting it become generally known that we have been turned down by our own government. It will be a hindrance to successful negotiations with any other government. We have not informed a single person outside of our own family, except yourself. We think it best to maintain secrecy as to the progress of all negotiations with governments.

. . . .

Wilbur Wright to Octave Chanute

December 19, 1905

We have no objection at all to a statement of our progress being made to the Am. Ass'n for the Advancement of Science, but as we are not members, and moreover refuse to reveal our machine and methods, a statement volunteered by us might be regarded as an impertinence. You may make a statement regarding our performances if you wish, but we prefer that nothing be said of our machine and methods, except that the machine is of the aeroplane type.

. . . .

Wilbur Wright to Octave Chanute

December 19, 1905

We are not sure but that the "friend," whose visit is announced by Capt. Ferber, will prove to be the representative of a syndicate of sportsmen instead of an army officer. If so, a deal with him would necessitate a change in our present plans for other countries. We would be very glad to have your advice as to what precautions we should take in negotiating with a professed agent of an unincorporated syndicate who might make public the terms discussed without entering into an enforcible contract. What credentials should we demand regarding the powers of the agent, and the reliability of the principals?

I enclose a clipping from *Les Sports* giving Mr. Archdeacon's view. We have had a good laugh at his assumed perspicacity and wisdom. If stealing is so easy, why has he not stolen something from the birds long ago?

.   .   .   .

Wilbur Wright to Octave Chanute

December 27, 1905

The idea of selling to a single government as a strict secret has some advantages but we are very much disinclined to assume the moral responsibility of choosing the proper one when we have no means of knowing how it will use the invention. And then it is very repugnant to think of hiding an invention of such intense human interest until it becomes stale and useless.

A letter just received from Ferber states that the "friend" is M. Fordyce, the representative of a syndicate which intends to purchase with a view to turning it over to the government.

. . . .

Arnold Fordyce, when he arrived in Dayton, said that he was secretary to M. Letellier, a member of the syndicate and owner of the Paris newspaper, *Le Journal.*

Wilbur Wright to Octave Chanute

January 2, 1906

It seems that Capt. Ferber realized that it would require a year or two for the French Government to act, and fearing another nation would anticipate it, he went to some wealthy friends and newspaper publishers and induced them to form a syndicate to purchase our invention and present it to the nation as a gift for war purposes. We have made an agreement by which the secret formulas are communicated, not to the syndicate, but to the government direct. We give a license to manufacture only for government use. The syndicate cannot exploit the invention commercially. The members are not Aéro Club people, and have no wish to make the machine public. Their idea seems to be to secure their return in the shape of army promotions, or decorations of the "legion of honor" &c, &c. They are to post a forfeit of 25,000

francs by Febr. 5th, and deposit one million francs in a New
York bank before April 5th, of which sum 750,000 frs is to
become ours absolutely as soon as we have delivered a machine to them, after a trial flight of 50 kilometers. The balance is to become ours absolutely after an interval not ex-
ceeding three months more, during which time we are to
exercise diligence in imparting instruction &c. . . .

We have just received a letter from the "Austrian Association of Builders" of Vienna, who, having seen that we are
offering the invention to the French for 1 million francs, write
to inquire whether they can not become the purchasers for
the purpose of presenting it to the emperor Franz Joseph on
the occasion of his 60 jubilee in 1908 as a national gift. The
idea is to make it the star feature of the Vienna Exposition.
If the idea of acquiring the machine in different countries
by popular subscription should spread, we may be able to
secure all the remuneration we care for, and establish free
trade in flying-machines within a year or two. Nothing would
suit us better, but we shall not begin counting our chickens
until we are sure of them.

· · · · · · ·

Wilbur Wright to Arnold Fordyce,
21 rue Joubert, Paris, France

January 8, 1906

We thank you for your two letters and a card from New
York, and also for the newspaper clippings. We sent to you
several days ago two clippings from Dayton papers, and
another today. A vivid imagination is characteristic of Amer-

ican journalism, but the French seem to be very similar. The continued story of Coquelle in the *L'Auto* December 22-26, is nearly all pure fancy. We laughed so loudly while reading it that you must have heard us half across the Atlantic ocean. The N. Y. *Herald* man's idea of the nature of our secret formulas was also very amusing. He seemed to think that we possessed a formula for compounding a wonderful elixir, two or three drops of which when rubbed on the wings were sufficient to overcome the force of gravity and allow the machine to soar aloft.

We hope that your passage proved less rough than you expected and that you reached home in good health and spirits. We shall begin work at once on the preparation of a machine for the earliest possible delivery. When you first disclosed your plan for raising money, we were not entirely sure of your success and felt some hesitancy in signing an agreement, but since we have had time to consider more carefully our doubts have vanished. A small part of the public may hold back in fear of being "hoaxed," but more will see that France would become for many years the laughing stock of Europe if it should now let slip this prize after having secured the very first chance at it. The risk of accepting the chance is infinitely small compared with the risk which would result from rejecting it. . . .

No doubt an attempt will be made to spy upon us while we are making the trial flight and teaching a French operator, but we have already thought out a plan which we are certain will baffle such efforts as neatly as we fooled the newspapers during the two seasons we were experimenting at Simms.

. . . .

Wilbur Wright to Octave Chanute

January 10, 1906

If the French deal goes through all right, we will have no difficulty in securing all the money we need without exploiting the invention commercially or assuming any business responsibilities. It will leave us entirely free to pursue a number of scientific studies which we have heretofore carried only far enough to settle practical points.

.   .   .   .

Wilbur Wright to Arnold Fordyce, Paris, France

Dayton, Ohio, January 15, 1906

We enclose a clipping from the N. Y. *Herald* of 7th January. If anything appeared in the N. Y. *World* it escaped our search. You will be much amused at the *Herald* interview. We have just been laughing over a number of clippings from foreign periodicals which Mr. Chanute sent to us. Is not Archdeacon an "amoosin cuss?" In his article in *La France Automobile* of 23rd December he offers to solve the flying problem in three months for only 200,000 francs. It is as funny as if a school boy who has not finished learning the multiplication tables should offer to calculate the eclipses of the sun for the next five years if some one will advance 20 francs to buy lead pencils and paper. It is quite evident that M. Archdeacon has never ventured to try a ride on an aeroplane himself. A few personal attempts at gliding merely would open his eyes to problems whose existence he knows nothing of. He would then know more and talk less.

Like all novices we began with the helicopter, [in childhood] but soon saw that it had no future and dropped it. The helicopter does with great labor only what the balloon does without labor, and is no more fitted than the balloon for rapid horizontal flight. If its engine stops it must fall with deathly violence, for it can neither float like the balloon nor glide like the aeroplane. The helicopter is much easier to design than the aeroplane but it is worthless when done.

. . . .

Wilbur Wright to Octave Chanute

January 19, 1906

We have no objections to the publication of information regarding the number, length, time, height and direction of our flights, nor anything relating to them which does not throw light on the construction of the machine or the methods and principles of operation. We do not object to saying that the machine is given initial speed by a run on a track before it rises into the air, and that it slides on the ground when it lands. Before the methods of control had been perfected some of the landings were rough, but in the later flights the machine landed easily and without damage. We think it would not be wise to either deny or confirm any published descriptions of the machine, or data of dimensions. You may say that the weights of the various power machines ranged from 750 to 925 lbs. and the horse power from 12 to 20. The speed of minimum power consumption is below that at which the machine usually flies. We think it best to say nothing about the patents for which we have applied. We make no concealment of our reasons for wishing to sell in some other way than as a patented commercial invention. We prefer to sell to governments because we can thus secure a sure return, sufficient to satisfy us, without delay, and without burdening our future with business responsibilities and the tedious law-suits which are always necessary to maintain a valuable invention by patent. We wish to be as free as possible for further scientific explorations.

We enclose another bunch of French papers in which the combat deepens. We have had an invitation to join in the fray but shall keep out of it entirely.

. . . .

The *Scientific American* of January 13, 1906, in an article headed "The Wright Aeroplane and Its Fabled Performances," commented skeptically on a letter written by the Wright brothers which had been published in a Paris automobile journal. In that letter the Wrights had given details of the long flights of late September and early October, 1905. In expressing its disbelief in the "alleged" flights described in the Wright letter, the *Scientific American* said: "If such sensational and tremendously important experiments are being conducted in a not very remote part of the country, on a subject in which almost everybody feels the most profound interest, is it possible to believe that the enterprising American reporter, who, it is well known, comes down the chimney when the door is locked in his face—even if he has to scale a fifteen-story skyscraper to do so—would not have ascertained all about them and published them broadcast long ago?"

A few weeks later, in February, 1906, the editor of the *Scientific American* wrote to the Wrights to inquire if there was any truth in reports that they were negotiating with the French Government. He enclosed in his letter a clipping of "The Wright Aeroplane and Its Fabled Performances."

Wilbur Wright to Munn & Co., publishers of the Scientific American, *New York*

February 7, 1906

Your letter of February 3rd and a copy of your paper containing an article entitled "The Wright Aeroplane and Its Fabled Performance" have been received and read with much amusement. As you profess to have obtained the data of what you term "alleged experiments" direct from a published letter signed by ourselves, and do not discredit the authenticity of the letter, but only the truthfulness of the statements, we are at a loss to understand why you should desire further statements from such a source.

No doubt many of your readers were surprised, in view of the reputation we have long maintained among scientific workers, that you should have found it necessary in publishing the data of our recent experiments to use forms of expression whose humorous side may not have been as apparent to them as to us. In their sight it would have had a better appearance if these expressions had been preceded by some evidence of a sincere effort to discover whether such terms were really justified.

.　.　.　.　.　.　.

Wilbur Wright to Octave Chanute

January 31, 1906

We regard the publication by Capt. Ferber of our private letter to him of November 4th (see last *Aérophile*) as simply outrageous. It is the worse from the fact that he deliberately includes the direct reference to Russia, Austria and the German Emperor, while striking out all embarrassing references to his "bluff," and making other changes in the letter.

.　.　.　.　.　.　.

The Wrights had written to Ferber: "With Russia and Austria-Hungary in their present troubled condition and the German Emperor in a truculent mood, a spark may produce an explosion at any time. No government dare take the risk of waiting to develop practical flying machines independently. To be even one year behind other governments might result in losses compared with which the modest amount we shall ask for our invention would be insignificant."

The editor of *L'Aérophile* had translated "in a truculent mood" to mean *"cherchant noise"*—seeking a quarrel.

Ferber's "bluff" was his implication that he himself was about to solve the flying problem. Though the Wrights felt sure it was only a bluff to try to induce them to lower their price, they wrote politely, saying: "France is indeed fortunate in finding a Ferber."

Wilbur Wright to Octave Chanute

March 2, 1906

Orville has been having his eyes examined and has not been able to read, so we secured a translation of the German editor's remarks from Prof. Werthner, of the High School, and enclose a copy. We did not really make the statement that the German Emperor was a "disturber of the peace" as the French translator has it, but we will not make a fight about it. Nor will we take any notice of the German editor's attack upon us. Possibly he will soon be so busy crawling out of the hole into which he has jumped, by disputing the credibility of our performances, that he will forget all about the "lese majesty" of our remark. The Vienna paper also expressed some doubt of the truth of the stories from America. I think this attitude is largely due to the fact that the news first appeared in France, and that France secured the first option on the machine. We consider the fight to establish the truth of our claims practically over.

Prof. Zahm* wrote us a very nice letter a few days ago in

---

* Albert F. Zahm, at that time a professor of mathematics in Washington and a student of aeronautics, made his first contact with the Wrights in a letter to Wilbur in March, 1902. At first he seemed to go out of his way to be friendly to the Wrights, but later became troublesome to them. See Orville Wright's letter to McSurely, February 5, 1946.

which he informed us that it was the intention of himself
and several others to present resolutions for adoption by the
Aero Club of America, congratulating us on the achievement
of the first successful human flights. As no request was made
for a "schematical" representation of the machine we are
not in any way embarrassed.

The newspapers report the death of Prof. Langley. No
doubt disappointment shortened his life. It is really pathetic
that he should have missed the honor he cared for above
all others, merely because he could not launch his machine
successfully. If he could only have started it, the chances are
that it would have flown sufficiently to have secured to him
the name he coveted, even though a complete wreck attended the landing. I can not help feeling sorry for him.
The fact that the great scientist, Prof. Langley, believed in
flying machines was one thing that encouraged us to begin
our studies. It was he that recommended to us, *Progress in
Flying Machines, The Aeronautical Annuals, Experiments*
in *Aero-dynamics,* Mouillard's *Empire of the Air* and Lilienthal's articles on gliding, and thus started us in the right
direction at the beginning. His honorable course in the Herring matter in 1902 also commended him to us.

.   .   .   .

At the time he made the foregoing comment, Wilbur
Wright had never seen the Langley machine, or even a drawing of it, and was unaware that fundamental errors in its
construction were too serious for it ever to have been
launched successfully. Also, Wilbur was either leaning back-
ward to be gracious, or else had forgotten that the reading

material from the Smithsonian Institution did not come from Langley, the Secretary and Director, but from Assistant Secretary Rathbun. The reply to Wilbur's letter was doubtless handled in a routine way and would hardly have required the attention of the head of the institution.

Wilbur Wright to Octave Chanute

April 1, 1906

I telegraphed to you this morning asking you to be present at the final conference with representatives of the French government. Mr. Fordyce arrived in America on March 18th without previous notice of his coming, accompanied by Comm. Bonel, chief of engineers of the general staff, who brought credentials authorizing him to conclude a final agreement in behalf of the Minister of War. Capt. Fournier, attaché at Washington and Mr. Berry, official legal advisor of the French embassy, were also made a part of the commission. They reached Dayton a few days later and took up the question of a few amendments to the former contract. The real object of their coming was to secure an extension of the exclusive feature of the contract. The other points were trivial and apparently were blinds. They demanded first 15 months and finally one year; we offered 5 months and finally six months. Two references of proposed agreements to the War Minister have kept the matter dragging for nearly two weeks. The commission is unanimously in favor of the acceptance of our final offer but they fear the Minister will not accept. An answer is expected today.

. . . .

Wilbur Wright to Octave Chanute

April 5, 1906

We neither saw nor heard anything from the Frenchmen after you left till this afternoon at about 3 o'clock, when they brought a telegram from the war minister insisting on his previous terms. As it still included rising to a height of 300 meters we at once rejected it. The deal is therefore off temporarily, but there is a strong probability that an agreement may be reached when the Comm. Bonel reaches home and makes his report. We have told them that we are willing to sign the present contract with a clause waiving the forfeiture and making the exclusive period one year, provided they extend the limit for delivery to October 1st and except the U. S. Government entirely from the exclusive feature of the contract. The commissioners think they can secure the acceptance of this proposition, which however is not an option in the sense of preventing us from making a conflicting contract elsewhere before their acceptance. The exclusive option terminates today.

We thank you very much for your kindness in coming to Dayton, and hope that it has not seriously disturbed your own affairs.

.   .   .   .

Wilbur Wright to Octave Chanute

April 13, 1906

We fully appreciated the probability that the French deal would fall through; but we felt that we did not care for a contract which called for a rise to 300 meters with the time limit of Aug. 1st. The time was too short for any preliminary practice, and almost too short for what we had already agreed to perform.

. . . .

Before leaving Dayton, the Frenchmen said they believed they knew what was back of the failure to close the deal— that it was probably the present attitude of Captain Ferber, the man who had been instrumental in starting the negotiations. Ferber, they thought, had now decided that with his knowledge of the Wright plane he could build one himself, and so become the French pioneer in aviation—a greater honor than being merely the instrument of introducing the airplane into France.

Wilbur Wright to Octave Chanute

April 28, 1906

Mr. [Patrick] Alexander spent a day with us and then started home by way of Washington and New York. As near as we can make out his trip was for the purpose of learning whether or not there was any truth in the reports that we had made a contract with the French. I think he was asked to get information on this point by the government authorities.

The U. S. patent has been granted on the gliding machine and will issue as soon as the final fee is paid.

. . . .

Wilbur Wright to Godfrey L. Cabot, Boston, Mass.

May 10, 1906

Previous to our entering into negotiations with foreign countries we brought the subject before our own government. The answers of the department officials were so insulting in tone as to preclude any further advances on our part.

.   .   .   .

Wilbur Wright to Octave Chanute

May 15, 1906

We have received a letter from the officers of the Vienna Aviation Society regarding the confirmation of the news of our successful flights. It is the irony of fate that after all our rejoicing because they addressed you instead of us, they should now write direct to us. However, as they only ask for a schematical sketch of our faces to decorate the diploma, and as their treatment of you has been most inconsiderate, we will be less embarrassed in making answer than if they had written to us as they did to you for a sketch of the machine.

There have been no new developments in any of the negotiations. We have no present intention of doing any more flying with the power machine until a deal is closed. For the present we are concerning ourselves with the prosecution of negotiations, and the preparation of parts for several machines. We wish to be ready to make a demonstration with the least delay whenever a deal is effected.

. . . .

Wright brothers to Godfrey L. Cabot, Boston, Mass.

June 21, 1906

If Gen. Crozier should decide to send a representative to Dayton we would be glad to furnish him convincing proof that a machine has been produced which by actual operation has been shown to be able to produce horizontal flight and to carry an operator. If the board of ordnance then desires a conference with us we will be pleased to appear before it and discuss in detail the capabilities of the different machines we could offer, and the terms on which we could supply them. We are ready to negotiate whenever the board is ready, but as the former correspondence closed with a strong intimation that the board did not wish to be bothered with our offers, we naturally have no intention of taking the initiative again.

We wish to thank you for the trouble you have taken in this case, and to assure you that we value it especially as an evidence of the unselfish interest you take in the success of ourselves and of the cause of human flight.

. . . .

Wilbur Wright to Octave Chanute

June 21, 1906

We have been much touched by the unselfish interest
which both Sam'l and Godfrey Cabot* have shown in our
success. The latter has recently interested himself at Washington as you will see from the enclosed letters. In reply to
his first remark about the situation there, we stated that we
had made offers to our own government before going abroad,
but that the insulting replies of the department officials pre-
cluded . . . further overtures. In reply to his last we said
that we would be glad to receive a representative from Gen.
Crozier or meet the board at Washington, but that we did
not feel ready to take the initiative in any renewal of the
negotiations, in view of the board's last letter to us.

Please thank Mr. Sam Cabot for us and tell him that we
finally decided to give up the trip East for the present. We
have no thought, as yet, of forming a commercial company.
We certainly very much appreciate the kindness of his offer
to assist us either on a business or on a strictly scientific
basis, and also his invitation to visit him at his home, though
we cannot at present accept any of them.

. . . .

---

* Godfrey L. Cabot, of Boston, to Dr. George W. Lewis, executive officer,
National Advisory Committee for *Aeronautics*.

August 29, 1940
my brother Sam and I myself, each of us, independent of the other, and
without the knowledge of the other, offered pecuniary assistance to the
Wrights, both of us in the year 1904, and the offer of each of us was declined. My offer was to buy any securities they might wish to offer. Sam's
was to give them funds; and it was two or three years before either of us
knew of the offer the other had made.

Wilbur Wright to Octave Chanute

July 25, 1906

Except a cable April 25th saying that the French war office was considering the matter of a contract with us, we have not had one word from either Fordyce or Bonel since they left Dayton. It is evident that the party opposing immediate action is in the ascendent for the present. Possibly the French also hope that we will turn our attention to commercial exploitation thus making the machine public. Other negotiations are progressing but have not reached the decisive point.

We have not definitely decided what course we will pursue if our present propositions are declined everywhere. My own idea is to stand pat and wait for something to happen which will bull the market. "All things come to him who waits." Excellent opportunities have been abundant in the past three years. I see no reason why similar chances should not occur within the next three. We certainly will not radically alter our present plane without first going to Europe and getting into personal contact with the various government officials.

. . . .

Wilbur Wright to Arnold Fordyce, Paris, France

September 11, 1906

We received your letter just as we had about given up hope of hearing from you. For four months we had not been able to get a word from France either in regard to our final proposition or the money in the bank in New York. . . .

We presume that the deal fell through because the higher officials at Paris were not as well convinced of the value of our flyer as were the members of the commission who investigated the subject at Dayton. If the men to whom the final decision was left had been here the negotiations would have been successful without doubt. In a year or two they will know that our invention is serious but the same opportunities will not then be open to them.

.   .   .   .

Wilbur Wright to Octave Chanute

October 10, 1906

Our friends do not seem to exactly understand our position in the matter of supposed delay. We are not delaying an instant more than we consider necessary. We merely refuse to let our hand be forced. Regarding the matter of price no two persons will have exactly the same view. There is really no such thing in the world as absolute value for anything. If there were, the air we breathe would be the highest priced thing in the world instead of the cheapest. From our own study of the situation and conversation with the French & English visitors we believe that the price or rather the amount of money is not directly an important issue. If it be assumed that some one else will produce a practical flyer in a year or two years at most, or that by refusing to buy, governments can force us to sell at their own terms, then the price we ask is undoubtedly too high. But if the governments know that there is only one way to get a practical flyer within five or ten years, and that there is no hope of beating down the price, then they will consider the price very low.

It all depends upon the point of view. If we had named $50,000 instead of $200,000 they would have cried "too much": "you must come down." It is not the amount involved but the possibility of getting it cheaper that makes them hesitate. We do not think that cutting the price in two would have any particular effect in securing contracts. If we would offer a lower price they would say to themselves, "The Wrights see that others will be flying in a few months and wish to work us for some money before it is too late, but we will wait and get it for nothing." If it were indeed true that others would be flying within a year or two, there would be reason in selling at any price but we are convinced that no one will be able to develop a practical flyer within five years. This opinion is based upon cold calculation. It takes into consideration practical and scientific difficulties whose existence is unknown to all but ourselves. Even you, Mr. Chanute, have little idea how difficult the flying problem really is. When we see men laboring year after year on points we overcame in a few weeks, without ever getting far enough along to meet the worse points beyond, we know that their rivalry & competition are not to be feared for many years. . . . We do not believe there is one chance in a hundred that any one will have a machine of the least *practical* usefulness within five years. If our judgment is correct undue haste to *force a sale* would be a mistake.

. . . .

Octave Chanute to Wilbur Wright

October 15, 1906

You are quite correct in saying that it is not the amount of money involved but the possibility of buying your machine cheaper which causes your clients to hesitate. The value of an invention is whatever it costs to reproduce it, and I am by no means sure that persistent experimenting by others, now that they know one success has been achieved, may not produce a practical flyer within five years.

The important factor is that light motors have been developed. As there are many shapes of birds, each flying after a system of his own, so there may be several forms of apparatus by which man may compass flight. Flapping wings for instance. I cheerfully acknowledge that I have little idea how difficult the flying problem really is and that its solution is beyond my powers, but are you not too cock-sure that yours is the only secret worth knowing and that others may not hit upon a solution in less than "many times five years" — It took you much less than that and there are a few (very few) other able inventors in the world. The danger therefore is that others may achieve success, and one (shall we say distressing) symptom is that, thus far, nobody seems to have been hurt in trying. This does not mean that I would advise you to "force a sale," but that I believe that if the only obstacle in the way was the question of price it would be wise to make a reduction.

. . . .

The notion that a flying machine would soon have come, regardless of the Wrights, because of the improvement in internal combustion motors, continues. Yet the motor played a minor part in the Wright's success; they had solved much of the problem in their 1902 glider with no motor at all. The equivalent of all the material in that glider had been available for a thousand years!

Wilbur Wright to Octave Chanute

October 28, 1906

I am not certain that your method of estimating probabilities is a sound one. Do you not insist too strongly upon the single point of mental ability? To me it seems that a thousand other factors, each rather insignificant in itself, in the aggregate influence the event ten times more than mere mental ability or inventiveness. The world does not contain greater men than Maxim, Bell, Edison, Langley, Lilienthal & Chanute. We are not so foolish as to base our belief, (that an independent solution of the flying problem is not imminent,) upon any supposed superiority to these men and to all those who will hereafter take up the problem. If the wheels of time could be turned back six years, it is not at all probable that we would do again what we have done. The one thing that impresses me as remarkable is the shortness of the time within which our work was done. It was due to peculiar combinations of circumstances which might never occur again. How do you explain the lapse of more than 50 years between Newcomen and Watt? Was the world wanting in smart men during those years? Surely not! The world was full of Watts, but a thousand and one trifles kept them from undertaking and completing the task. . . . We look upon the present question in an impersonal way. It is not chiefly a question of relative ability, but of mathematical probabilities.

. . . .

In other words, a serious mishap, an illness, or anything which encroached too much upon the time they devoted together to the flying problem might have prevented the Wrights' triumph. Suppose one or the other of them had got married!

Wilbur Wright to Octave Chanute

November 2, 1906

Yours of yesterday containing a telegraph news report of a flight of a kilometer by Santos-Dumont is received. You say "I fancy he is now very nearly where you were in 1904." This report gives such an excellent opportunity for exercising our powers as prophets that I can not resist making a forecast before the details arrive.

From our knowledge of the subject we estimate that it is possible to *jump* about 250 feet with a machine which has not made the first steps toward controlability and which is quite unable to maintain the motive force necessary for flight. By getting up good speed a machine can be made to rise with very little power, and can proceed several hundred feet before its momentum is exhausted. Several seconds are required to change the direction of a large machine. One turn up and one down will require several seconds within which time, at 50 ft. per second, several hundred feet may be traversed. From our knowledge of the degree of progress that Santos has attained we predict that his flight covered less than 1/10 of a kilometer, and that he has only jumped. If he has gone more than 300 ft. he has really done something; less than this is nothing. Maxim made a machine lift 12 years ago, and immediately quit in despair.

You have possibly forgotten that we stayed in the air 59 seconds in a wind of twenty miles velocity in the year preceeding 1904 and that we made four flights in one day and incidentally carried 63 lbs. to the horsepower. That was three years ago. We have not been wasting our time since then. When some one goes over three hundred feet and lands safely in a wind of seven or eight miles it will then be important for us to do something. So far we see no indication that it will be done for several years yet. There is all the difference in the world between jumping and flying. We have never considered light motors the important point in solving the flying problem.

. . . .

Chanute was completely wrong in thinking that Santos-Dumont was now where the Wrights were in 1904. As the Wrights surmised, the reported flight was a hop of about 200 feet. It was to be a long time before anyone could surpass the Wrights. Indeed, the basic principles of flight that the Wrights discovered are still used in every airplane that flies.

The Wrights were to face long delays, however, both in France and the United States before receiving full recognition.

Octave Chanute to Wilbur Wright

November 4, 1906

Did I write you that there is to be a meeting in memory of the late Secretary Langley in Washington on Dec. 3rd? . . . I have been asked to deliver an address on his contributions to aerial navigation. . . . Kindly advise me soon how much you feel that you have been assisted in your own work by Langley's publications and labors, and give me such hints as may occur to you.

.   .   .   .

Wilbur Wright to Octave Chanute

November 8, 1906

The knowledge that the head of the most prominent scientific institution of America believed in the possibility of human flight was one of the influences that led us to undertake the preliminary investigation that preceded our active work. He recommended to us the books which enabled us to form sane ideas at the outset. It was a helping hand at a critical time and we shall always be grateful. Of his actual work, his successes and his failures, it is perhaps too soon to make an accurate estimate, but entirely aside from this he advanced the art greatly by his missionary work and the inspiration of his example. He possessed mental and moral qualities of the kind that influence history. When scientists in general considered it discreditable to work in the field of aeronautics he possessed both the discernment to discover possibilities there and the moral courage to subject himself to the ridicule of the public and the apologies of his friends. He deserves more credit for this than he has yet received. I think his treatment by the newspapers and many of his professed friends most shameful. His work deserved neither abuse nor apology. Even his final experiment was as worthy of honor and praise as the failures of Dr. Nansen and Lt. Peary. His fellow scientists will yet be proud of his work in this field, and thankful that he, with a very few others, saved their profession the disgrace of being unrepresented when a great scientific problem was being solved, for it was really scientific rather than mechanical. As you know, his methods and ideas were very different from ours, so his direct assistance to us was less than that of several others, but his accounts of the troubles he had encountered and overcome, put us on our guard and enabled us to entirely avoid some of the worst of them. He painted so vividly the troubles resulting from excessive lightness that we have been as men vaccinated against that disease. Though we have rarely followed his lead, we have always found a study of his writings very profitable, especially at the time when we were trying to find out what the real sticking points of flying were. Those who count his successes only in estimating his contribution to the cause of human flight, omit some of the most valuable parts.

. . . .

Wilbur Wright to George A. Spratt

Dayton, Ohio, November 10, 1906

Since our last letter we have scarcely been out of Dayton at all. All our work has been in the shop. I think I told you

that we had given an option to the French for the government use of our flyers in that country. Later a commission
from the government came to this country and asked for
some modification of the original contract. The important
points were an extension of the time, during which their
rights should be exclusive, from three months to 15 months;
and an agreement that during a flight we should rise to a
height of 1000 ft. We rejected the first point but finally
agreed with the commission on six months. The second we
rejected because they refused to give us more time for making the demonstrations and delivering the machine. The
commission however decided to waive the point and an
amended agreement was drawn up which the commission
recommended for acceptance by the home authorities, but
some one evidently raised an objection for the recommenda-
tion of the commission was turned down. They however offered $120,000 if we would go ahead on the old terms but
we rejected the offer. So the option lapsed. We got $5,000
on the forfeit. Several members of the commission have urged
us to renew the negotiation, but we decided to make more
thorough preparations before taking it up again. We have
spent the last six months in building some new motors of
greater power than the old ones and slightly lighter. We will
now be prepared to offer a two man machine which can carry
fuel for two hundred miles. This is what the different governments have wanted and we thought it best to get the goods
before pushing sales further.

.   .   .   .

Wilbur Wright to Octave Chanute

November 18, 1906

It is the complexity of the flying problem that makes it so difficult. It is not to be solved by stumbling upon a secret, but by the patient accumulation of information upon a hundred different points some of which an investigator would naturally think it unnecessary to go into deeply. That is why we think a quick solution impossible. . . .

In speaking of Prof. Langley you say that "he also gave great service by his data as to the power required for aerial support." . . . If you mean his "two-hundred pounds to the horse power" demonstration, it would probably be wise to avoid calling attention to it again, for it was a great blunder, resulting from a false assumption, and was not warranted by the experiments on which it was based. I think it probable that he became aware of the slip himself, and would have corrected it at a convenient time. He must also have discovered the error of the so called "Langley law," but it is only natural that he should have wished to make his corrections at a time when he should have raised his prestige to an unassailable point by the success of his big machine. I can well understand what the failure of the latter must have meant to him.

The newspapers contain reports of further experiments by Santos-Dumont, including a flight of two hundred meters. I see nothing unreasonable in this report and presume it is substantially correct. It is the first real indication of progress that has been displayed in France in five years. When we remember that within two hours of our first attempt at free flight we succeeded, in 1901, in remaining in the air for 19 seconds in a wind of about 12 miles an hour, it seems almost ridiculous that the French have never made any success at gliding in all these years. Whether M. Santos will find the motor an aid or an encumbrance in his attack upon the real problems of flight only the future can tell.

. . . .

Wilbur Wright to Octave Chanute

December 20, 1906

Flint & Co. now offer us $500,000.00 for our rights outside of the United States. We reserve the latter. The money to be paid in cash upon the delivery of one machine after a demonstration consisting of a flight of 50 kilometers. We are to have the privilege of going for prizes, &c. and to publish anything we choose after a limited time. Their idea seems to be to depend on getting possession of the market by being first in the field rather than by depending on patents alone, or, secrecy alone. Orville has just returned from New York where he had a conference with them this week. We have not committed ourselves. What do you think of it? Do you think them safe people to deal with under proper precautions? The price and terms are satisfactoy and we would accept if we felt sure of their character.

. . . .

Charles R. Flint, New York banker and promoter, was often called "the father of trusts." His company became interested in the Wrights after a few references to them had appeared in New York newspapers. The deal worked out with the firm was that they should be the Wrights' business representatives, on commission, in all countries except the United States. A little later it was arranged that the Wrights should manage their own affairs also in Great Britain and its colonies.

The Flints proposed that they would have the Czar of Russia and certain other crowned heads request private demonstrations of the flying machine. But the Wrights were not impressed by such suggestions and in a letter to the Flints said they thought it would be better for them to "look the ground over first before making arrangements with the Czar."

Wilbur Wright to Octave Chanute

December 29, 1906

We are not apprehensive that Flints will sell exclusively to Russia if they secure the foreign rights. We can guard against danger in that direction by reason of our reservations. At present there seems to be a pause in the negotiation apparently due to the fact that the Paris agent has been impressed by the French talk that we have nothing patentable and has raised the question of whether any dependence can be placed in patents or whether it will be necessary to depend on superior knowledge & experience entirely. We expect to know their intentions soon.

. . . .

Wilbur Wright to Octave Chanute

January 28, 1907

We returned from New York Saturday after a conference with Mr. Flint. The original proposition was that they purchase outright the foreign rights, but Mr. Flint found some of his foreign associates opposed to this and we on our part found that we would necessarily grant things that we were indisposed to give up. They next proposed to become selling agents for foreign countries with the condition that we receive everything until $500,000 had been reached and that beyond that they receive half. We did not like the idea of giving them full control of the selling department without some guarantee of results. They next proposed that if we would consent to give a private exhibition before the Czar of Russia they would guarantee to pay us $50,000 whether any business followed or not; and that of any business, we should receive 90% and they 10% up to $500,000 and an equal division thereafter. They to pay all expenses of the exhibition. We have this offer now under consideration. It includes a provision that in case the profits are less than $100,000 for each six months we are at liberty to terminate their agency. We also discussed with them a proposition according to which we retain full control of the terms and places of selling and they work under our directions so far as we choose to give any. We to be entirely free to handle the American business with absolute freedom, and to maintain secrecy or not as we wish. In this case they to receive 20% of foreign profits up to $500,000 and 40% thereafter. They to forfeit agency if the business amounts to less than $200,000 in six months, if we desire its forfeiture. We are more favorably disposed toward this plan than the others proposed, as we retain full control in every respect and merely utilize their services and assistance.

Mr. Flint has become very much interested in the matter and is very anxious to do something. He will attend to the business in Russia himself. In Germany and Austria he expects to operate through the Mauser gun people who have signified their readiness to take it up. His French associates were very lukewarm. In England also he would expect to cooperate with a large gun company. In the proposition which included the exhibition before the Czar it was understood that Russia was to be offered exclusive rights for two years, with England and America excepted. We did not like this, even with the exceptions named.

At first we were indisposed to consider any agency proposition, but in thinking it over we see some advantages over attempting to handle the foreign business entirely alone. They would pay all expenses connected with selling and delivering the machines, give any needed assistance in manufacturing if we wished it, and make things move in all quarters at once. The fact that we had the support of such influential people would make the governments less disposed to ignore us, with the intention of stealing our invention later.

. . . .

Wilbur Wright to C. R. Flint, New York

February 16, 1907

When we discontinued our experiments at Dayton we gave the shed to Mr. Huffman, on whose land it stood, and he tore it down and used the lumber elsewhere. In order to give a demonstration some time would be required to find a suitable location, provide shelter, and set up the machine.

We appreciate that in some respects it would be very advantageous to make some further demonstrations before a select company. We would have done so before this [except for] the danger of the private demonstration becoming really public. The newspapers now watch us closely, and we would have no soldiers to guard us.

We are not sure that any risk of publicity ought to be taken until after arrangements have been made for exploiting the invention openly in case we were badly caught. At present we have only a few elementary features patented, and no arrangements at all for manufacturing and exhibiting.

．　．　．　．　．　．　．

Wilbur Wright to C. R. Flint, New York

February 28, 1907

We have been thinking over the matter of a demonstration before a select company, and are of the opinion that the advantages to be derived from it will not pay for the disadvantages. If we find that the machine can not be sold without first creating a more general enthusiasm among the nations by some demonstration, we shall then change our plan of selling secrets, take out additional patent protection, and come out into the open, in part. In that case the business would have to be conducted on the usual commercial basis. We are watched so closely by the newspapers and some others that a secret flight in the East would be impossible. We therefore think it best to let that matter rest for the present until we see what can be done along the lines on which you are now working.

If the prize that is being raised by the Aero Club for a flight from New York to Chicago is intended as a stimulus to the development of endurance and daring in flying machine operators, it will no doubt have its effect after the flying machine has once come into every-day use. If it is intended to stimulate invention, it is doubtful whether it will have any effect. Of the people who have done serious work upon this problem, very few have possessed the physical requirements necessary to enter into a contest of endurance.

We believe more would be done for the promotion of aeronautics in America in placing a smaller prize that would go as a reward to invention, rather than a large one as a reward to endurance and daring after the machine has been invented. It is only the flying machine "crank" who hopes to win such a prize except after years of experiment and practice.

Since the flyer must be invented before there is any use of the operator, the early prizes should be given to stimulate invention. The conditions of winning should be severe enough to prove the value of the invention, but a flight of more than 100 miles is not necessary to do that. In fact, the most important use of the flyer, military scouting, will not require flights of more than 100 miles. Of course, under like conditions, the larger the reward, the greater will be the effort to win it.

. . . .

Wilbur Wright to Barnum & Bailey, Bridgeport, Conn.

March 1, 1907

We are the inventors of the Wright Flyer, a power-pro-pelled aeroplane, of which some account is given in the inclosed Bulletin of the Aero Club of America. . . .

Although we are not now, and will not be for some time, ready to begin the exhibition part of our program, yet we are desirous of getting into communication with parties that would be able to handle that part of the business when the time comes.

If you think you would be interested in such a proposition, we would be pleased to have one of your representatives call upon us when he passes through our city; or, if more con-venient, we may be able to call upon you when we are next in the East.

Please treat this communication as strictly confidential.

. . . .

The Wrights foresaw that exhibitions would be an im-portant part of aviation business at first. As will appear, Barnum & Bailey showed interest later, when the Wrights were in Europe.

Wilbur Wright to Octave Chanute

April 9, 1907

Negotiations are in progress with several foreign govern-ments, but no agreements have been reached as yet. I learn that Mr. Herbert Parsons, the Republican leader in New York city, has recently been bringing the flying machine to the attention of Pres. Roosevelt. I think the department officials would be very glad if we would reopen negotiations, but we are inclined to let them make the first move.

Our newest engine just completed gives more than 30 horse power, or 50% more than we used in our 1905 flights. It is enough power for two men, fuel, and a hundred pounds of extras. It weighs 160 lbs.

· · · · · · ·

Wilbur Wright to Reginald A. Fessenden,
Brant Rock, Mass.

April 13, 1907

The story published in the newspapers so often that we cannot get patents on our invention is not correct. The trouble has not been in the getting of patents, but in deciding whether patents would be of much value to us after we have them. We have always thought that our best market would be with the governments, and it has been a very serious question with us as to whether patents would give us adequate protection against governments—especially foreign governments. . . . We have a patent on our early gliding machine, but have not applied for protection on any of our work of the past five years. We have generally been informed that secrets were worth more to governments than patented articles. For that reason we have taken out no patents since we found there was any practical use in our invention.

· · · · · · ·

Wilbur Wright to Octave Chanute

April 22, 1907

Major Moedebeck [editor of a German aeronautical magazine] is quite right in thinking that practice in time of peace is essential to the attainment of the best results in time of war, but this is a matter for governments to be concerned about rather than ourselves.

Fear that others will produce a machine capable of practical service in less than several years does not worry us. We have been over the course and understand how much yet remains for them to do. The real disturbing element is the general *belief* that they will accomplish wonders shortly. As a hindrance to business this is almost as bad as reality. So long as the foreign experimenters build their machines for calms, they will advance very slowly in the development of a serviceable flyer. They may make flights sufficient to excite hopes, but the real task will remain. So far no foreigner has shown any thing near the control we displayed as early as August 9, 1901, when we made flight after flight of some fifteen seconds each in a wind of almost twenty miles an hour. Yet it took four years more before we attained satisfactory mastery of a flyer. But while we do not fear competition we, of course, realize the disadvantage of permitting others to hold the center of the stage so far as present practice is concerned, and therefore aim to push business negotiations as rapidly as possible so that we may resume actual flights again. . . .

There is a little sparring, between the U. S. government & ourselves, now in progress, through the medium of Mr. Parsons, but no direct communication has been established,

and I am not expecting that it will be, or that results would
follow if it were. Unless there is a real prospect of business
we would prefer to let matters remain as they are for the
present. The army officers do not seem to enjoy present conditions as well as we do.

. . . .

Wilbur Wright to Octave Chanute

May 12, 1907

We offered our flyer to the U. S. Government before offering it elsewhere, and repeated the offer before entering upon
the French negotiation of 1905-6. We also, some weeks since,
expressed to Mr. Parsons, who was in communication with
the war department, a willingness to have a conference with
Gen. Bell if it at any time seemed desirable, but declined
to make the first move again. Our consciences are clear, and
we will keep them so.

. . . .

Wilbur Wright to Orville

en route to New York, May 16, 1907

In the U. S. correspondence be careful not to give them
any chance to put us in a bad light as very unreasonable, etc.
If they say that they will have no authority to purchase upon
demonstration, until authorized by congress, that will be

sufficient excuse for letting the question of a demonstration go over till shortly before congress meets. Even they could not claim any advantage in an immediate demonstration under such circumstances.

VII

TWO YANKEES AND EUROPE

Wilbur Wright to Octave Chanute

May 16, 1907

We received a telegram from Flint yesterday morning requesting that one of us sail for Europe Saturday, so I grabbed a few things and started the same evening. I think that there is nothing special on, but that some of them are going and thought it desirable one of us be on hand for consultations. We had thought it probable that one or both of us would go over after a while, but the decision to start immediately was rather sudden. . . .

Before leaving home we received a communication from the U. S. Board of Ordnance & Fortification notifying us that the board had under consideration several propositions for the construction and testing of flying machines, and that we could take any action in the matter we chose.

. . . .

The Flints had an associate in Europe, Hart O. Berg, who in 1899 had helped to introduce American electric automobiles on the continent. He had acted, too, for Simon Lake, inventor of the submarine, in dealing with Russia and other foreign governments. They thought Berg might be able to start negotiations for forming a European Wright company. But Berg, not knowing the Wrights and feeling scant confidence in what they were reported to have done, was less than lukewarm over the idea. Flint suggested that it would be well for at least one of the Wrights to go to Europe, with expenses paid, to discuss their invention with Berg and give him more faith in it. The Wrights themselves, said Flint, could do more than anyone else to implant in Berg the wholehearted enthusiasm he would need to convince possible buyers.

Wright Brothers to U. S. War Department

May 17, 1907

We have some flyers in course of construction, and would be pleased to sell one or more of them to the War Department, if an agreement as to terms can be reached.

These machines will carry two men, an operator and an observer, and a sufficient supply of fuel for a flight of two hundred kilometers. We are willing to make it a condition of a contract that the machine must make a trial trip before Government representatives of not less than fifty kilometers at a speed of not less than fifty kilometers an hour, before its acceptance by the Department, and before any part of the purchase price is paid to us.

If the War Department is in a position to purchase at this time, we will be pleased to have a conference for the purpose of discussing the matter in detail, or we are willing to submit a formal proposition, if that is preferred.

. . . .

Wilbur Wright to his sister

R.M.S. Campania *May* 18, 1907

I sailed this morning about 9 o'clock and we are now something near 200 miles out. . . . The list of passengers . . . is rather small—only about half the ship's capacity. That is how I came to get a $250 cabin for $100.

. . . .

Berg and Wilbur went together from London to Paris where they were joined by F. R. Cordley, a member of the Flint firm.

From Hart O. Berg, London, to Flint & Co., New York

May 26, 1907

At 12:30 yesterday I met Mr. Wilbur Wright at Euston Station. I have never seen a picture of him, or had him described to me in any way, still he was the first man I spoke to, and either I am a Sherlock Holmes, or Wright has that peculiar glint of genius in his eye which left no doubt in my mind as to who he was. . . . He arrived with nothing but a bag, about the size of a music roll, but mildly suggested

, . . he thought it might be advisable for him to buy another suit of clothes. I fortunately found a shop open in the Strand, for it was Saturday afternoon, and fixed him up, at least for evening wear, as he came to the conclusion that he'd "guess he'd better have a swaller-tail coat." We spent the entire afternoon together. . . .

The company idea did not seem to please him very much, as he first wanted to know himself exactly what the attitudes of the several governments were. After a long talk, . . . I believe, please note that I say distinctly "I believe," that I made something of an impression as regards the impossibility of getting any sort of action in the near future from any government. He agreed that he did not think the British Government would do any business. He also stated that perhaps it would be very hard to do anything with the French Government, as the French were so chauvinistic that their specialist officers in Commission would probably turn down the suggestions of even the Minister of War. There was only the German Government left, and even there I assured him that the government would do nothing, but we must look to the power greater than the government, that is, the Emperor himself. I proceeded to explain to him that even if the Emperor did recommend a full examination of his apparatus I was fearful that the Aeronautic Officers in the German Army would be apt to put all sorts of difficulties in the way, and I was fearful that it would be a long winded affair.

About 5 o'clock in the afternoon, I think, you will distinctly note that I say "I think," I brought about some sort of action in his mind, and I think he was on the point, you will note that I distinctly say that "I think he was on the point," of veering around from the government to company methods.

I told him further that I had made an engagement to take him to see Deutsch [de la Meurthe] on Tuesday, and that Deutsch had stated that he wished to see Wright before anyone else saw him. I think he agreed, you will note that I distinctly say "I think he agreed," to go to Paris with me Monday. I am to see him again at 1 o'clock today, Sunday, and I think I shall be able, you will kindly note that I distinctly say that "I think I shall be able," to get a more distinct expression from him of what he wants than resulted in my efforts of yesterday.

He made the argument that if we offered to private individuals at present, and our overtures were refused by them our chances with the governments would be greatly diminished. I could not agree with this. I think just the contrary, that we must not go so far with governments as to get an absolute negative from them, otherwise our chances in organizing a company would be diminished, as we could not offer the hope that the company would get government business. The idea being refused by private individuals would have no influence on governments, but being refused by governments would have a great influence on private individuals. I think Mr. Wright eventually looked at it in this light —you will note that I distinctly say that "I think Mr. Wright, etc."

I am much pleased with Wright's personality. He inspires great confidence and I am sure that he will be a capital Exhibit A.

.   .   .   .

Orville Wright to Wilbur

Dayton, Ohio, May 27, 1907

A few days ago the following came from the Ordnance Board:

"In reply to your letter of the 17th instant, I am directed to request that, as suggested by you, you will submit a formal proposition for furnishing a dirigible flying machine in such detail that the Board may take definite action thereon.

"The subject of aerial navigation being still in the experimental stage, no requirements have been formulated by the Board, and it is therefore suggested that you state what specifications you can fulfill, incorporating the conditions already named by you for a machine capable of carrying fuel supply for a flight of two hundred kilometers and two men in free flight at the rate of 50 kilometers an hour, for a sustained flight of 50 kilometers, and with reasonable dirigibility and safety in flight and in landing.

"Your proposition should also include a time of delivery and a stated price for the complete apparatus, payment to be made contingent upon agreed performance.

"If you have a machine constructed with which you can make flights, the Board would be interested in witnessing tests and could visit your establishment for the purpose.

"The next meeting of the Board will be held in this city on June 6th and a reply to this letter is requested prior to that date."

I intend to answer that we will furnish one machine, etc. for $100,000; that additional machines will be furnished at a reasonable advance over the cost of manufacture. That the time of delivery will be dependent upon what other engagements we have at the time of signing a contract, but that a contract entered into now could be filled within three to six months. I will probably answer their suggestion to come here and witness a flight something like this: Since many of the important features of our flyer have been kept secret— and are not now properly protected by patents—it would not be prudent to show the machine in advance of a contract. But in order to protect the purchaser we are willing that such specifications be entered in the contract as may be necessary to guarantee the dirigibility of the machine and its structural strength; and that as an additional safeguard to the purchaser, we are willing that no part of the purchase price be paid to us until the trial flight has been made in accordance with the requirements of the contract. I think I will propose to make the minimum speed forty miles an hour, provided $5,000 is allowed us for each mile above the speed performed in the trial flight; we to forfeit $5,000 of the purchase price for each mile below forty miles.

. . . .

Wilbur Wright to Orville

Paris, May 30, 1907

This afternoon I spent a couple hours in the Louvre, mostly in the picture galleries. On the whole, good prints give a very good idea of them. I liked the Rembrandts, van Dycks, Holbeins, Dous, Jordaens—a whole lot better than the Rubens, Titians, Raphaels and Murillos, though each of the latter has a few features I like very much. There seems to me to be a great difference between different pictures by the same man.

In one room they have a row consisting of a sample of several of the most celebrated painters, Tintoretto, Titian, Leonardo (Mona Lisa), Raphael (Portrait of Balthasar), and Velasquez and Corregio. The Raphael seems to me the best of the lot and the best of all the Raphaels. The Velasquez . . . is killed by the others. The Mona Lisa is no better than the prints in black and white. I must confess that the pictures by celebrated masters that impressed me most were not the ones that are best known. I like Leonardo da Vinci's "John the Baptist" much better than his "Mona Lisa." Holbein paints his portraits about the color of an Indian but they look like real people. Van Dyck is really the best portrait painter as a whole, though his "Children of Charles I" is not near as good as the prints, and his celebrated portrait of Charles is inferior to some of his other paintings.

.   .   .   .

Wilbur Wright to his father

Paris, June 4, 1907

The French understand how to place public buildings. There is always an open space. . . . And in addition there is nearly always a broad avenue leading directly up to it, giving a view from a long distance. It is this as much as the buildings and monuments themselves that makes Paris such a magnificent city. If the fine public and business buildings of New York could be arranged in the same way it would equal or surpass Paris, . . .

In Paris the parks are the play grounds of the people. In day time they are filled with children wearing little black silesia aprons or rather coats coming about to their knees, to keep their clothes clean. It is very amusing, but shows French thrift.

.   .   .   .

Wilbur Wright to his sister

Paris, June 5, 1907

This afternoon I spent a couple of hours in the Louvre. I went through the galleries of antiquities, Greek, Roman, Egyptian, Assyrian, Persian, etc. and also of the Middle Ages. There was really more art and sculpture during the period from 1000 to 1500 than I had supposed.

I also visited the rooms containing the French paintings of the 19th century. Troyon, Daubigny, Delacroix, Fromentin, Corot, Millet, Dupré, Regnault, Courbet, Meissonier, etc. While I do not pretend to be much of a judge I am inclined to think that in five hundred years it will be recognized as some of the greatest work ever done. Corot and Millet have styles peculiar to themselves. Corot nearly always uses a very light background of sky with the greatest light close to the ground. His trees are hazy and stand between you and the light, so that the latter comes through the trees instead of falling on them. In this he to some extent follows Claude Lorrain, but his light is very much bluer and he always shows trees instead of the Roman buildings which nearly always occupy one side of the Claude Lorrains. The pictures of Millet are usually figures of peasants or workmen not very clearly outlined on a dark background. The "Angelus" and the "Gleaners" are really not in his most common style.

Troyon always puts some cattle or other farm animals such
as sheep or chickens in his foreground.

.   .   .   .

Wilbur Wright to his sister

Paris, June 8, 1907

I stopped to have a look at the inside of the Notre Dame.
It was rather disappointing as most sights are to me. My
imagination pictures things more vividly than my eyes. The
nave is seemingly not much wider than a store room and
the windows of the clere-story are so awfully high up that
the building is very dark. The pillars are so heavy and close
together that the double aisles on each side form no part of
the room when you stand in the nave. The latter is so high
that the length seems shorter than it really must be.

.   .   .   .

Orville Wright to Octave Chanute

June 8, 1907

According to the newspapers Santos-Dumont has just tried
an experiment with an aeroplane attached to a gas bag, and
has had a very narrow escape from a serious accident. On
the whole, I have thought the design of Santos' machine
better than that of Delagrange or Kapferer; I can not just
now recall the design of the Zens' Brothers, though I have
seen it. But I do not feel uneasy that any of those that we can

read about in the papers are pursuing us too closely. It is now more than a year since Santos made his first trial; his longest flight was only 20 seconds; the next best less than ten seconds. In less than a year from the time we made our first trial, we had made thirty-seven flights of over twenty seconds —the thirty-seven amounting to a little over forty-one minutes, or on an average more than a minute and six seconds each. It would not appear from this that their progress is as rapid as ours was.

In the matter of wind their experiments will not compare at all with ours. As far as we can learn from the newspaper accounts, no flight has as yet been made in Europe in a wind of as much as five miles an hour. Our flights of 1903 were made in a wind of over twenty miles, and many of those here in Ohio were in winds of over ten miles an hour. In our early experiments we could not get a start unless we had a wind of at least ten miles, for lack of sufficient track. Our slowest flights were at a speed of thirty miles an hour. The best speed made in France is as yet less than twenty-five miles.

In the flights of 1903, we carried 63 lbs. per horse power at a speed of 30 miles an hour; and in 1905, 47 lbs. at a speed of 38½ miles an hour. Multiplying the weight per h.p. by the speed in miles per hour, it will be seen that the number of lbs. carried a mile per h.p. by Santos is but 350 as compared with 1860 in our flights of 1903.

From what Wilbur says in a letter just received, Kapferer is earnestly in favor of the formation of a company to take over our invention. From this I would infer that the French are not so sanguine of success as they were some months ago.

. . . .

Orville Wright to Wilbur

Dayton, Ohio, June 9, 1907

Cable dispatches from Paris say that you have bought several light French motors . . . or rather that *we* have— for according to the dispatches I am over there too! I also see that you have just sold several machines to the German government at $10,000 each, and I am being congratulated on our good luck!

I would give three cents to see you in your dress suit and plug hat!

. . . .

Wilbur Wright to Orville

Paris, June 11, 1907

It is possible that we may be compelled to agree to rise to a height of 300 meters, but the more I think of the matter the more certain I am that this feature is a matter of little risk to us.

. . . .

Orville Wright to Wilbur

Dayton, Ohio, June 11, 1907

If we organize a [European] company, we must take precautions against being frozen out. If they have control of the business, they could dispose of us in a very short time. . . .

It should also be understood that we are to have the privilege of taking in the smaller prizes that are up—even if we do not keep the money—so that we can have the glory of it.

. . . .

Orville Wright to Wilbur

Dayton, Ohio, June 15, 1907

I think it quite important that we should have a full half of the stock; otherwise the majority stockholders can elect themselves to all of the offices and thus consume all profits in salaries. If we have half the stock we can keep half the offices.

I have just answered the U. S. Ordnance Board, and I inclose a copy which you can destroy when you are through with it. I thought that if they still persist in a demonstration, that I would suggest the next time that we would have no objections if they have the power to contract for a machine immediately upon the demonstration, at the terms we have proposed.

. . . .

Wright Brothers (by Orville) to U. S. War Department

June 15, 1907

The price quoted in our letter of May 31 should be understood as the price of the first flyer delivered to the Government and the instruction necessary to enable a representative of the War Department to operate it. The price does not include any period of time during which the use of the invention would belong exclusively to the United States, since a recent contract precludes our offering such right.

We believe that the principal use of a flyer at present is for military purposes; that the demand in commerce will not be great for some time. It is therefore our intention to furnish machines for military use first, before entering the commercial field; but we reserve the right to exploit our invention in any manner we think proper.

In view of the abundant evidence already available, we do not regard the actual sight of the machine a prerequisite to the formulation of terms of contract; but on the other hand, we do think that some agreement should be reached as to price, etc., before any part of the invention is disclosed, since it provides the only guarantee that a sale on satisfactory terms will follow a demonstration that the machine is all that has been claimed for it.

We are able and willing to furnish proper presumptive evidence of ability to fulfill a contract. When a contract has been signed we will produce a machine at our own expense and make flights as specified in the contract in the presence of representatives of the War Department before any money whatever is paid to us. We do not ask for such payments as are customary in the building of battle ships, nor for any assumption of risk on the part of the Government.

We propose this method of doing business for the reason that it is the only way we see that will protect us against disclosing secrets to the idle curious, and at the same time protect the serious purchaser against imposition.

. . . .

Wilbur Wright to his father

Paris, June 18, 1907

As I have not been able to get back to London where I had ordered a dress suit, I have ordered another one here, and also a Prince Albert. They will cost about a hundred dollars. Please have Orville send me an American Express money order for $150. I cannot hob-nob with the Emperor when I go to Berlin without some clothes. We are expecting to go there within a few days. . . .

I have had numerous invitations to attend dinners, etc. in my honor but so far I have declined to make any promises. Unless it becomes necessary from a business point of view I shall wait about such things till Orville comes over.

June 20

In France the houses are built on the street solidly, and the courts are in the center where only the owners can enjoy them. Likewise in the country the road runs between high stone walls and resembles an alley, but inside, out of the traveler's sight, are beautiful grounds. It is not the American way.

. . . .

Wilbur Wright to Orville

Paris, June 18, 1907

Germany is now in the international [patent] agreement, which is good for us. In that country the law does not provide for patenting principles as we thought. It provides for patenting technical results. For instance if a man should be the original discoverer of the whip and should patent it for the purpose of making horses go faster, another man could get a patent on exactly the same thing for use in beating the dust out of carpets. But the third man, who might try to patent an improved form of whip for either purpose would be turned down by the patent office unless he could show that he achieved a new result, rather than a new construction.

In France the original inventor is given one year to make improvements, and any patents on improvements which he may file before his year is up, take precedence over patents covering the same improvements filed by others during the year. The other fellow's patents are no good, even though filed first.

. . . .

To Wilbur Wright in France from his father

Dayton, Ohio, June 22, 1907

It behooves you to be watchful of your interests, and to be certain in any move you may make. And you may be sure that all dealing with you will try to reach into you as far as possible. Men of wealth generally have exercised their shrewdness pretty well.

. . . .

Wilbur Wright to Octave Chanute

Paris, June 24, 1907

I arrived in London on the 25th of May and on the 27th came over to Paris for the purpose of a conference with Mr. Deutsch, who had indicated a desire that I should take up with him a proposition to form a company to take over the European business. With Mr. Berg and Mr. Cordley I called on him the day after my arrival. He expressed a readiness to join in the formation of a company, or to take us to the Minister of War. We finally decided to take the matter up with the war office before forming a company. Our proposition provides for a flight of 50 kilometers, rising to a height of 300 meters with one man on board. The price to be a million frances. The Minister of War had indicated to Mr. Deutsch that such a proposition would be acceptable. If this is not accepted without substantial modification we will probably go to Berlin to see Mr. Loewe and the German authorities.

If we close a deal Orville will come over with machines. Until something definite is done I do not know when I shall return to America.

As I have been very busy I have aimed to avoid social engagements, but have met most of the leading men interested in aeronautics,—Besançon, Ferber, Archdeacon, Da La Vaulx, Tatin, Malet, Surcouf, Delagrange, Zens, Masfrond, Esnault-Pelterie, &c, &c.

. . . .

Wilbur Wright to Orville

Paris, June 25, 1907, 3 P.M.

There are interesting developments. Certain parties whose identity is not clearly defined, and whom it would not be wise to name in a letter anyhow, have intimated that it would be best for us to raise our price to the F. gov't to 1,250,000 fr. and give the extra part to them. As I have taken the position that any payments to persons in any way representing the government must appear in the contract . . . it is probable that they will block us if they can, out of spite. I am very much surprised that such conditions obtain in this country. . . . If it appears that these people persist in their demands, we will file our offer with the Minister of War and if nothing is done promptly, will proceed to Germany.

. . . .

Orville Wright to Wilbur

Dayton, Ohio, July 2, 1907

A man representing a number of big Cincinnati machine companies in Japan was here yesterday to see about taking up our business with the Japanese government. I can't think of his name now, though I have his card somewhere. He married the daughter of Smith, the editor of Cincinnati *Tribune*. He was a consul in Japan under appointment from Harrison. I told him Flints were representing us in our foreign business. He said he knew of them very well but he did not care to take hold of the business through them.

. . . .

Wilbur Wright to Orville

Paris, July 2, 1907

I received your cable turning down the French government deal this morning. At noon the government also turned it down, so I am turned down on both sides, after both sides had, as I thought, indicated their approval.

. . . .

Wilbur Wright to Orville

Paris, July 5, 1907

As to the terms offered France (Flight of 50 kilometers, one man; rise 300 meters, one man; carry two men 10 kilometers; 6 months exclusive use; make the trials in France; do it within 7 months,) I studied all these points very carefully and I am sure that if we had offered less we would certainly have failed to secure a contract. We may fail even as it is. . . . I do not, myself, believe the 300 meters (height) feature will add materially to the danger, or to the time necessary, or to the chance of failure. If we put on a vane to show the angle of incidence and watch it to see that it is maintained approximately at 8 degrees or so, we are bound to rise at the maximum speed, even if the ground is out of sight. No special training is required. . . .

I am sorry that I did not insist stronger on your taking this end of the job, . . .

I realize fully that the nervous strain of sitting at home waiting for news, agitated by hopes and fears based on incomplete knowledge of the actual situation, not only unfits a man for work, but makes it difficult to give sound advice. Mine has been much the easier task.

．　．　．　．　．　．　．

Orville Wright to Octave Chanute

July 14, 1907

Our European negotiations have developed some very interesting situations in the past few weeks. I believe I told you in a former letter that Deutsch had had a conference with the ministers of marine and war, and that the Minister of War had expressed a willingness to purchase if we would agree to rise to a height of 300 meters.

A day or two after this conference, Deutsch received word from the Minister of War that Letellier had raised objections to the part Deutsch was taking in the matter, and asking that Deutsch withdraw. Letellier was the man that sent Fordyce here a year ago. He is the proprietor of the *Journal*, and the minister evidently was afraid of his influence. Letellier thought that the honor of bringing the invention to France should belong to him.

M. Deutsch withdrew and the road to an early contract appeared clear, when suddenly the negotiations were brought to a stop by certain parties, whom Wilbur does not care to mention in a letter, demanding that we raise the price several hundred thousand francs in order to furnish them an opportunity for graft.

Wilbur told them that we would not consider such a propsition, and that if they insisted on standing in our way, we would take the matter out of the ordinary channel, and offer it directly to the Minister of War for his acceptance or rejection, and that in that case, unless our proposition was accepted at once, we would proceed to Berlin. The bandits withdrew.

I received a cable last night from Wilbur asking me to ship goods and to come on to Paris at once, as they were ready to close.

.   .   .   .

Wilbur Wright to his sister

Paris, July 17, 1907

I am sorry that you are all so worn down by excitement. Strangely enough I myself am feeling much better than at any time in the past two years. Within a few days after reaching Europe I felt that I could handle the situation. . . .

When I first came over, Berg & Cordley thought that they were the business men and I was merely a sort of exhibit. But their eyes have gradually opened, and now they realize that I see into situations deeper than they do, that my judgment is more often sound, and that I intend to run them rather than have them run me. . . . Now I control everything and they give advice and assistance. . . .

It is amusing to me to see that Cordley and Berg are afraid to leave Orville and me to settle the commission business with Flint in New York. They feel certain that we could do as we pleased with him, if Cordley was not there to steady him. Cordley is really the best business man of the crowd. Flint and Berg are merely "hustlers."

You people at home must stop worrying! There is no need

of it. Orville & I can take care of ourselves all right, and we will be found on top when the smoke has cleared away.

. . . .

Wilbur Wright to his sister

Paris, July 18, 1907

Yesterday being the national holiday, I went out to Long-champs to help Pres. Fallières, Premier Clemenceau, and Gen. Picquart review the troops. We did a good job of it, reviewing some thirty thousand troops in a couple of hours. On the way home a poor fellow fired a toy pistol at us, but none of us were hurt. I was a mile or two away at the time, but from all accounts I was in about as much danger as the President.

. . . .

From Wilbur Wright's Diary

July 19, 1907

In afternoon wrote out a comparison of airships vs. flyers to send to Loewe [in Berlin]. He had asked for it.

. . . .

Both the Germans and the French were still pinning their hopes of air navigation to dirigible balloons rather than to heavier-than-air craft. The French had built the airship "La Patrie." The comparison Loewe had asked for would be useful, Hart O. Berg told Wilbur, in dealings with others who might be induced to invest in a flying-machine company.

. . . .

Wilbur Wright on Airships vs. Flyers

The cost of an airship of the type "La Patrie," including its equipment, is fully ten times as great as that of a flyer with its equipment, and there is a similar disproportion in the cost of upkeep.

It results that airships must necessarily be used in small numbers and for that reason under conditions which preserve them from danger of destruction by the shots of the enemy, while the cheap aeroplane flyer can be supplied to the army in such numbers that they can be used with the greatest freedom without fear of great monetary loss or of exhaustion of the supply if one is destroyed by the shots of the enemy now and then. . . .

The real advantage of the aeroplane flyer over the gas-bag airship lies in its enormously greater speed and serviceability. . . . But the flying machine has still another advantage of the greatest importance. It is so small and inconspicuous, and moves so fast that it is safe from the shots of the enemy at comparatively short distances. It comes and goes before the gunners can train their pieces and get the range. Moreover shots piercing the cloth do no serious harm. . . . At critical times 20 or even 50 flyers can be sent out at once to obtain knowledge of the enemy's movements. . . . If only one half should return bringing the desired news, the cost in life and money would be less than that of an ordinary reconnaissance. . . .

Attention is also called to the fact that the flying machine is in its infancy, while the airship has reached its limit and must soon become a thing of the past. The future is for the speedy, cheap and hardy flyer.

.   .   .   .

Having in mind the probable need to select a place for the demonstrations in France, Wilbur Wright made the same kind of investigation of weather conditions that he and Orville had done before going to Kitty Hawk.

From Wilbur Wright's Diary

Paris, July 20, 1907

Went to Tour St. Jacques and saw wind records and anemometer charts showing wind. Also went to Central Bureau and obtained special pamphlet on winds at Central Bureau and at Eiffel tower.

July 22, 1907

Bought a copy of French meteorological records giving wind, temperature, and rains for different parts of France and Colonies.

.   .   .   .

Wilbur Wright to his sister

Paris, July 24, 1907

I have not been devoting much time to sight seeing for some time, but this morning I spent an hour in the Louvre again. I was especially interested in the Dutch & Flemish pictures which occupy a row of little rooms on each side of the grand salon of Rubens. I had not been in these rooms before. The pictures of van Ostade, Brouwer, Wouverman, Mieris, Dou, Cuyp, &c, are very wonderful in their way but I should scarcely call them great. They are very lifelike in their fine detail and brilliance, but when you stop to think whether or not they really look like the things they profess to picture, it must be confessed that they do not. But the landscapes of Ruysdael and Hobbemma (I have inserted enough letters so you can take your choice) are about the finest things I have seen. They possess one characteristic in common. Their trees are not like pressed flowers pasted on canvas, but they stand out each branch for itself with the air circulating all through. They have a little the appearance of Corot's landscapes but are free from the indistinctness of the latter. There are several pictures by Franz Hals but they did not particularly impress me. The pictures of Rembrandt have been removed into the large salon except a few. The same is true of the Rubens pictures. The Flemish and Dutch schools are badly mixed in these rooms so that I have to stop and think sometimes whether Paul Potter and Teniers and van Eyck are Dutch or Flemish. It has always been my impression that Rubens, van Dyck, Teniers, Snyders, Jordaens are Flemish; and that Rembrandt, Hals, Paul Potter, Cuyp, Dou, the van Ostades, and the Ruysdaels, &c were

Dutch. I suppose I really ought to get a Baedecker and get these things straight in my mind, but this business of walking through picture galleries merely for education and not for pleasure does not suit my present needs.

I suppose Orville will be here within four days so I am trying to avoid any definite action on our offer to the French government till he arrives. I am sure that we could close the deal by giving them a year's exclusive time, but this I have positively refused, as Orville was not satisfied even with my offer of six months. The probability is now that the negotiation will be fruitless like that of last year's, as neither side will yield the last inch necessary to reach common ground.

.   .   .   .

Wilbur Wright to Octave Chanute

Paris, July 24, 1907

I have met Capt. Ferber several times, but we are not very intimate. I find that after working hard last year or rather in 1905-6 winter to secure our flyer for France, he became infected with ambition before the end, and was largely responsible for the failure of the final negotiation in March 1906. Since then he has done all he could to prevent us from doing business here.

.   .   .   .

Wilbur Wright to his father

Paris, August 2, 1907

Orville arrived in Paris last Sunday morning pretty well tired out. He looked rather thin but is fattening up a little, I think, now. From what he says it seems he supposed I had come over here merely to talk, or for fun, rather than for business. . . .

One or both of us will almost certainly go to Berlin about the end of this week and spend a few days there, talking with Mr. Loewe, who is the head of the firm that supplies Germany and many other countries with small arms.

.   .   .   .

Wilbur had cabled to Orville to join him in Paris. And with the prospect that it might be necessary to make a demonstration, a plane was crated and shipped from Dayton to France.

Orville arrived in Paris around the first of August. Charles Taylor, the Wrights' chief mechanic, came a week later.

In conferences when both brothers were present, Wilbur was likely to do most of the talking. Orville felt that the older brother should take the lead.

Orville Wright to his sister

Paris, August 2, 1907

I arrived in Paris Sunday morning at five o'clock. . . . I engaged a porter to carry my trunk to a cab, explaining to him in English that I had no French money. . . . When he got the trunk on the cab, I offered him a dime. Then you never heard such jabbering. I asked whether that was not enough, to which he replied and continued to jabber in French. I had no idea of what the trouble was, but I handed him another dime. To my astonishment he handed this back with a lot more jabber, of which I could only make out *"assez"* and, smiling, he waved me off. I have been wondering ever since what all his talk was about.

.   .   .   .

Orville Wright's Diary

August 6, 1907

Humbert [head of budget committee of French Senate, at lunch with Fordyce and General Targe] said that he had no faith in the Wrights—that they were frauds.

.   .   .   .

Wilbur Wright to Orville

Berlin, August 6, 1907

We reached Berlin at 7:30 yesterday and put up at Hotel Bristol on Unter-den-Linden. My room is #236.

Berg went to see Herr Loewe [arms manufacturer] and got an appointment for 5 P.M. with him. In conversation with Berg he said that the German officers were prejudiced on account of the reference to the Emperor, in the doctored letter which Ferber published in 1906. He also said that they talked that our machine would be useless even if it did all we claimed. At five we went to see Herr Loewe together, and remained with him for over an hour. He had made an appointment to have Hauptman von Kehler, (who is managing the airship society which the Emperor instigated last year,) meet us at his office Tuesday at 10 o'clock. . . .

Capt. von Kehler came about 11 o'clock. He had arisen at 4 o'clock to attend a flight of the minister of war in the new airship, but unfortunately there was a wind of seven or eight miles and it was necessary to postpone the demonstration. . . . Having thus fortunately met the minister of war, he mentioned my presence in Berlin and his engagement to see me. The minister asked him to take us to see the chief of the department of means of communication at once. The minister also said that it would be impossible to talk business on the basis of a million francs, as he had no such sum on hand at present for such purpose, but he sent his personal assurance to Herr Loewe and us that if we trusted them and the machine proved important we would not be cheated out of a proper reward. Such an assurance from the minister himself, communicated to both us and Herr Loewe, is of course a very different thing from a similar assurance from some minor official with no authority to speak or power to make good his promise. Captain von Kehler is becoming very much excited. In fact I think we will soon have the whole pot boiling. Herr Loewe is evidently becoming more and more interested and he has the position to get us to the right people. Berg also has a very wide acquaintance with the prominent arms people of Germany and gets them to talking about us.

. . . .

Orville Wright to his father

Paris, August 23, 1907

We have been real good over here. We have been in a lot of churches, and haven't got drunk yet!

. . . .

Wilbur Wright to his father

Paris, August 27, 1907

As to drinking and dissipation of various kinds you may be entirely easy. All the wine I have tasted since leaving home would not fill a single wine glass. I am sure that Orville and myself will be careful to do nothing which would disgrace the training we received from you and from mother.

. . . .

Wilbur Wright to his sister

Paris, August 27, 1907

I am sorry that all three of you could not have been here all summer prancing up and down the Champs Elysées and rue de Rivoli and through the Louvre with red Baedeckers in hand, like the other teachers I have seen. It is so rich to see that look of ravenous thirst for knowledge; and combined expression of heavenly satisfaction and sore feet. Ha! Ha!

. . . .

Orville Wright's Diary

August 27, 1907

Cash on hand $59. . . .

. . . .

Wilbur Wright to Octave Chanute

Paris, September 2, 1907

I spent two weeks in Berlin early last month and found a much readier spirit to negotiate than expected. Capt. von Kehler who is manager of the Emperor's motor airship society has shown himself exceptionally friendly and interested in advancing negotiations with his government. It was thought best however to withdraw our offers to France before starting there.

We had a pledge from the minister of war, Gen. von Einen, that if we would come to Germany we would receive fair treatment. As we found a very different spirit cropping out in the French negotiations, we finally decided to withdraw here and try countries we could trust further. We will probably go to Berlin before the end of this week. The future negotiations will not contain any provision for a period of exclusive use. We will thus be free to negotiate with more than one government at a time.

The French aeroplanists are busy, but up to the present we see no indication of a practical machine in the near future. . . .

Some of the American newspapers recently contained a

story regarding our American negotiations which very much misrepresent the facts, and particularly misrepresent our sentiments. We have never thought of excluding America from the use of our invention. Neither did our resentment of the treatment our early communications received ever extend beyond insistence that the government should voluntarily reopen the door it had slammed in our faces. It has done this, and we are as ready to reach an agreement as though the incident had never occurred. We are sorry that a direct conference could not have been arranged before we were called to Europe.

. . . .

To Wilbur Wright in France from his father

September 5, 1907

I did not anticipate that either of you would become intemperate or debauched, but I want you to show the foreigners that you are teetotalers, and in every way maintain that high character which it is most proper to have, and which in the eyes of the best in America is the most approved.

. . . .

Orville Wright to his sister

Paris, September 20, 1907

Bleriot tried his aeroplane day before yesterday and made a flight of a little over 500 feet and rose to a height of 60 ft.

according to the papers! The machine made a sudden dart and was badly smashed up. They even blamed the motor for the dart. They seem to have almost perfect machines, but very cantankerous motors!

．　．　．　．　．　．　．

Orville Wright to Wilbur

Paris, September 21, 1907

I took dinner at the Lahm's last evening. . . . The Lieutenant is taking a great deal of interest in airships, . . . He is evidently expecting to have some work of that kind—having been transferred to that department in the U. S. Army.

．　．　．　．　．　．　．

It was Frank S. Lahm, an American businessman living in Paris and a member of the Aéro Club, who had arranged with a relative at Mansfield, Ohio, some time previously to investigate the claims of the Wrights. After going to Paris the Wrights soon became friendly with him, and with his son Lieutenant Frank P. Lahm. The younger Lahm's transfer to the Signal Corps at Washington became important to the Wrights, since he had strong faith in them and enthusiasm for the airplane's possibilities. At last there would be a man in the War Department at Washington who believed in the Wrights.

Wilbur Wright to his father

Berlin, September 27, 1907

We are in communication with the owner of the Barnum
& Bailey show business but do not yet know whether anything will come of it.

.   .   .   .

Wilbur Wright to Orville

Berlin, September 28, 1907

I write to London thinking possibly you may be called
there to have a conference with Mr. Stewart [representing
Barnum & Bailey circus]. If so you will need to consider the
following plans.

(1) A gliding machine raised by a balloon and dropped.
It could be operated in any ordinary weather, and if a suitable place for landing could be found within a mile of the
show grounds it could be easily reached. It would even be
practicable to come back and land on top of the big tent as
the weight would be less than that of two men and well
spread out. It could land in a crowd without killing any one
as the weight is light and the speed could be reduced to
nothing almost.

(2) Exhibitions at such places as large race tracks where
admission could be charged. Followed by exhibitions of the
machine in an exhibition hall up town.

(3) Exhibition of short straight flights on such grounds

as are used for Buffalo Bill shows and in connection there-with.

(4) Exhibitions at fairs, pleasure resorts, &c, &c, and big celebrations.

. . . .

Wilbur Wright to Orville

Berlin, September 29, 1907

It is not probable that anything can be done with Stewart strictly on exhibition lines until we have our other plans definitely settled upon. . . . It would be all right certainly to tell him that we offered to go to Washington last spring in order to have a heart to heart talk with the war department, to see if some plan could not be found on which we could get together, but they did not approve our suggestion, and so we never had a chance to find out whether they really wished to do business or not. But if they would give us a chance to talk over matters with them we believe some basis of agreement could be found, as we are not disposed to make our first flight abroad, if our own government really wishes to enter the flying game. Tell him that our proposed con-tracts have contained the clause leaving us free to furnish machines to our own country whenever it wished to have them.

. . . .

Orville Wright to his family

London, October 1, 1907

Mr. Stewart wanted to exhibit our machine at an Exposition to be held here at London next year. He wants the machine to start from inside an amphitheater, like that at the St. Louis fair. He proposed to have Chevelier, one of the French automobile racers, operate the machine; but I do not think the plan feasible. He says he can make scads of cash out of it if we can operate it under such conditions.

.   .   .   .

Orville went from London to join Wilbur and Berg in Berlin. The German officials, though greatly interested, could not believe that what the Wrights offered to do could be possible. They were afraid to sign their names to a contract, because it seemed almost as risky as signing up for a perpetual motion machine, and they didn't want to become laughing stocks of the world.

On the other hand, if the invention was really as good as represented, they did not want this opportunity to slip through their fingers. They therefore gave, instead of a signed contract, their solemn promise that if the Wrights would make a flight before them, under conditions set forth in a proposed contract, they would buy planes on the Wrights' terms. The Wrights expected to return to Germany in the spring of 1908. They could not foresee that by then they would have too many other engagements in definite contracts.

Wilbur Wright to his sister

Berlin, October 13, 1907

In the evening we usually go to a restaurant down on the Leipsiger strasse, about a half mile away and afterward walk for an hour on our way back to the hotel. About the most amusing thing we have seen in these walks was the Cash Register office. . . . The room was full of people going about playing with the machines as though they were toy pianos or something of the kind. . . . I joined in like any Dutchman and punched a couple of tickets as souvenirs of the occasion. . . . The signs explained so clearly and convincingly the advantages of cash registers in selling all kinds of goods, that we came near getting one to help sell our flying machines.

. . . .

Wilbur Wright to his sister

Berlin, October 22, 1907

One of the German papers had a cartoon on us a few weeks ago, that is about the best thing we have seen. Orville will send you a copy if he has not already done so. The Gebruder Wright are represented as bargaining over the sale of a "cat in a bag." Orville is at one end bargaining with France while I am working Russia at the other end. France has a wheelbarrow full of money and is down on its knees begging us to accept it. The pile is marked 3,900,000 francs. Orville with

a pipe in his mouth leans indifferently against the bag containing the wonderful machine, and with a bare glance at the
3,900,000 fr. holds up four fingers to indicate that 4,000,
fr. is our bottom price. At the other end I am almost equally
indifferent, though Russia is represented as pulling its last
rouble out of its pocketbook.

As soon as France scrapes up another 100,000 fr. we will
sell out and come home.

. . . .

Orville Wright to his sister

Paris, November 15, 1907

I went with Mr. Berg to the Automobile Show, and there
met several of the prominent automobile people. . . . While
we were looking at the exhibit of the Antoinette motors,
Capt. Ferber came up and I had a little talk with him—a very
little talk—for he couldn't understand my English and I
couldn't understand his French. Berg would occasionally tell
us what we were talking about!

. . . .

Orville Wright to his father

Paris, November 19, 1907

I went out to see Farman go for the Deutsch-Archdeacon
prize yesterday. Mr. Berg took Walter Savage Landor and
me out in his automobile. We were not much more than out

of the automobile when Mr. Archdeacon happened to spy Berg and rushing up to him said in his loud, squeaky voice, "Now, where are your Wrights?" With a sweeping gesture to me and to Landor who was with me, Berg said, "There they are." Archdeacon did not seem to understand, or thought Berg was fooling, so he shouted louder than ever, "Where are the Wrights?" It was not more than fifteen seconds till I was surrounded by newspaper men. There were several hundred cameras on the grounds and Berg and Savage say there was not one that failed to take a snap at us. . . . Berg enjoyed hugely the attention we attracted, and was right in for going out today again, but I objected.

. . . .

Wilbur Wright to his father

On board R.M.S. Baltic, *November* 22, 1907

I left Paris on Monday the 11th and after spending two days in London sailed on the 14th from Liverpool. We expect to reach New York about 6 o'clock tonight. . . .

Orville is still in Paris getting drawings ready for having some engines built in France. . . .

We will spend the winter getting some more machines ready for the spring trade. Then we will probably put out a sign, "Opening day, all goods below cost." We will probably return to Europe in March, unless we make arrangements with U. S. Government before that.

. . . .

Wilbur Wright to Octave Chanute

December 9, 1907

When I arrived in Europe last Spring, Mr. Berg in accordance with an engagement already made with Mr. Deutsch, took me to Paris at once for a conference with him. Mr. Deutsch after some conversation said he was very much interested and would be pleased to join in the formation of a company to exploit our invention if we could present a proposition of a sound business character. He also offered to see the minister of war in regard to our machine. After a few days he called on the minister who sent for the Wright "dossier" and the Comm. Bonel, and after examination said the matter was one of evident importance and that if machines were offered for sale he would be disposed to buy some. Mr. Deutsch was very much pleased with the interview and again asked us to present a proposition. After obtaining Orville's consent to the formation of a company, we proposed a company with a capital of $700,000 of which $600,000 was to represent the value of the invention and $100,000 was to be working capital. $350,000 of the stock was to be sold for cash. Of the proceeds, $100,000 was to remain in the treasury of the company as working capital, and the remaining $250,000 was to be ours. We were also to retain the unsold stock. In other words we were to receive $250,000 in cash and a half interest in the company, for the European rights in our inventions. Mr. Deutsch after considering the proposition agreed to take $70,000 of the stock, one-fifth of the amount offered for sale. Mr. Loewe, of Berlin was to have taken an equal amount, and Messrs. Flint had agreed to put their commission back in with enough additional cash to bring their share up to the same amount. We expected to secure large subscribers in England, Italy and possibly Austria for most of the remaining two-fifths. It was not the intention to have many small stockholders. With such men in it the company would have been strong enough to command the respect of any government or person disposed to pirate our inventions, and it is my belief that the profits of the business would have amounted to several million dollars within a half dozen years.

But while the lawyers were preparing the articles of incorporation an event occurred which blocked the whole plan for the time. When Fordyce and his master Letellier learned that we were in conference with Mr. Deutsch they were very angry and though we offered to let the latter subscribe for the same amount as Mr. Deutsch if he wished, he insisted that he should be the sole French member on a large scale. As an attempt to drop out Mr. Deutsch would have meant the probable withdrawal of Mr. Loewe and the Messrs. Flint & Co., it was impossible to accede to this demand, even though we had been willing. But we were not willing and told him it would be much better to have Mr. Deutsch with us also. When Letellier found he could not gain his end with us, he went to the minister of war and made a fuss. He said he had spent money sending Fordyce to America and securing an option which had been assigned to the former minister, and that he did not propose to let Mr. Deutsch come at a late day and get all the credit. He claimed that a paper given to Fordyce by the former minister at the time Fordyce transferred his option, gave him certain rights, the nature of which I do not clearly understand. He demanded that the business should be done through him. As Letellier's father is the owner of *Le Journal* the minister did not wish to have trouble, and sending for Mr. Deutsch told him that he wished the business done through Letellier. Mr. Deutsch was naturally very much mortified and at once sent us word of what had occurred, and of his withdrawal from the company project. He at first supposed that we were really bound to Letellier and were culpable for coming to him at all, but later in the season we found opportunity to explain the true situation and he became quite friendly again.

Without a strong company back of us we did not feel it safe to begin selling machines one by one, so it became a question of attempting to put through a deal with France on the old basis or of trying Germany. As it had become known that we were in negotiation with Mr. Deutsch and that the latter had been to see the minister of war, we felt it hopeless to go to Germany with the apparent discredit of a flat turn down by both the government and private capitalists, in France. We could not make known the real facts. Under such conditions it seemed preferable to try France. We had reason to believe that the minister was not hostile and that some of his most trusted advisers were positively in our favor.

As the negotiation was carried on through Fordyce as intermediary, it moved very slowly, two or three weeks being consumed with each interchange of papers. We soon saw that unless we could get face to face with the officials so as to understand each other clearly, the negotiation might last a year or two. We tried twice to get the war office to let us deal directly, but each time were assured by Targe, the minister's assistant, that the minister wished the business done through Letellier. After the second attempt we decided to send in notice of the withdrawal of all propositions, and get out. This we did, although Fordyce assured us that the deal would certainly be made in a short time longer. I think a bargain could have been made if we had been willing to trust the other side a little further.

In Germany the autumn maneuvers prevented us from getting a negotiation well under way till the latter part of September, but we were very favorably received, and within a few days after Gen. von Lyncker, chief of "inspection," and Major Gross, of the balloon section were free, we had come to an agreement as to the requirements in the trials. Major Gross was very anxious to see the negotiation succeed. We also had the support of Capt. von Kehler, the active head of the Emperor's airship society, as also of Mr. Loewe, of the Mauser gun concern and other important companies, and Mr. Rathenow, head of the "Allgemeine Electrisch Gesellschaft"—these two men being directors and the chief contributors to the funds of that society. Von Moltke, chief of staff, was favorable also. There seemed to be no active opposition anywhere, but as they were under no apprehension of being beaten by the French, they finally decided to reject our proposition for an outright sale. However we received assurances that if we would furnish machines one by one we would be fairly treated. We however thought it best to wait till the opening of a new season before entering upon such a plan of doing business. We did not like to disclose our machine at the tail end of the year and give imitators all winter to manufacture copies of it. We do not wish to get into lawsuits before we get the business properly organized and started. Our plan is to spend the winter building a half dozen new machines for the spring trade. We do not fear any serious competition until after we show our machine.

. . . .

Wilbur Wright to Octave Chanute

January 1, 1908

I note from several remarks in your recent letters that you evidently view the present situation in aviation circles with very different eyes from what we do. I must confess that I still hold to my prediction that an independent solution of the flying problem would require at least five years. The two years that have passed since Archdeacon, Santos and Ferber predicted that the feats of the Wrights would be surpassed in France within three months, have seen all other predictions than ours overturned or repeatedly amended. I have confidence that our prediction will still stand solid after the scythe of time has reaped several fresh crops of French predictions. . . .

This question however is now becoming one of little practical importance. We had all the time we needed for negotiations on the line of secrecy, and at no time were our plans overturned or seriously affected by the work of other experimenters. If there was a possible exception to this statement it was due to the fact that some of the people with whom we were in negotiation may have been rendered more skeptical of the usefulness of aeroplanes by the ups and down of aeroplane inventors during these years. The things actually accomplished by them were a negligible factor so far as effects on our negotiations were concerned.

As to the matter of price we have always felt that it is impossible to fix a definite price on an invention of this kind and then say, "More, would be too much; less, too little." Of one thing I feel very certain—the result of every negotia-

Wright Brothers Memorial at Kill Devil Hill, N. C.,
near Kitty Hawk.

Orville Wright, 26 years old. Before he raised his mustache.

7 Hawthorne Street, about 1900. Here the Wrights lived while inventing the plane.

Wilbur Wright, 1907.

The house at Hawthorn Hill, where Orville Wright lived
after 1912.

Katharine Wright, 1898.

Bishop Milton Wright, 1889.

Manufacturers of Van Cleve
Bicycles **Wright Cycle Company**
St. Clair
1127 West Third Street.

DAYTON, OHIO, *May 13, 1900*

Mr. Octave Chanute, Esq.
Chicago, Ill.

Dear Sir; For some years I have been afflicted with the belief that flight is possible to man. My disease has increased in severity and I feel that it will soon cost me an increased amount of money if not my life. I have been trying to arrange my affairs in such a way that I can devote my entire time for a few months to experiment in the field.

My general ideas of the subject are similar those held by most practical experimenters, to wit: that what is chiefly needed is skill rather than machinery. The flight of the buzzard and simi

Opening page of Wilbur Wright's first letter to Octave Chanute.

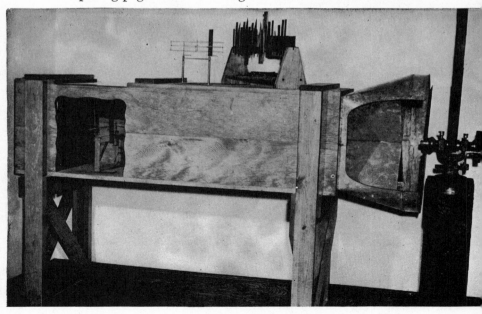

Replica of Wrights' wind tunnel. Having no electricity in their shop they used a one-cylinder gasoline engine to operate the fan.

Kitty Hawk camp and plane, 1903.

The life saving station at Kill Devil, whence came most of the spectators of the first power flight.

Wilbur Wright in 1902 glider, in which most of the problems of human flight were solved, with Wright's Kitty Hawk camp to be seen below.

2—161.

DEPARTMENT OF THE INTERIOR,

No. ___

United States Patent Office,

Washington, D. C., *Mar -14-*, 190 *3*.

Informal.

SIR:

I have to acknowledge the receipt of the petition, specification, oath, and

drawing of your alleged *Improvement* in _____

Flying machines.

_____

_____

with **Fifteen Dollars** as the first fee payable thereon.

The papers are ~~duly filed, and your application for a patent will be taken up for examination in its order~~ *returned for formal oath, blank form sent. please return all papers sent herewith*

_____

You will be duly advised of the examination.

Very respectfully,

F. J. Allen.

Commissioner of Patents.

O. Wright & W. Wright

_____

_____

NOTE.—In order to constitute an application for a patent, the inventor is by law required to furnish his petition, specification, oath, and drawings (where the nature of the case admits of drawings) and to pay the required fee.

No application is considered as complete, nor can any official action be had thereon, until all its parts, as here specified, are furnished in due form by the inventor or applicant.

Acknowledgment of basic patent application—nearly nine months before the first flight in powered machine. The patent was based on the system of control demonstrated in their 1902 glider.

east corner of the paper. Finally we got to the top and thought that our troubles were over but they were only begun for after riding about half a mile the road began to "wobble up and down something after the following fashion.

Centerville

As Boyle Roache would have said "Just when she had climbed to the highest of all possible hills she

A part of one of Wilbur's letters to his sister showing "illustrations."

Wreck of Wright plane at Fort Myer, September, 1908, when Lieutenant Selfridge was killed and Orville Wright injured.

First flight of the Wright power plane, December 17, 1903.

Orville Wright setting new world's record for gliding,
at Kitty Hawk, 1911.

The Wright brothers, 1910.

Cartoon by Homer Davenport drawn in 1909, autographed to "The sister of men who have won the admiration of all of us, even to the birds of the air."

L'Aviation en 1908

I'll tie a string to you
next time to keep you from
going too high or too far.
Its too much trouble to
break your records.
Will.

Photo J. Bouveret Le Mans

Postcard sent from France by Wilbur Wright to Orville during
Orville's sensational flights at Fort Myer.

Orville Wright, 1944.

Presentation of Wright brothers' first airplane, after its return
from exile, to custody of National Air Museum,
December 17, 1948.

tion would probably have been the same if the price named had been one-half as great, or, even one-fourth as great as it was. Other points were the real stumbling blocks, and a moderate reduction in price would not have removed them. We considered it the better plan to vary our plans to meet the real issues. This is what we are doing.

. . . .

Wright Brothers to U. S. War Department

January 9, 1908

We thank you for your letter of January 3rd informing us of the action of the Board of Ordnance and Fortification in authorizing the Chief Signal Officer to modify the specifications for heavier than air flying machines in such manner as to permit any bidder to reserve as confidential such features of his machine as he wishes to keep secret.

We note that the specifications require that a bond equal to the amount of the bid be filed at the awarding of the contract. As the nature of some of the requirements in the specifications are different from anything with which we have had experience—such as, that the test of the machine be limited to three trials, all to be made within one month—we would like to inquire as to what extent bondsmen would be liable in case the machine fulfilled most of the requirements within the prescribed time, but should fail in one or two particulars to meet every requirement. Would the bond be absolutely forfeited, or would the bondsmen be liable only for the damage done the government by such failure?

We would also beg to inquire whether it is probable that the certified check deposited with the bid will be held for a considerable time, or whether it is the intention of the Board to take definite action soon after the opening of the bids.

. . . .

Lieutenant Thomas Selfridge, Secretary of the Aerial Experiment Association,* to the Wright brothers

January 15, 1908

I am taking the liberty of writing you and asking your advice on certain points connected with gliding experiments, or rather glider construction, which we started here last Monday.

Will you kindly tell me what results you obtained on the travel of the center of pressure both on aerocurves and aeroplanes?

Also, what is a good, efficient method of constructing the ribs of the surfaces so that they will be light and yet strong enough to maintain their curvature under ordinary conditions, and a good means of fastening them to the cloth and upper lateral cords of the frame?

I hope I am not imposing too much by asking you these questions.

. . . .

---

* The Aerial Experiment Association had been formed by Alexander Graham Bell and others, with headquarters first in Nova Scotia and later at Hammondsport, New York, where Glenn Curtiss lived. Curtiss became a "Director of Experiments." See letter from Orville Wright to Fred C. Kelly, November 9, 1940.

Supposing the information asked for would be used only for scientific purposes, the Wrights obligingly replied at once.

Wilbur and Orville Wright to Lieutenant Thomas Selfridge, secretary of the Aerial Experiment Association

January 18, 1908

You will find much of the information you desire in the addresses of our Mr. Wilbur Wright before the Western Society of Engineers, published in the Journals of the Society of December, 1901, and August, 1903.

The travel of the center of pressure on aeroplanes is from the center at 90 degrees, toward the front edge as the angle becomes smaller. The center of pressure on a curved surface is approximately at its center at 90 degrees, moves forward as the angle is decreased until a critical angle is reached, after which it reverses, and moves toward the rear edge. The critical angle varies for different shaped curves, but is generally reached at some angle between 12 and 18 degrees. With the angles used in gliding flight the travel will be between the center of the surface and a point one-third back from the front edge.

The methods of construction used in our gliders are fully described in an article by Mr. Chanute in the *Revue des Sciences* in 1903 (we do not remember the month) and in the specifications of our United States patent, No. 821,393.

The ribs of our gliders were made of second growth ash, steamed and bent to shape.

. . . .

The data the Wrights gave them must have been useful to the Aerial Experiment Association, for early the following summer Glenn Curtiss, director of experiments, had a power-driven airplane called the "June Bug" in which he made a flight on July 4, 1908, at Hammondsport. That flight created the belief in the minds of many who were not fully informed that the Aerial Experiment Association had done an amazing job of original research. This belief was encouraged by the fact that after the Aerial Experiment Association began building and experimenting with flying machines, using the information obtained from the Wrights, they neglected in public statements about their work to mention the Wright brothers.

Wilbur Wright to Octave Chanute

January 16, 1908

Of course it is not possible to know just how the financial end of our flyer will come out until the event shows, but I think the prospects as good now as at any time since Fordyce and Letellier spoiled things for us. It would have been a great advantage if we could have organized our company before beginning business, but we will still do very well unless we are much mistaken. The governments will each spend many times $200,000 on flying machines within the next fifteen years, and we think we will have patents, knowledge and business associations sufficient to insure a good share of it coming our way. Yet we may be mistaken.

The belief that others would soon succeed in attaining results equal or superior to ours has of course been one of the serious obstacles we have always had to contend with. It has never been stronger than in the first few months after our announcement of success. It was based on the general principle that what one can do, others can do. The actual progress made by others was much slower than was expected and tended to dispel the belief that we would be overtaken almost at once.—I do not think that very much respect is paid to Archdeacon's opinions. He is such an ass. In any event the day when much talk could do us serious harm is now past. For nearly a year we have worked on the plan of selling to governments for a lump sum, only when forced to it. Our real idea has been to get a proper organization for doing a regular business with governments first and the general trade afterwards.

. . . .

Wilbur Wright to Octave Chanute

January 27, 1908

I . . . note that your views do not in all respects coincide with our own. You think a serious accident in the French camp would benefit us. We do not think so. Our *real* difficulty has been to convince army officials that an aeroplane could be made practical. If they had been certain on this point, all questions of price, &c, would have been settled in short order. The troubles of the French experimenters made *us* much more trouble than their successes by throwing more and more doubt on the practicability of any aeroplane. If Farman should be killed by a fall, it would injure us to the extent of thousands of dollars, we believe.

Neither can we feel that a mistake was made in failing to organize a company at the beginning. It is true that we could have made big money by selling stock to ignorant gullible investors, but we never considered it proper to do such a thing. We might have sold some stock to persons like yourself, Mr. Root, and Mr. Cabot, who would have invested for other than sound business reasons, but we did not care to do that. As for selling to real business men on a strictly business basis, we feel certain that we can do much better today than we could have done at the beginning. In organizing a company the patents are the important things. They are fully as valuable now as at the beginning. The reason we have never worried for fear we would be overtaken, was because we have felt that no machine depending on dihedral [v-shaped] angle would ever be practical, while our patents would protect our own system broadly. We have never seen any indication of a new solution of the problem of lateral stability. Of course if the dihedral angle furnishes a satisfactory solution of this problem we have not now, and never had the basis on which to found a company. But we had such confidence in this reserve, that we have always felt safe in taking all the time we needed for attempting sales on other than company plans. If these special plans failed, we would be no worse off than before we tried them. Meanwhile the increase in general interest in aeronautics would make our patents more salable rather than less salable.

VIII

WORLD RECOGNITION

The U. S. War Department finally got around to dealing with the Wrights and on December 23, 1907, advertised for bids for an airplane. Since the Wright machine was the only one in existence that could meet the requirements, and a price of $25,000 was understood in advance, advertising for bids may have been superfluous but was considered necessary to meet demands of red tape. The Wrights' bid was accepted on February 8, 1908.

Less than a month later, on March 3, the Wrights closed a contract for the formation of a company in France. A member of the French syndicate was M. Deutsch de la Meurthe who had some time previously taken steps to form a French company. For the syndicate in France, as well as for the U. S. War Department, a satisfactory demonstration of the machine was required.

Now with two contracts on their hands, the Wrights had much preliminary work and practicing to do before they could make the required demonstrations. Though they had done no flying since October, 1905, they had been improving both plane and engine. Their newest engine, capable of producing about thirty-five horsepower continuously, was so much better as to reliability that now long flights could be made without danger of failure of the motive power.

During all their experiments of the Huffman pasture they had continued to ride "belly-buster," as a boy usually does when coasting on a sled. Lying flat and controlling the mechanism partly by swinging the hips from one side to the other was good enough for the experimental stages of aviation; but the Wrights knew that if a plane was to have practical use the pilot must be able to take an ordinary sitting position and do the controlling and guiding with his hands and feet, as in an automobile. The brothers therefore had adopted a different arrangement of the control levers, for use in a sitting position, and added a seat for a passenger. Moreover, the machine could be steered from either seat and thus was suitable for training other pilots. (The plane sent to France for possible trials in 1907 was thus equipped.) They now revamped the machine they had used at the Huffman pasture in 1905 and installed their later improvements; the engine had vertical instead of horizontal cylinders. With this machine they would go to Kitty Hawk and gain needed practice in handling their new arrangement of the control levers.

The United States Government tests would be made at Fort Myer, Virginia, near Washington. Delivery of the machine had to be made by August 28, and the tests themselves were to begin shortly afterward, in September. At about that same time, one of the brothers would make a demonstration in France. They had not yet decided which of them would fly at Fort Myer and which should go to France. But both had to be well prepared and there was no time to lose. They must be established at Kitty Hawk as soon as possible.

Wilbur Wright to Octave Chanute

Elizabeth City, N. C., April 8, 1908

I am on my way to Kitty Hawk to get a camp in shape for a little practice before undertaking the official trials at Washington and in France. I am not sure that I mentioned the fact that we have been in negotiation for the sale of our French rights for several months past, and that we finally accepted the offer of M. Lazare Weiler who is the head of many large enterprises in France. The contract was closed on the basis of 500,000 fr. cash and one half the founders' shares, the founders' shares being entitled to one half the profits, after interest has been paid on the cash capital. We are to make two flights each of 50 kilometers within an hour. The flight in each case must be made within four days of the time we may designate for the first attempt, and must be not later than five months from the first of June. In case of high wind or breakage of machine the time required for return of flying conditions is omitted in counting the four days.

We would have preferred to leave the arrangement of European sales rest till after the U. S. business had been finished, but when it came to accepting or refusing a direct offer, we thought on the whole, it would be safer to accept it. It includes both government & commercial rights for France & its colonies. The contract also provides for the sale of four additional machines beyond that used in the demonstration; we are to have an extra 20,000 fr. each for these machines, 80,000 fr. in all. About half will be profit. We are a little worried for fear one of us will have to go to France before the U. S. work is finished.

. . . .

Wilbur Wright to Orville

Kitty Hawk, April 9, 1908

I reached K.H. last evening about 7 o'clock. . . . This
morning I went down to camp . . . and found everything in
ruins. The side walls and rafters of the old building are still
standing but the paper and sheeting are off the roof and the
north door is gone. The floor is several feet underground. The
new building is clear down. The worst feature of the situation is the lack of any place to live while putting up the new
building. . . . It will be a big job getting the lumber down to
the old neighborhood. The best place except for mosquitoes
would be near the old fish landing but the bugs that bite
would probably eat us up before we fairly got to experimenting, so I think now that I will go down near the old place
again. . . . I will expect you to arrive with relief Saturday.
I am not sure I can hold out much longer than that.

. . . .

Wilbur was joined within a week by Charles W. Furnas,
a mechanic from Dayton. Both the plane and Orville reached
Kitty Hawk on April 25.

Wilbur Wright to his sister

Kill Devil Hills, April 14, 1908

I reached Kitty Hawk on the motor boat belonging to
Capt. Midgett on Thursday evening about 7 o'clock and put
up for the night with the Captain. . . .

Saturday we went down with two carts and spent the day hauling the lumber to camp. Monday, with the assistance of two semi-carpenters, I began work on the new building and put in the foundation posts and part of the sills. . . . The new building is to be 22 ft. wide and 48 ft. long so it is about a half larger than any we have used before. There will be plenty of room for kitchen, dining room, reception hall, parlor, and bed rooms, with bath accommodations, &c, &c, in one corner of the large building. . . .

I am staying at the life saving station and have the best the place affords. . . . The men are very friendly. . . .

I fear we will have trouble getting the big box ashore but it must and will be done somehow or other.

. . . .

Wilbur Wright to his father

Kill Devil Hill Station, April 16, 1908

This is my eleventh day from home and only one day's work has been done on the new building. Two days were spent getting to Elizabeth City. Two were lost at Elizabeth City waiting for the boat. One was spent on the sound en route to Kitty Hawk. Friday and Saturday were spent selecting a location, landing and hauling lumber to it. Monday was spent putting in foundation and sills. Tuesday, Wednesday, and today, Thursday, have been spent in waiting for more lumber to arrive, and storms to pass. We hope to get down to work tomorrow.

Just before noon yesterday Charlie Furnas [Dayton mechanic] showed up. I was not particularly pleased to see him, as there was no way to keep him except at the Station where

I already about exhausted accommodations, and there was nothing for him to do. He said Orville would start Thursday so I telegraphed him to wait till next week. We can not keep three men until the building is up, and the camping outfit on hand. I am making every effort to push things as fast as possible but there are many delays. Once we can get the necessary lumber four of us ought to put the building together in four or five days. The wind has been above twenty miles an hour most of the time since I arrived. It may be troublesome to put on tar paper unless we can find a quieter day.

.   .   .   .

Orville Wright to his father

Kitty Hawk, April 28, 1908

I reached Kitty Hawk Friday evening, and camp about noon the next day. I brought our shipments of materials, groceries, etc. on the boat with me. They had reached Elizabeth City several days ahead of me, but had been left in the depot there, as Will was not ready for them. He had the building just about completed when I reached here, so that we began unpacking and setting the machine together Monday morning. We now have the surfaces set together and will begin installing the machinery tomorrow. . . .

Our new building is large so that we are not so crowded as heretofore. We will have the machine together before the end of the week, unless we decide to arrange it now so that two men can be carried. This will necessitate some changes in the center part of the machine, and may delay us a little.

Since looking over the ground I feel pretty sure that we will get practice much faster than we could at a place like Simms. We have seen nothing of newspaper men so far, and will probably succeed in making some flights before any news of what we are doing leaks out.

. . . .

Orville Wright to his sister

Kitty Hawk, May 7, 1908

We got the machine out for trial yesterday afternoon for the first time. A slight wind was blowing, seven to ten miles. The engine and machinery worked finely, but we do not know how much power we had as we took no measurement of the speed of the engine.

The flight was not quite equal to that described in the Norfolk papers a week ago, probably not 1/200 as long. The account in the paper did not attempt to give the exact length of the flight any more than to say that we went 10 miles to sea and back and did a lot of maneuvering over ground. This flight of yesterday measured only one thousand feet. If our timing is correct the speed averaged 41 miles.

. . . .

Orville Wright to his sister

Kitty Hawk, May 13, 1908

Today a man and his wife and ten or fifteen children came over from Collington Island to see us fly. They arrived about one o'clock just after we had made one flight and remained all afternoon. They were so interested, and had walked such a long way lugging some of the smaller children, that we would have liked to fly while they were here, but the wind had risen to 20 to 25 miles, which we thought a little too strong to attempt circles at present.

. . . .

Orville Wright to his father

Kitty Hawk, May 15, 1908

Yesterday morning we tried carrying two men for the first time. Will made a flight of about 500 ft. with Chas. Furnas on board, but was unable to steer the machine around the hill. A little later I took him a complete circle, covering a distance of 4120 meters (according to anemometer) in 3 minutes and 40 seconds. Will then made three attempts to get off, but he seemed a little rattled, for every time he made some mistake in operating the handles and failed to get off.

After dinner he started alone. After making one circle and about half of another, and when running exactly with the wind at a speed in the neighborhood of 52 to 54 miles an hour, he suddenly turned the front rudder down by mistake and plunged into the ground. I was watching with the field glass. The machine turned on end—the front end—with the tail in the air. There was a big splash of sand—such a cloud that I couldn't see from where I was exactly what had happened, but I thought the machine had rolled a complete summersault. We were somewhat excited at camp for a few seconds. It was probably thirty seconds before Will appeared. As we found out afterwards he was not badly hurt —only a few bruises. Instead of coming out where we could see him, he spent a half minute or so examining the damage done the machine. The time of the flight was seven minutes and a half.

As the accident occurred at a distance of over a mile from camp we had considerable difficulty in getting the machine back last evening, and we were all very tired when we went to bed last night.

The reporters have been hanging about the hills and woods for a week or so. Arthur Ruhl, of *Colliers Weekly*, who visited us at Dayton about a year ago was here yesterday. Today Gilson Gardner, who wrote the article on Flying Machines a few years ago for the *Technical World*, and a man representing the London *Daily Mail* came over from Manteo, and found us just bringing in the last of the wreckage. They had visited the camp in our absence and had taken a few photographs of the outside but claimed to have no picture of the interior.

We are now expecting to start home immediately upon receipt of money.

. . . .

Newspapers had finally discovered that the Wright brothers were newsworthy, and a number of reporters had arrived at the Tranquil House at Manteo on Roanoke Island. Among them was Byron R. Newton of the New York *Herald*, later Collector of Customs in New York.

The newly arrived correspondents, noting the desolate isolation of Kitty Hawk, thought it probable enough that the

Wrights must prefer to be let alone. Perhaps, they thought, if intruders came the Wrights wouldn't fly at all. They decided that if the Wrights were secretive, they themselves would be no less so. They would hide in the pine woods, as near as possible to the Wright camp, and observe with field glasses what happened. That meant a short walk to a wharf on Roanoke Island, five miles by sailing boat to Haman's Bay across the sound and then a walk of a mile or so over the sand to the place where they should secrete themselves. They made a dicker with a boatman to take them all back and forth each day and act as their guide. Provided with food and water, field glasses, and cameras, they set out about four o'clock each morning from May 11 to May 14 to keep their vigil. Hour after hour they fought mosquitoes and woodticks and sometimes were drenched by rain. But to their astonishment they several times witnessed human flight. The first flight any of them witnessed was early in the morning of May 11. On May 14 the correspondents saw what no person on earth had ever seen before—a flying machine under complete control carrying *two* men. First Wilbur made a short flight with Charles W. Furnas as passenger, and then Orville flew with Furnas for nearly three minutes. Newton predicted in his diary just after that: "Some day Congress will erect a monument here to these Wrights."

The ending of these trials brought no grief to the correspondents who had been getting up before daylight each morning and returning to Manteo late each afternoon, footsore and tired, with their dispatches still to be written.

"What would you have done," Orville Wright was asked, afterward, "if all those correspondents had come right to your camp each day and sat there to watch you?"

"We'd have had to go ahead just as if they weren't there,"

he replied. "We couldn't have delayed our work. There was too much to do and our time was short."

That the Wrights would have treated the correspondents politely enough was indicated in a letter from Orville Wright to Byron Newton, dated June 7, 1908. Immediately after his return to New York, Newton had written graciously to the Wrights, enclosing clippings of his dispatches to the *Herald*, and expressing his admiration for them and their achievements.

"We were aware of the presence of newspapermen in the woods," Orville wrote; "at least we had often been told that they were there. Their presence, however, did not bother us in the least, and I am only sorry that you did not come over to see us at our camp. The display of a white flag would have disposed of the rifles and shotguns with which the machine is reported to have been guarded."

Wilbur Wright to Orville

New York, May 20, 1908

I am to sail on the *Touraine* tomorrow morning at ten o'clock. . . .

I stopped a few moments at the *Century* office and told them that I was going abroad and that it was probable that we would be doing business publicly before an article could be furnished them as heretofore talked of; but that if they wished they could communicate with you in regard to getting something ready; but intimated that you probably would not have time to do so now. However it is my opinion as firmly as ever that we need to have one true

story told in an authentic way at once and to let it be known
that we consider ourselves fully protected by patents. One
of the clippings which I enclosed intimates that Selfridge is
infringing our patent on wing twisting. It is important to
get the main features originated by us identified in the
public mind with our machines before they are described
in connection with some other machines. A statement of our
original features ought to be published and not left covered
up in the patent office. . . .

If you think best, prepare to follow me to France within
a few weeks and get some practice there before we undertake to go to Ft. Myer. We can settle then which shall return
for the trials in U. S. in case it is found impossible for both
to return. This plan would . . . help ward off an approaching financial stringency which has worried me very much
for several weeks.

.   .   .   .

Wilbur Wright to Orville

New York, May 20, 1908

It seems we had the newspaper men [at Kitty Hawk]
thoroughly convinced that if they attempted to approach at
all closely that we would not fly. It is a good thing sometimes
to have a fierce reputation, like a school teacher.

When I got to New York a *Herald* man met me at the train
having been warned from Norfolk. He acted very decently
and gave a fairly good report of our talk, though he got all
balled up on the motor question. About a dozen reporters
and members of the Aero Club have been besieging Flint &

Co. today trying to find me but I am supposed to have left
yesterday.

. . . .

Wilbur Wright to Orville

Paris, June 3, 1908

I found our affairs here about like Peter Cartwright
reported religion to be on one of his circuits, "Looking upward," in other words flat on its back. . . .

Our position is improving rapidly as it always does when
one of us is here to meet people and infuse a little confidence
in them. At first there was a tendency of the French papers
to be hostile, but I think it is about over. A similar tendency
among the leading aeronautical and automobile people
seems to be melting away too. Every one is getting more and
more interested and enthusiasm will follow when we get to
doing something. . . .

I am to visit another ground near Paris early tomorrow
morning, and then go down in the auto beyond Orleans
where the Commandant Bonel says there is a lot of flat sandy
ground very suitable for our purpose. I am looking for a place
where we can practice, train operators, &c, instead of a
ground merely for a demonstration.

. . . .

Orville Wright to Wilbur

Dayton, Ohio, June 3, 1908

On my way back from Kitty Hawk I stopped at Washington. On account of the bad weather I could not get around much, tho I took a pretty good look over the grounds at Fort Myer and the country for some distance around. That is about as tough ground to fly over as one could well expect. . . .

I found the ground at Fort Myer much smaller than you reported it. It is not nearly so large as the field at Simms, but much smoother.

I am of the opinion that I had better prepare for and begin demonstrations here as soon as possible.

Our mail has increased about ten fold. Several letters have come from [Arthur] Ruhl. His account in *Collier's* of the movements of the newspaper reporters in the woods is the best thing I have ever read about our experiments. He is a fine writer.

Newton writes us a nice letter, and says that when we need any affidavits to substantiate our claims he would be glad to help us. . . . A letter from the *Century* company says they will give $500 for an article.

Salley, the Norfolk reporter met me at the train. I had a time getting away from him without giving away where I was going.

It has been a hard job to get work done since I came back on account of everyone wanting to talk. . . .

The New York *Herald* stirred up considerable commotion by advertising on its wagons in big letters that it would the next day—May 29th—give a full description of the secrets of the Wright invention. They published the drawing and description from our French patents. All the other papers began telegraphing trying to either get something for themselves or to discredit the *Herald* story.

. . . .

Orville Wright to Wilbur

Dayton, Ohio, June 7, 1908

I had a letter from Ruhl a couple days ago, saying that Mr. Collier would like to buy a flying machine, and asking for a price. I have answered that our present contracts will take all our time for several months, but that as soon as we are through with these, we would be glad to take up the matter with Mr. Collier. What do you think about prices? and shall we try to sell machines to individuals now?

I see by one of the papers that the Bell outfit* is offering "Red Wings" for sale at $5,000 each. They have got some nerve.

. . . .

Wilbur Wright to Orville

Paris, June 7, 1908

Tomorrow . . . I will go down to Le Mans a hundred kilometers or so west of Paris. M. Leon Bollée the well known automobile maker has been very kind and has sent

---

* The Aerial Experiment Association.

us several invitations to locate in that vicinity and offered us the facilities of his factory which is located there. There is a race course and also several large private grounds in the vicinity. . . .

I believe the French opened our boxes and examined them last year. The customs officers evidently have leanings toward scientific investigation!

. . . .

Wilbur Wright to his sister

Paris, June 9, 1908

Since my last letter we have been continuing our search for suitable grounds. . . .

Monday Berg and I went down to Le Mans about 200 kilometers west of Paris. . . . M. Leon Bollée, the auto manufacturer, met us at the station and took us to his factory which is very pretty as well as well fitted to its use. He took us to see three or four grounds in the neighborhood any one of which would answer very well. He was very kind and not only offered us any facilities his factory afforded but placed at our disposition a large room in which we can proceed at once to assemble the machine, without waiting to construct a shed on the grounds chosen for experiments. I think it will be wise to avail ourselves of the chance. . . .

I have no word from Orville since leaving Kitty Hawk. Does he not intend to be partners any more?

. . . .

Wilbur meant that last line as a joke; he knew something had happened to the mails from home. Letters from Dayton had been sent in care of Hart O. Berg without adequate address.

Wilbur Wright to Orville

Paris, June 14, 1908

We have decided to locate at Le Mans. We get exclusive possession of the race course at 250 francs per month and 15% of gate receipts if we charge admission at any time. The course is entirely enclosed by trees and is 800 meters long and 300 meters wide. The ground is not at all smooth but will do for landing all right. There are several trees at one corner which will prevent following the track all the way around unless I go over them. It is not an ideal grounds but I think it will answer our purpose. . . .

Bleriot called the other morning and offered us his shop at Neuilly and his shed at Issy if we wished to use them. A more friendly spirit is being manifested on all sides.

I saw Mr. Rolls* the other day. He wishes to be the first to fly one of our machines in England. He did not propose to buy one himself but thought he could get a wealthy friend to buy one if we would sell one, and let him run it. I said I would consult you as to price and date of delivery. If we can get an order I think it might be well to take it. When could you have a machine ready to ship? And what should be our price without training operators? What do you say to

---

* Charles S. Rolls, British Aeronautical Society member, was founder of the Rolls-Royce automobile firm.

$10,000 each? We ought to do something in England. Do not fail to inform me when our patent there must be worked.

. . . .

Orville Wright to Wilbur

Dayton, Ohio, June 15, 1908

Chanute had an article in the *Independent* last week criticizing our business methods, and saying that we have always demanded an exorbitant price.

I have another letter from Newton, of the N. Y. *Herald,* saying that he has severed his connection with the *Herald* on account of the sensational way they try to palm off old stuff as revealing our secrets. . . .

I am now planning to set the machine together before shipping to Fort Myer. I think it will be policy to try to make the flights in the early part of August. The winds will probably be lighter then than later, and the sooner the trials the more lenient the [War] Department will be, it's my opinion.

. . . .

Wilbur Wright to Orville

Le Mans, France, June 17, 1908

A note came from Farman asking to meet me, so Berg invited him to take lunch with us. . . . He is a pretty nice sort of fellow and disposed to be friendly. He is much better looking than his pictures make him out to be. . . . The newspapers in general are giving us a lot of advertising and on the whole in a much more favorable way than heretofore. *Les Sports* is about the only one to hold out in its pretended unbelief and it is getting shaky.

. . . .

Wilbur Wright to Orville

Le Mans, June 17, 1908

I opened the boxes yesterday and have been puzzled ever since to know how you could have wasted two whole days packing them. I am sure that with a scoop shovel I could have put things in within two or three minutes and made fully as good a job of it. . . . Did you tell Charley not to separate anything lest it should get lonesome? Ten or a dozen ribs were broken and as they are scattered here and there through the surfaces, it takes almost as much time to tear down and rebuild as if we could have begun at the beginning. One surface was so bad that I took it completely down. Never again pack anything else in the surface box. The cloth is torn in almost numberless places and the aluminum has rubbed off of the skid sticks and dirtied the cloth very badly. The radiators are badly mashed; the seat is broken; the magneto has the oil cap broken off, the coils badly torn up, and I suspect the axle is bent a little, the tubes of the screw supports are mashed and bent. . . . Please bear in mind hereafter that everything must be packed in such a way that the box can be dropped from a height of five feet ten times, once on each side and the other times on the corners. The boxes must be cleated outside, and the lids must be put on with screws as they must be opened by the customs authorities. Such things as magnetos and other articles of similar size must not be thrown loosely into a box fifteen feet long, but must be put into medium size boxes and enclosed in the bigger boxes if desired. To be brief, things must be packed at least ten times as well as they were last time. And everything must be listed and the net weights taken of the stuff in each box.

In looking over the materials I notice that the rear wire is sometimes not inside both cloths; there are no blocks to keep the end ribs on each section from slipping inward when the surfaces are taken apart; the little washer on the rear wire is on the wrong side of the rib and therefore useless; the rear spar is not wrapped with glued cloth where the screw frames fasten on, and the screws are only 1 inch instead of 1¼ inch as heretofore. There are no nuts on the 1/4″ bolts which fasten the tubes of the screw axle supports to the central tube. The bolts for fastening sections of surfaces were not put back in the holes, and are lost or returned to America. We have been delayed because we have been unable as yet to get anything to replace them. It is going to take much longer for me to get ready than it should have done if things had been in better shape.

.   .   .   .

Orville was much amused by Wilbur's scolding letter. In a later letter he explained that the trouble was caused by customs officials. He realized full well how many troubles and annoyances Wilbur was having to endure, but he knew, too, that Wilbur often talked to him as to a "kid brother." For years afterward Orville would show this letter to friends and chuckle over it. These comments apply also to a later letter from Wilbur dated July 9, 1908.

Wilbur Wright to Orville

Le Mans, June 20, 1908

I have had an awful job sewing the sections together. We have had regular French weather for the past four days, and the cloth is shrunk about a foot, and as you failed to put blocks to hold the end ribs of each section, and also put the little washer on the rear wire outside instead of inside the rib, we had trouble enough. I was the only one strong enough in the fingers to pull the wires together tight, so I had all the sewing to do myself. It took a day and a half. My hands were about raw when I was not half done.

. . . .

Wilbur Wright to Orville

Le Mans, June 20, 1908

In putting the machine together I have to do practically all the work myself as it is almost impossible to explain what I want in words to men who only one fourth understand English. I doubt whether I can get ready to fly within three weeks.

Farman said he . . . would like to get one of our machines as soon as we have them to sell. Keep this mum for the
present.

. . . .

Wilbur Wright to his father

Le Mans, June 21, 1908

When I was in Paris this time I was so busy that I had no
time for sightseeing, the only thing of interest I visited being the Ste Chapelle. . . . This is the chapel which St. Louis
built about the 13th century, I think, within the enclosure of
the royal palace on the island about a furlong from Notre
Dame. It is one of the most remarkable specimens of Gothic
architecture in existence, though not very large. There are
no walls except the buttresses, thus leaving the sides an almost solid mass of brilliant stained glass windows. Unfortunately the ceiling and the buttresses have been decorated
in the blue and gold of Napoleon's time and this makes the
interior effect too gaudy, and detracts from the effect of the
wonderful windows. Within the last half century it has become somewhat common to construct buildings with walls
mostly glass, but to the people of the middle ages, accustomed to heavy walls and mere peep holes for windows,
this must have been a most wonderful building. . . .

The electric trolley street cars are about the most amusing
thing here. The track is single and narrow gauge. The street
makes a bend every half square and if by chance a longer
straight occurs, a switch is put in the middle of it. When
people are in a hurry they walk. The fare is two cents ("dix

centimes") but should be reduced to one cent unless the
service is improved.

. . . .

Wilbur Wright to his sister

Le Mans, June 23, 1908

I have never been as comfortable away from home as I
am here. No one in the hotel understands my English or my
French, but they do their best to serve me well.

. . . .

Wilbur Wright to his sister

Le Mans, June 28, 1908

This morning I went down to the cathedral at the 10
o'clock service. The only part of the service I could really
understand and participate in was the collection. . . .

I was a little astonished and disturbed the other evening
when I sat down to dinner to find my soup, which was a sort
of noodle soup, turning into all sorts of curious forms and
even letters of the alphabet. I began to think I had the "jim
jams." On close investigation I found that the dough had
been run through forms so as to make the different letters of
the alphabet and the figures too! It was like looking into the
"hell box" of a printing office. . . .

. . . .

Wilbur Wright to Orville

Le Mans, June 28, 1908

In the *Century* article you should say in the text or in a foot note, that the article in the *Independent* of — 1904 entitled "The Experiences of a Flying Man" by Wilbur Wright was a forgery; that many pretended interviews in newspapers have been absolute fabrications; and that reports of real interviews have almost invariably contained more than was said. . . .

You should also call attention to the fact that the European revival of interest in aviation dates from 1903 in which year Mr. Chanute who had been our guest at Kitty Hawk in 1901 and 1902 gave an address before the aeronautical societies of Paris in which he gave a full account of the results of our work, with photographs of many of our flights with motorless gliding machines. Moved by this address M. Archdeacon employed a couple of young mechanics, the Voisin brothers, to build a gliding machine . . . of the Wright type.

.   .   .   .

Wilbur Wright to Orville

Le Mans, June 28, 1908

I have been at work eight days now and have the machine about a fourth done. . . . I have a man but . . . his vocabulary is limited. When I say to him, "Hand me the screw driver," he is liable to stand and gawk or more often rush off as though he really understood me, and it is only after I have

waited a long time and finally get it myself that I realize that
he does not understand the special meaning of the word
"hand" as I used it.

. . . .

Orville Wright to Wilbur

Dayton, Ohio, June 28, 1908

Curtiss et al are using our patents, I understand, and are
now offering machines for sale at $5,000 each, according to
the *Scientific American*. They have got good cheek!

. . . .

Soon after the report of the flight of the "June Bug" by
Glenn Curtiss on July 4, 1908, a statement appeared in the
newspapers that Curtiss was going to do exhibition flying.
That news led Orville Wright to send to Curtiss the following letter:

I learn from the *Scientific American* that your "June Bug"
has movable surfaces at the tips of the wings, adjustable to
different angles on the right and left sides for maintaining
the lateral balance. In our letter to Lieutenant Selfridge of
January 18th, replying to his of the 15th, in which he
asked for information on the construction of flyers, we referred him to several publications containing descriptions
of the structural features of our machines, and to our U. S.
patent No. 821,393. We did not intend, of course, to give

permission to use the patented features of our machine for exhibitions or in a commercial way.

This patent broadly covers the combination of sustaining surfaces to the right and left of the center of a flying-machine adjustable to different angles, with vertical surfaces adjustable to correct inequalities in the horizontal resistances of the differently adjusted wings. Claim 14 of our patent No. 821,393 specifically covers the combination which we are informed you are using. We believe it will be very difficult to develop a successful machine without the use of some of the features covered in this patent.

The commercial part of our business is taking so much of our time that we have not been able to undertake public exhibitions. If it is your desire to enter the exhibition business, we would be glad to take up the matter of a license to operate under our patents for that purpose.

. . . .

Curtiss replied that he did not expect to do anything in the way of exhibitions; that his flights had been in connection with the work of the Aerial Experiment Association. By the next year, however, Curtiss had joined with A. M. Herring to form a commercial company, The Herring-Curtiss Co., to make or exhibit airplanes.

Wilbur Wright to Orville

Le Mans, France, July 5, 1908

I have been taking some pains to have the chief points of our patents well published so as to let the general public become accustomed to linking these ideas with us before others attempt to steal them.

. . . .

Orville Wright to Wilbur

Dayton, Ohio, July 5, 1908

I inclose a letter from Prof. Zahm. . . . I had half a notion to accept the proposition for you. My power of attorney seems of little use for anything else!

. . . .

Professor Zahm had undertaken to become a matchmaker and wrote of a beautiful heiress he wanted Wilbur to meet.

Wilbur Wright to his father

Le Mans, France, July 9, 1908

I have had a little trouble . . . recently. A rubber tube came off of the upper water connection of the engine when it was running with water boiling, at 1500 rev. per min. I was standing just in front of it taking the speed, and the stream under pressure of the pump struck me in the side and upon the arm at my elbow.

. . . .

Wilbur Wright to his sister

Le Mans, France, July 7, 1908

. . . my burns were not very serious and I will be at work again today. In order to avoid any chance of my arm getting sore I had a "docteur," . . . probably a "hoss doctor," come to dress my arm Sunday. He sent for a bale of cotton and a keg of oil, and after soaking the former in the latter made a vain attempt to plaster it on to my arm and side before more than half the oil had dripped out. When he was done he had two wash bowls, six towels and a dozen or two newspapers soaked with oil, not to speak of the table cover, the rug and my clothes. The oil ran down my arm and began dropping off my finger tips and down my legs till my shoes were half full. As I had no tin handy to make eave troughs I got a dozen newspapers and spreading them on the bed, tried lying down. But the oil went through all the newspapers, the sheet and into the mattress. I thereupon removed all the stuffing, like the fat man in A. Ward's show, and dressed the burns myself with more sense.

I fired the "docteur" after his first visit. If you ever get burned do not waste your money on doctors, but get a barrel of oil and fill up your bath tub and crawl in and stay till you are well.

. . . .

Wilbur Wright to Orville

Le Mans, July 9, 1908

I would really save time by getting into bed and staying there till entirely well, as nothing is done down at the shop except irritate my arm and nerves. If you had permitted me to have any anticipation of the state in which you had shipped things over here, it would have saved three weeks' time probably. I would have made preparations to build a machine instead of trying to get along with no assistance and no tools. If you have any conscience it ought to be pretty sore. . . . If I had known in advance what I would be up against I could have saved much time & worry by making proper preparation. I would have secured a real mechanic and one who really understood English, and I would have provided a full set of tools (American) and got material together before I started.

I think you had better go to Washington as quick as possible. My fear all the time has been that you would not be fully ready. Go in time to get sufficient practice, and opportunity to make necessary alterations.

For work in the small field I intend to operate the tail and wings entirely independent of each other. I think it the only safe plan for the present.

. . . .

Wilbur Wright to Orville

Le Mans, July 10, 1908

It might be well to write to Curtiss that we have a patent covering broadly the combination with wings to right and left of the center of a flying machine which can be adjusted to different angles of incidence of vertical surfaces adjustable to correct inequalities in the horizontal resistance of the differently adjusted wings.

Say that we do not believe that flyers can be made practical without using this combination, and inquire whether he would like to take a license to operate under our patent for exhibition purposes. I would not offer any manufacturing rights.

.   .   .   .

Wilbur Wright to his sister

Le Mans, July 11, 1908

Not very much work has been done in the past week as my arm was in such shape that I did not dare to abuse it any. . . . As I have had more leisure than heretofore I have had time to ride on the street cars instead of walking. The whole system reminds one strongly of the game of wood tag which we used to play. The cars all seem to think themselves safe only when standing on switch. You remember how "Billy" Wagner used to walk up to a corner and take a look before making the turn? That is the way the cars do here. They look to see if the switch is full. If there is room for one more, they make a rush for the place. About once in so often they make a stop to take a cash register on board. The cash register walks up and down the aisle inspecting tickets to see whether the conductors are knocking down fares. From the amount of the fare (two cents) and the seedy looks of the conductors I think that making a living stealing fares would be sufficiently hard without being bothered with cash registers like this. The animated cash register is very amusing, but it is quite characteristic of the French to find ingenious ways of making human labor take the place of machines.

. . . .

Wilbur Wright to Orville

Paris, July 14, 1908

I have a very nice letter today from Gelett Burgess who wishes to come down from Paris to see me. I have told him it would give me pleasure to meet the author of the book which I have probably read through more times than any other in the world.

. . . .

Burgess was much pleased, assuming that Wilbur referred to a book of philosophical essays; but Wilbur was thinking of a book of verses for children that his nieces and nephews had compelled him to read over and over.

Wilbur Wright to his sister

Le Mans, July 15, 1908

I have just received Prof. Zahm's letter. [About the beautiful heiress!] . . . When Orville gets down to Washington I fear my chances will be gone, so far as the young lady is concerned. But I will console myself with the thought that "my loss is his eternal gain," as they say at funerals.

. . . .

Orville Wright to Wilbur

Dayton, Ohio, July 19, 1908

I had been thinking of writing Curtiss. I also intended to call the attention of the *Scientific American* to the fact that the Curtiss machine was a poor copy of ours; that we had furnished them the information as to how our older machines were constructed, and that they have followed this construction very closely, but have failed to mention the fact in any of their writings.

I am sorry you are having such a hard time getting the machine together, but I believe on the whole it will be a good lesson. I foresaw the difficulty of attempting to set machine together away from home, and with foreign workmen. . . .

I notice that Chanute has written an article for the *Mittheilungen,* in which he again criticises our business methods, says we have spent two years in fruitless negotiations, because we have asked a ridiculously high price, but that now we have gone to the other extreme in making a price to our own government. . . . I think I will write him. He has also become a convert to airships, and thinks they are going to have great value in war. He says the use of the flyer is greatly overestimated, generally, and that its uses will be very restricted. He seems to be endeavoring to make our business more difficult. . . .

I am expecting every day to hear that you have begun experiments. Be very careful in the first flights. I think there will be little danger after you get accustomed to the new levers, though I infer from what I have read that your field is very limited and not very smooth.

. . . .

Orville Wright to Wilbur

Dayton, Ohio, July 25, 1908

I see by *l'Aérophile* that Capt. Ferber is cutting loose again. He says that none of our patents are worth anything, although our discoveries are of the greatest importance. The patents are invalid because we had given away twisting the wings before the patents were taken out. He produces a photograph—one of Mr. Chanute's taken in 1902—showing the pulley on one wing. He says that it could easily be seen what that was for. That a front rudder—(he thinks we claim patent on placing the rudder in front)—is old, since carriages and bicycles are steered from in front. We gave away the wing twisting when in some article it was said that we "steered with the wings." He also quotes from your addresses. It looks to me that the strongest point he makes is the importance of our inventions.

. . . .

Wilbur Wright to his sister

Le Mans, July 27, 1908

The doctor comes tomorrow for the last time, but it will be a week before my arm is entirely well. . . . I have been receiving letters from patent medicine people, faith healers, &c. and so much literature that I have half a notion to scald my other arm just for the luxury of seeing it get well almost instantly.

. . . .

To Wilbur Wright from his father

Dayton, Ohio, August 2, 1908

I think that, aside from the value of your life to yourself and to ourselves, you owe it to the world, that you should avoid all unnecessary personal risks. Your death or even becoming a cripple or an invalid, would seriously affect the progress of aeronautical science . . . Soon, others can do the flying, but you have a field for truth and science that no one else can fill. I think that you and Orville ought to take especial care of your health, as well as of your lives.

. . . .

Wilbur Wright to his sister

Le Mans, August 2, 1908

We took all our stuff except the flying machine itself, from Bollée's to the race course* a day or two ago, and will begin living there tomorrow. There is a little restaurant where we get very good meals, just as we turn in from the main road. We have a little outfit of cooking and eating utensils so that we can make coffee at any time. . . .

There is a farm house within a hundred feet of our shed, so we can get milk and water very handily. A little boy about five or six years old talks English and German. At least he replies very politely *"Oui Monsieur"* when I say *"Parlez vous Anglais"* . . . and he looks like a truthful little chap. . . .

I have had several amusing experiences with officers connected with the Camp d'Auvours which lies a few miles east of Le Mans. It is the finest place for flying experiments I have seen and we may try to get the privilege of using it later. Accordingly, I was very polite to an officer who requested to see the machine, but found out later that he was a bookkeeper in the commissary department. But a few days ago we had a visit from the commander in chief of this department. When he left he said that he was to be transferred to another department in a couple of days and therefore had dropped in to see the machine before going!

. . . .

---

* The Hunaudières course, used for his early flights in France

Wilbur Wright to Orville

Le Mans, August 2, 1908

Two Russian officers are in Paris waiting to see some demonstrations, and Prince Borghese is coming up from Italy, with the head of the Italian aeronautical department. I think we will get a Russian order almost immediately if all goes well.

.   .   .   .

Wilbur Wright to his father

Le Mans, August 5, 1908

The newspaper men have already camped down to wait for me to begin experiments. Their attitude is much more friendly than when I first reached France. The *Daily Mail* had a little scamp here, but we saw the manager and had him called off.

.   .   .   .

Wilbur Wright to his sister

Le Mans, August 8, 1908

I am afraid that you are doing too much worrying. You will soon have us worrying about you. You may depend upon it that if anything very serious happens I will let you know of it, so you need not pay too much attention to newspaper talk. . . .

Night before last we folded the front framing back against the machine and set a couple of automobile wheels under the skids of the machine and hitched one wing tip to the rear of an automobile, and ran the whole business down to the race course, a distance of about five miles, in about a half hour. We fooled the newspaper men completely. Not one was on hand.

. . . .

Wilbur Wright to Orville

Le Mans, August 9, 1908

I finished the machine yesterday far enough to enable me to make a little flight. Neither my arm nor the machine was really finished but a report had got out that I would make the first trial yesterday and a number of people had come down from Paris, including two Russian officers who have been waiting there for several weeks by instruction of their government. As the day was the finest for a first trial we have had for several weeks, I thought it would be a good thing to do a little something. . . .

I made two rounds of the field in a little less than two minutes and landed in front of the grand stand.

. . . .

Hart O. Berg reported that Wilbur's first flight in France was all the more dramatic because of his undramatic appearance—ordinary street clothes, with the usual white starched collar.

Wilbur Wright to Orville

Le Mans, August 15, 1908

Last Saturday I took the machine out for the first time and made a couple of circles. On Monday I made two short flights. In the first I wound up with a complete 3/4 of a circle with a diameter of only 31 yards, by measurement, *and landed with the wings level.* I had to turn suddenly as I was running into trees and was too high to land and too low to go over them. In the second flight I made an "eight" and landed at the starting point. The newspapers and the French aviators nearly went wild with excitement. Bleriot & Delagrange were so excited they could scarcely speak, and Kapperer could only gasp, and could not talk at all. You would have almost died of laughter if you could have seen them. The French newspapers, *Matin, Journal, Figaro, L'Auto, Petit-Journal, Petit Parisien,* &c., give reports fully as favorable as the *Herald.* You never saw anything like the complete reversal of position that took place, after two or three little flights of less than two minutes each. Deutsch telegraphed to inquire whether he could have the 100,000 fr. stock and definitely took it. The English Mercedes-Daimler Co. have written to know whether they can have England on same terms as the published Weiler contract. They also would like to arrange the German business, I presume through the German Daimler Co. I have asked them to send a man to talk over matters.

We certainly cannot kick on the treatment the newspapers have given us, even *Les Sports* has acknowledged itself mistaken. I thought the first accident might bring out a different turn from some of them, but there has been little tendency that way yet. On Thursday I made a blunder in landing and broke three spars and all but one or two ribs in the left wings and three spars ends of the central section, and one skid runner. It was a pretty bad smash up, but Kapperer who was present pronounced it as fine a demonstration of the practicability of flying as the flights themselves. . . .

In your flights at Washington I think you should be careful to begin practice in calms and *keep well above the ground.* You will probably be unable to cut as short curves as I do here, but you will have it easier on your speed test in a straight line. . . .

Be awfully careful in beginning practice and go slowly.

. . . .

Wilbur Wright to his father

Le Mans, August 15, 1908

In my experiments I have my two men and in addition a special corps of high priced assistants consisting of M. Bollée, & M. Pellier the richest men in Le Mans, who come out every day and work twice as hard as common laborers. Pellier is one of the largest manufacturers of canned goods in France and has factories in a number of different towns. He has sent me for my lunches all kinds of the finest sardines, anchovies, asparagus, &c, &c. you ever saw. The people of Le Mans are exceedingly friendly and proud of the fame it is giving their town. I am in receipt of bouquets, baskets of fruit &c., almost without number. The men down at Bollée's shop have taken up a collection to buy me a testimonial of their appreciation. They say that I, too, am a workman. I wish Orville could have been here, but I presume he will find similar treatment at Washington. Only he will miss seeing Bleriot, Delagrange & Kapperer so excited that they could scarcely talk, gasping that nothing like our flights had ever been seen in France. Yet I have made flights of only a few minutes each so far.

. . . .

Wilbur Wright to his sister

Le Mans, August 22, 1908

The newspapers have told every thing I have done and still more that I have not done so you know pretty well how things are going. The way the French have thrown up the sponge and made a grab for the band wagon is a great surprise. M. Peyrey the aeronautical editor of *Auto* has been favorable to us ever since I met him on my arrival in France, and he has almost outdone himself since I began flying. Several others are not much behind. All question as to who originated the flying machine has disappeared. The furor has been so great as to be troublesome. I cannot even take a bath without having a hundred or two people peeking at me. Fortunately every one seems to be filled with a spirit of friendliness and this makes it possible to deal with them without a fuss. . . .

We have even been set to music, and every one is singing a song "Il Vol" [he flies] of which I will send you a copy as soon as I can get one. You really can have no comprehension of the enthusiasm with which the flights have been greeted, especially in France, but almost equally in the rest of Europe. The dangerous feature is that they will be too enthusiastic and that a reaction will set in. I do not like such conditions. But in any event it has resulted in advertising us ten times more than anyone has been advertised before in connection with flying and settled all questions of priority.

. . . .

Orville Wright to Wilbur

Washington, D. C., August 23, 1908

Yesterday I went over the grounds for five miles in several directions from the Fort. I have about decided on a course directly towards Alexandria. There would be quite a number of good landing places on this course, though there is one large forest of over a mile wide in which there are no breaks whatever. The starting point at Ft. Myer is 240 ft. above sea level. The ravines are sea level, and the turning point 160 ft. Three of these deep ravines must be crossed. The low lands are more cultivated and therefore more open and suitable for landings. . . .

I am not looking for much trouble, if I can get the practice which I expect. The parade grounds are rather small, but I think quite as large as the part of the grounds which you could use at Le Mans. . . .

I am now at the St. James but I expect to change to the

Cosmos Club within a day or two. Mr. Zahm is taking me there.

I expect to begin the first flights about the first of September. I may be ready a day or two before that. I can choose my man that goes with me in the trials. If Lieut. Lahm wants to go I think I will ask him, or maybe Lieut. Foulois* whom I like very much. He is a little fellow, only weighing 130 lbs.

The goods came through in perfect shape. They were packed exactly as were the goods sent to Europe. Our trouble there is with the Customs House tearing everything loose and not fastening them again.

. . . .

Wilbur Wright to Orville

Le Mans, August 25, 1908

The excitement aroused by the short flights I have made is almost beyond comprehension. The French have simply become wild. Instead of doubting that we could do anything they are ready to believe that we can do everything. So the present situation is almost as troublesome as the former one. People have flocked here from all over Europe, and as I wish to practice rather than give exhibitions it is a little embarrassing. But I tell them plainly that I intend for the present to experiment only under the most favorable conditions. If the wind is more than five miles an hour I stay in. In a calm you can detect a mismovement instantly, but in winds you do not know at first whether the trouble is due to mistakes or to

---

* Benjamin D. Foulois became an early Army flyer.

wind gusts. I advise you most earnestly to stick to calms till after you are sure of yourself. Don't go out even for all the officers of the government unless you would go equally if they were absent. *Do not let yourself be forced into doing anything before you are ready.* Be very cautious and proceed slowly in attempting flights in the middle of the day when wind gusts are frequent. Let it be understood that you wish to practice rather than give demonstrations and that you intend to do it in your own way. Do not let people talk to you all day and all night. It will wear you out, before you are ready for real business. Courtesy has limits. If necessary appoint some hour in the day time and refuse absolutely to receive visitors even for a minute at other times. Do not receive *any one* after 8 o'clock at night. . . .

A few days ago I was presented with a medal of the International Peace Society of which Baron d'Estournelles de Constant is president. Another for you was also given into my charge.

That English crowd, Daimler Mercedes, is ready to make a contract similar to the Weiler contract but at a higher price. However I fear that they are more interested in selling stock than doing regular business and I am waiting to make further investigations, and consider other offers.

It is not probable that I will be able to go to Washington unless absolutely needed. I can only say be extraordinarily cautious. Choose your own times. Good Luck.

. . . .

Orville Wright to his sister

Washington, August 27, 1908

I haven't done a lick of work since I have been here. I have to give my time to answering the ten thousand fool questions people ask about the machine. There are a number of people standing about the whole day long. . . .

I find it more pleasant here at the [Cosmos] Club than I expected. The trouble here is that you can't find a minute to be alone. . . .

I have trouble in getting enough sleep.

.   .   .   .

Too many wanted to talk with him!

Wilbur Wright to Orville

Le Mans, August 29, 1908

It has rained and stormed all week and I have not made any attempt to fly. I should have gone out several times if it had not been for the crowds and reporters, but I did not care to take it out and then come back without a trial. I fear you will have trouble at Ft. Myer with the crowds. They are an awful nuisance here, though they are friendly and good tempered. . . .

I have been feeling around a little regarding English business but do not feel sure things are ripe yet. The Daimler Mercedes crowd of promoters would take the business at a good price, but I am afraid they are merely stock jobbers. I have talked with Rolls but doubt whether he is in position to do anything.

The papers here continue to devote considerable space to us every day. We are more advertised than is really desirable, but it is almost impossible to control such things. I fear they will raise too high expectations. . . .

I see from the papers that you have the machine about ready, and will begin experiments next week. Be careful of your electrical connections.

. . . .

Orville Wright to his sister

Washington, D. C., August 29, 1908

I meet stacks of prominent people here at the club, who are very friendly. Last evening I met Mr. Steward, the chief examiner at the patent office, who was just as friendly as he could be. He told me, if we had any patents pending, over which we were having any trouble, to come in and see him; that he might be able to at least give advice which would help us.

I think I will be able to begin flights Monday or Tuesday.

. . . .

Wilbur Wright to Orville

Le Mans, August 30, 1908

The papers today report an accident to your transmission in which the chains apparently whipped around the axle. It may have been due to running new chains too loose and letting them climb the sprockets, but I do not see how any trouble was really possible if everything was properly assembled and locked. . . .

With the machine I have here I can turn easily in four or five hundred feet diameter. The accident was due to pulling the lever the wrong way. . . .

Be exceedingly cautious as to wind conditions and thorough in your preparations. I wish I could be home.

. . . .

The accident referred to was not a serious one.

Wilbur Wright to his father

Le Mans, August 30, 1908

Crowds of people have flocked here from all over Europe. . . . Ambassador White and Senator Lodge had arranged to come down but we stopped them by telegraph as the weather made a flight impossible. . . . I tried to make a rule that I would receive no visitors before 5 P.M., but every day several people whom I can not well refuse come to see me, and keep me pretty well tired out, though I am feeling better than last week. I learn from the newspapers that Orville is in Washington and almost ready to begin flying. I fear he will have trouble with over-attention from reporters, visitors . . . &c. It is an awful nuisance to be disturbed when there is experimenting and practicing to be done. I am treated with wonderful kindness on all hands, but too much time is wasted and too much nervous energy expended.

. . . .

Orville Wright to his sister

Washington, D. C., August 31, 1908

I don't know whether you have seen the Washington papers or not. The reporters seem to think I am not in the least uneasy about fulfilling our contract. They say that I do no boasting of what I can do; that they can get but little out of me as to what I expect to accomplish, but that I have the air of perfect confidence! . . .

I am meeting some very handsome young ladies! . . . I will have an awful time trying to think of their names if I meet them again. . . .

I think it quite probable that I will make an attempt to fly tomorrow evening. The grounds are 700 ft. at one end by about 900 to 1000 feet on the other sides. If I get a good start I think I will have no trouble in keeping within the space.

. . . .

Orville's first flight was on September 3. There were no taxicabs in Washington in 1908, and he went from the Cosmos

Club to Fort Myer by street car. It is doubtful if any of the others on the car suspected that this fellow passenger was about to perform a miracle. When he reached Fort Myer, Orville got the impression that not all the Army officers present thought he would succeed in meeting the tests required by the contract. The area from which the flights would be made was only about 700 by 1,000 feet. Neither of the Wrights had ever before made flights within so small a space.

Orville circled the field one and one-half times on that first test and was in the air only one minute, eleven seconds; but the crowd "went crazy." When he landed, it was Orville's turn to be astonished. Three or four supposedly "hardboiled" newspapermen who rushed up to interview him had been so stirred by the drama of witnessing the "impossible" that each of them had tears streaming down his cheeks.

(Those who witnessed this flight might have been prepared for what they saw and less surprised, since Wilbur Wright for more than a month had been making flights in France. Some of these were reported in the newspapers, but the brief accounts seldom if ever had first-page display and were not treated as important news.)

Wilbur Wright to Orville

Le Mans, September 6, 1908

The newspapers continue exceedingly friendly and the public interest and enthusiasm continues to increase. The Voisin brothers, Esnault-Pelterie, Gastambide, & Archdeacon do all they can to stem the tide but the other aviators, Kapperers, the Zens boys, Faber, Bleriot, Delagrange &c, are very decent. . . .

I see by the papers that the women & men are kissing you in genuine French fashion. The report about Berg kissing me after the first flight was of course a fake. Dickin [reporter for Paris *Herald*] put it in as a joke on Berg.

. . . .

Orville Wright to Wilbur

Washington, D. C., September 6, 1908

It is now nearly two weeks since I have had a letter from you. I see in the papers something of what you are doing, though some of the reports seem pretty unreliable. . . .

I made a flight of 4 minutes and 15 seconds Friday afternoon. . . . I find it easy to make short turns—the greater difficulty is to turn slowly. . . .

Lieutenants Selfridge and Foulois are detailed to operate the dirigible at St. Joseph, Mo. the latter part of the month. Lieut. Lahm will stay here. I like Foulois very well, but I will be glad to have Selfridge out of the way. I don't trust him an inch. He is intensely interested in the subject, and plans to meet me often at dinners, etc. where he can try to pump me. He has a good education, and a clear mind. I understand that he does a good deal of knocking behind my back. All the others I think are very friendly. . . .

The reports published in the New York *Herald* are the best I have seen. Mr. Claudy, who is making their reports, is a very nice man of much more intelligence than most of the others.

. . . .

Lieutenant Thomas Selfridge, twenty-six-year-old West Point graduate from San Francisco was the same Selfridge who in January of that year had written to the Wrights on behalf of the Aerial Experiment Association for information on how to build an airplane, and received the data he asked for. Inasmuch as that information had enabled Glenn Curtiss, another member of the Aerial Experiment Association, to build an airplane that flew, but without any credit ever being given to the Wrights, it was natural enough that Orville Wright did not feel happily inclined toward Selfridge, even without anything further to stir his suspicions.

Orville Wright to his sister

Washington, D. C., September 7, 1908

I will probably take a passenger on board in a few days. I would like to take Lieut. Lahm, but I am afraid it will cause jealousy among the young officers. Selfridge is doing what he can behind our backs to injure us. . . .

I have been feeling better than when I left Dayton. My only trouble is in getting more than five or six hours' sleep, on account of visitors and correspondence that must be attended to at nights.

. . . .

Orville Wright to his father

Washington, D. C., September 7, 1908

I do not allow myself to become worried over the business, and am consequently in pretty good condition for carrying on the experiments.

The grounds are quite small so that I am compelled to be turning the entire time. Most of the circles are of but six or seven hundred feet diameter. I can turn, however, in two or three hundred feet when necessary. . . .

Flint was down Saturday night and a part of yesterday. As usual he has started a lot of embarrassing reports.

. . . .

To Wilbur Wright from his father

Dayton, Ohio, September 9, 1908

Indeed they treat you in France as if you were a resurrected Columbus; and the people gaze as if you had fallen down from Jupiter. Enjoy fame ere its decadence, for I have realized the emptiness of its trumpet blasts.

> "And false the light on glory's plume,
> As fading hues of even."

You and Orville are, however, secure of a place with Fulton and Morse and Franklin in the temple of fame. "Conquerors of the Air." Its extensive results are, as yet, uncomprehended and undreamed of, even by yourselves. Did Fulton have any

vision of an ocean greyhound, or Franklin of wireless teleg-
raphy? . . .

Some Specifications (confidential) came to Orville's address, here, after he was away. They were from the British
War Department. . . . They only ask that an applicant
should jump over the moon! through a hoop!! six times!!!

I wish it were so you could be in the home circle. Milton
[son of Lorin Wright] says his uncles will be in business,
and he can not have fun with them as in the past. You are so
alone, if not lonely.

.   .   .   .

Bishop Wright sent a similar letter to Orville.

On the morning of September 9, Orville circled the field
fifty-seven times in fifty-seven minutes, twenty-five seconds.
Later in the day, he circled the field fifty-five times in one
hour, two and one-quarter minutes. Then he surprised and
delighted his friend, Lieutenant Frank P. Lahm, by inviting
him to go with him for a flight. They were in the air six
minutes, twenty-four seconds, and circled the field six and
one-half times. All three of these flights on the ninth established new world endurance records; two of them for flights
with pilot alone, and the third for pilot with passenger.
Orville made a flight of one hour, five minutes, fifty-two seconds on September 10, rising to a height of 200 feet and ex-
ceeding the world endurance record made by himself the
day before. On the next day he again broke the one-man
endurance record by flying for one hour, ten minutes, and
twenty-four seconds, while circling the field fifty-seven

times and describing two figure eights. On the twelfth, he increased the two-man endurance record by taking with him Major George O. Squier, Acting Chief Signal Officer, for a flight of nine minutes, six seconds. Immediately after that, Orville made a flight alone. He circled the field seventy-one times in one hour and fifteen minutes—again breaking the endurance record for one-man flight.

Wilbur Wright to his sister

Le Mans, September 10, 1908

I received word last evening of Orville's flight of 57 minutes, and today learn of his having passed the hour in a second flight later in the day. It is a record for sure! I have not done much for several weeks, partly because of windy weather, partly because of accidents which have necessitated repairs, and partly because I have been so nervous and worried that I have not felt like doing much hustling. You can scarcely imagine what a strain it is on one to have no one you can depend on to understand what you say, and want done, and what is more, no one capable of doing the grade of work we have always insisted upon in our machines. It compels me to do almost everything myself and keeps me worried.

. . . .

Orville Wright to Wilbur

Washington, D. C., September 13, 1908

I have just received a letter from the Dayton *Herald* in regard to a reception upon our return to Dayton. I will endeavor to suppress the "spontaneous" uprising of our fellow citizens.

.   .   .   .

Wilbur Wright to his sister

Le Mans, September 13, 1908

I have had almost as many congratulations on Orville's success as I had a month ago. I suppose Orville must be overwhelmed with them. . . .

I have been making short flights almost every day this week as the weather has been much better. They have ranged from about five minutes to twenty minutes. Most of them have been interrupted by the heating of the motor. I did not care much as I merely wished to practice and did not wish to fatigue myself. However I must now get the motor into shape and get down to business. The new system of levers was rather difficult to learn to operate and I made many blunders, only two of which damaged the machine however. But with no competent assistance and a dearth of materials these two were enough. I think now that I will have no further trouble, and that I will have an exactness of control such as we have never had before.

M. Weiler and M. Deutsch were here yesterday. I made

a couple of flights of about 5 minutes each but the motor compelled me to stop. Next week Weiler will bring down the minister of navy and several other officials. . . .

An artist has been around the place trying to make a portrait of me for one of the big illustrated papers. I have given him a few "standings" but I have been too busy for "sittings." He will go to America to get one of Orville to accompany it. He has tried to catch that enigmatic smile which the papers talk so much about, but I fear you will raise an awful fuss when you see it. It is worse than shirt sleeves! We will soon have a picture you certainly can not kick about on the score of shirt sleeves. Yesterday it was rather cold and to shut out the wind during the flight I slipped on a blue jumper or overhaul jacket. It left about two inches of my coat sticking out at the bottom. After the flight Mr. and Mrs. Weiler and Mr. Deutsch came up to congratulate me and the . . . photographer slipped up and snapped us. Mrs. Weiler laughed heartily when I told her how you objected to shirt sleeve pictures and how pleased you would be to see that I had on two coats.

. . . .

Wilbur Wright to his father

Le Mans, September 13, 1908

Orville's fine flights are making more of a sensation than my first flight over here and I thought then people would go crazy they were so excited. Well it will be a relief to me to have some of the responsibility removed from my mind. While I was operating alone there was the constant fear that if I attempted too much and met with a serious accident we would be almost utterly discredited before I could get the machine repaired, with no materials and no workmen. The excitement and the worry, and above all the fatigue of an endless crowd of visitors from daylight till dark had brought me to such a point of nervous exhaustion that I did not feel myself really fit to get on the machine. But I am much better now and our position is so secure that I can work with less strain than when I felt that I was surrounded by a pack of jealous & chauvinistic Frenchmen who would be glad of the least excuse for stopping their cheers & beginning to hoot.

However I must say that here in the district of La Sarthe every one from the prefect or governor down to the humblest citizen has seemed a genuine friend from the beginning almost. They look on me almost as an adopted citizen and show their friendliness in a dozen different ways. For instance, the old green cap which Orville brought home last fall and which I have been wearing over here when at work has set a new style and the stores have their show windows full of "Wright" caps. Some of the other manifestations are not so pleasant. From daylight till dark a crowd hangs about the building peering in at every crack. Almost every evening a crowd of two or three thousand people comes out to see if I will make a flight, and goes home disappointed if I do not. Some of them have come twenty, forty or even sixty miles on bicycles and a few from foreign countries. One old man of 70 living about 30 miles away made the round trip on a bicycle every day for nearly a week. I sometimes get so angry at the continual annoyance of having the crowd about that I feel like quitting the whole thing and going home, but when I think of the sacrifices some of them have made in the hope of seeing a flight I cannot help feeling sorry for them when

I do not go out. If I can get through this season in such a way
as to make a reasonable competence secure I am done with
exhibitions & demonstrations forever. I can't stand it to have
people continually watching me. It gets on my nerves.

Mr. Lahm is immensely proud of the fact that his son made
the first trip with Orville.

.   .   .   .

Wilbur Wright to Orville

Le Mans, September 13, 1908

The newspapers for several days have been full of the
stories of your dandy flights, and whereas a week ago I was
a marvel of skill now they do not hesitate to tell me that I am
nothing but a "dub" and that you are the only genuine cham-
pion skyscraper. Such is fame! Your flights have naturally
created an immense sensation in Europe and I suppose that
America is nearly wild.

.   .   .   .

Orville Wright to Wilbur

Washington, D. C., September 13, 1908

I suppose you have had full reports of the flights I have
been making this week. . . .

The Navy department seems much interested. Lieut.
Sweet, who was detailed by the Navy department to witness
and report on our flights, is very enthusiastic. He says he

believes that every war vessel will soon be equipped with machines. They will want machines to carry two men, fly for four hours, and carry floats so that they will not sink in case the engine stops. . . .

Every one here is very enthusiastic, and they all think the machine is going to be of great importance in warfare.

.   .   .   .

Orville Wright to his sister

Washington, D. C., September 15, 1908

I have received a letter from the [Dayton] *Herald* in regard to a reception on our return home. I enclose a copy of my answer. . . .

The Packard Automobile Company have a couple of their principal men here. They are very much interested and want to get into the business.

.   .   .   .

*Orville Wright to C. J. Geyer, Herald Publishing Co.,
Dayton, Ohio*

Washington, D. C., September 15, 1908

I am in receipt of your letter of the 12th with clipping from the *Herald* inclosed. I am unable to express my gratitude for the honor given my brother and myself in these expressions of admiration and affection.

I would not wish to so interfere with plans as to wound the feelings of our fellow-townsmen in their desire to do us honor; yet I know that my brother, as well as myself, would prefer to quietly return and live among you as we have in the past.

I think that any definite arrangement should be deferred until my brother, who is now in France, can be consulted, as I could not consent to receive any honor in which he would not be an equal participant.

. . . .

The celebration was delayed until the next year.

Wilbur Wright to his sister

Le Mans, September 15, 1908

Commander Bonel is our warmest friend in France and seems to have a personal affection for us. You will notice his picture in one or two of the photographs I sent home. The boy about 14 or 15 years old in the same pictures is his son, an awfully nice boy. I have several youthful friends over here. The Baron d'Estournelles has a little boy about 10 and a little girl of 6 who are great partners of mine. They both speak English very well, and are sweet, well trained little folks.

. . . .

On September 17, Lieutenant Selfridge was assigned at his own request to go with Orville as passenger. Though Orville had his reasons for not fully approving of Selfridge, probably he never was so eager to have the machine behave well—to demonstrate to a possible infringer the futility of trying to equal it. But the flight ended in tragedy. Before they had been in the air more than three or four minutes, and while in the fourth round at a height of about 125 feet over the field, Orville heard or felt a light tapping in the rear part of the machine. He thought it was in the chain drive. A hurried glance revealed nothing wrong there, but he decided to shut off the power and descend. Hardly had he reached this decision when two big thumps which shook the machine violently, followed by the machine swerving to the right, showed that something had gone wrong. He immediately shut off the motor. Directly ahead was a gulley filled with small trees, a dangerous landing spot. He decided to make a half circle to the left, and to land on the parade grounds. It was then that he discovered that the tail was inoperative. By twisting the wings to give the greatest possible resistance to the left one, he did succeed in turning the machine until it faced directly into the field. In this maneuver the machine had descended about one-third of the way toward the ground without any indication of serious trouble. Orville moved the lever to straighten the wing tips in order to proceed straight ahead. Then the machine suddenly turned down in front. For fifty feet it was headed almost directly toward the ground, although the front elevator was turned to its limit. When about twenty-five feet from the ground the machine began to right itself, and if there had been another twenty feet to go, or possibly even ten feet, it might have landed safely.

But the recovery of control came too late. The machine hit the ground with such impact that Lieutenant Selfridge was fatally injured and died a few hours later. His skull had been fractured by a blow against one of the wooden uprights of the framework. Orville, though at first believed to be perhaps fatally hurt, had miraculously escaped with what then appeared to be only a fractured left leg and four broken ribs. He never lost consciousness and his first concern was about Selfridge.

Wilbur Wright to his sister

Le Mans, September 20, 1908

I received the news of the awful accident at Washington only on Friday morning about eight o'clock, just as I was finishing preparations for an official trial for the Michelin & Commission de Aviation prizes. The death of poor Selfridge was a greater shock to me than Orville's injuries, severe as the latter were. I felt sure "Bubbo" would pull through all right, but the other was irremediable. The weather was ideal, a day of a thousand, but in view of the positive news of Selfridge's death, I did not feel that it would be decent to proceed as though I was indifferent to the fate which had befallen him as a result of his trust in our machines. So the trials were postponed till next week.

I cannot help thinking over and over again "If I had been there, it would not have happened." The worry over leaving Orville alone to undertake those trials was one of the chief things in almost breaking me down a few weeks ago and as soon as I heard reassuring news from America I was well again. A half dozen times I was on the point of telling Berg that I was going to America in spite of everything. It was not right to leave Orville to undertake such a task alone. I do not mean that Orville was incompetent to do the work itself, but I realized that he would be surrounded by thousands of people who with the most friendly intentions in the world would consume his time, exhaust his strength and keep him from having proper rest. When a man is in this condition he tends to trust more to the carefulness of others instead of doing everything and examining everything himself. A man can not take sufficient care when he is subject to continual interruptions and his time is consumed in talking to visitors. I cannot help suspecting that Orville told the Charleys [mechanics] to put on the big screws [propellers] instead of doing it himself, and that if he had done it himself he would have noticed the thing that made the trouble whatever it may have been. If I had been there I could have held off the visitors while he worked or let him hold them off while I worked. But he had no one to perform this service. Here Berg helps to act as a buffer and gives me some chance to be alone when I work. People think I am foolish because I do not like the men to do the least important work on the machine. They say I crawl under the machine and over the machine when the men could do the thing well enough. I do it partly because it gives me opportunity to glance around to see if anything in the neighborhood is out of order. Hired men pay no attention to anything but the particular thing they are told to do, and are blind to everything else. When we take up the American demonstration again we will both be there. It is much easier to do things when you have some one at hand in whom you have absolute confidence.

Tell "Bubbo" that his flights have revolutionized the world's beliefs regarding the practicability of flight. Even such conservative papers as the London *Times* devote leading editorials to his work and accept human flight as a thing to be regarded as a normal feature of the world's future life.

The comments of the newspapers on the disaster are almost all very sympathetic and hopeful for the future. I have had dozens of telegrams expressing sympathy and confidence in us and our machines. Offers to accompany me are more numerous than ever. Mr. Nernst the inventor of the Nernst lamp was here Thursday evening and saw me fly in a golden sunset, thirty-two minutes, at about 80 ft. height. He had seen Delagrange make a flight of about twenty-five minutes in the morning before leaving Paris. He nearly went crazy with enthusiasm over my flight. "It was so different," he said. The next morning when he heard of Orville's accident he sent me a long telegram and said he would like to go with me, whenever I was ready to fly. Every one takes almost as much interest in Orville's recovery as I do myself. He has certainly won the sympathy and admiration of the world all right.

I am awfully sorry that you have had to pass through so much trouble of a nerve wracking character this summer. However I am sure that as soon as Orville is well on his way to recovery you will enjoy yourself immensely at Washington. Orville has a way of stepping right into the affections of nice people whom he meets, and they will be nice to you at first for him and then for yourself, for you have some little knack in that line yourself. I am glad you are there to keep your eagle eye on pretty young ladies. I would fear the worst, if he were left unguarded. Be careful yourself also.

I presume that poor old Daddy is terribly worried over our troubles, but he may be sure that . . . things will turn out all right at last. I shall be not only careful and more careful, but also most careful, and cautious as well. So you need have no fears for me. I promise you that I will be as careful of myself as I was in 1900 when I gave you a similar promise. It is a pity that Orville is not with me as he was then. I like to keep promises when I can do it conveniently.

.   .   .   .

Wilbur Wright to his father

Le Mans, September 22, 1908

I received the news of Orville's accident. . . . I know that you will be more cut up over the affair than even we are. Young people are shocked for a moment but soon recover themselves. You need not fear that such a thing will happen again. It is the only time that anything has broken on any of our machines while in flight, in 9 years' experience. I feel sure we can keep such a thing from happening again. I think the trouble was caused by the feverish conditions under which Orville had to work. His time was consumed by people who wished to congratulate and encourage him when the thing he really needed was time to rest and time to work. He is too courteous to refuse to see people, and he had no one to act as a buffer as Berg does for me. I will never leave him alone in such a position again.

.   .   .   .

Wilbur Wright to Orville

Le Mans, September 23, 1908

I received your letter of Sept. 13th yesterday. It confirms the fear I had that you would be overtaxed by well meant friendliness. I have been refusing all invitations, and all but a few visitors for six weeks nearly. I found it was necessary to take the bull by the horns or break down. . . .

I had noticed in the papers that you had been rising to 150-200 ft. but supposed it slightly exaggerated. I have been up close to a hundred feet several times, but not higher.

There has been some talk of a public subscription for us in America. If the subscription were really *spontaneous* and of sufficient size to justify it I would be willing to make our American patents free. But I would not care to receive any money which was not absolutely at our disposal. And I would not let it be known that we had thoughts of making the patents free until the success of the subscriptions was already assured. It would be our response to a voluntary gift, and not a matter of bargain and sale.

.   .   .   .

To Wilbur Wright from his father

Dayton, Ohio, September 24, 1908

You may rest assured that I have deeply felt for your situation in France. The loneliness of so far from home and friends, your difficulty in getting suitable workmen, your defective supply of parts of your machine, your burned arm, your overwork and unaided cares, the annoying attentions of the multitude, the inconsiderate attention and requirements of notables, the immense responsibilities on your lone shoulders—all joined to make it hard on you. And the thunders of the world's applause could but ill comfort you under the handicaps and mishaps and depressions you had to encounter. It took good metal to stand the strain. Most of men under it, would have been like your broken propeller-shaft, at Kitty Hawk, in 1903. But you will come through all, safely and gloriously. We shall yet see you here in triumph. . . .

The friendship of the officials and people of Sarthe is a beautiful thing—toward a stranger. I hope you will ever maintain and cherish it. . . .

The distance overcome and perseverance, to see the flights is pathetic. What compassion Jesus showed toward the multitude drawn out by curiosity!

No doubt, not a few would have welcomed a chance (by your mishap) to hoot, though they cheered your success along with the multitude. Men are savage.

Our folks like Lieut. Lahm and his father. Orville wrote that he would like to take the Lieutenant up first, but feared jealousy among the officers. He adroitly managed to give him the preference.

We look forward to the time when you can be again in the home you have always so loved. All Dayton awaits your coming.

.   .   .   .

Wilbur Wright to Orville

Le Mans, September 28, 1908

Today I made a flight of an hour and seven minutes, making 24 circuits of the two poles a kilometer apart, 48 kilometers in all. . . .

If I swipe the 5000 franc prize of the Commission of Aviation I will try to send some home.

.   .   .   .

Wilbur Wright to Orville

Le Mans, October 4, 1908

The newspapers report that you will be out next week and that you will be flying again in fifteen days. I had come to the belief that the French newspapers were worse than the American, but this belief gets jarred a little sometimes. However, I hope you are doing well, and that you will not be seriously lamed. I understand that it was your right side that was injured, but I have cautioned Kate to guard against internal injuries under the ribs of your left side. Hospitals are awfully dangerous places for bachelors.

Over here things are moving very well. Weiler would be satisfied to go ahead on the organization of the company on the showing already made, but I shall make the official trials as they have been publicly announced. It is probable that we will have to take half of our pay in stock but on the whole I think we want some stock as I am certain it will pay big dividends with Weiler and Deutsch the other big stockholders. Weiler is really a very level headed and smooth business man who will handle the government end of the business in a way that scarcely anyone else could.

After putting up a record of 48 kilometers around two posts and thus winning the prize of 5000 fr. offered by the Commission of Aviation of the Aéro Club, I took the motor off and overhauled and tested it at Bollée's shop. It was using up a tank full of oil in an hour. . . .

Our supremacy in flying is no longer questioned over here. Even Archdeacon has given up. It is amusing to see the scramble for the band wagon. The Aéro Club has voted us a gold medal. . . . Prade who wrote so many things against us in *Les Sports* is now one of our strongest boomers.

I have won one 5000 fr. prize. The council general of the
Sarthe has voted 500 fr. to start a prize for encouraging
aviation in the district, and it is intended to bring the amount
up to 2500 fr. maybe 5000 fr., for a flight of 30 meters height.
It is intended for me, of course. It is probable that the *Daily
Mail* and *Matin* will offer me $5000 for a flight across the
channel. There is already $2500 up for such a flight and the
Graphic prize of $5000 is still standing I think. I may swipe
in there before returning to America.

Well! hurry up and get well and get another machine
ready so we can finish the American business when I get
home. . . .

I took Bollée (240 lbs) for a couple rounds of the field
this morning. . . . It created more astonishment than anything else I have done.

.   .   .   .

Octave Chanute to Wilbur Wright

October 7, 1908

When I left Orville . . . he was pronounced quite out
of danger. . . .

He had so endeared himself to all the Army officers and
men with whom he had come into contact, as well as to the
hospital attendants, that they were eager to do all they could
for him, but, of course, a military hospital is not as comfortable as one's own home. At the Cosmos Club, where he had
been staying, he had become very much liked and the members kept continually asking about him, only regretting that
the surgeon's orders prevented calling upon him.

Your sister has been devotion itself. Fearing that he might lack something she stayed up at the hospital every night and deprived herself so much of sleep that I ventured to remonstrate with her about it. . . .

I congratulate you heartily upon the magnificent success which you have achieved in France, upon the recognition which is now accorded you and upon the prospect that you will reap a fortune from your labors.

. . . .

Wilbur Wright to Orville

Le Mans, October 9, 1908

Every day there is a crowd of people here not only from the neighborhood, but also from almost every country of Europe. Queen Margherita of Italy was in the crowd yesterday. Princes & millionaires are as thick as fleas.

. . . .

Wilbur Wright to Orville

Le Mans, October 18, 1908

You have probably learned that we convoked the scientific commission for the official trial a week ago on Saturday. The day opened with a pouring rain, but it cleared up toward evening so I got out the machine and took M. Painlevé, vice pres. of the commission and a member of "the Institute" for a trip of an hour and ten minutes. He wished to be taken as he intended to prepare a paper to read before the Institute. This finished the official trials. . . .

I had been bothered all week. The motor would run perfectly for about three minutes, and then begin kicking like anything. Nothing I could do helped it any though I used several different magnetos and a dozen or two plugs of various kinds. Finally I took the motor off and went down to Bollée's and took it all apart, even taking the crank out. I made up my mind to assemble it from the beginning and see that everything was in good order. . . .

The real trouble with the motor came from the intake pipe which . . . [a Paris firm] made. They made it of copper and failed to fasten in the rivets properly. About once in so often a rivet goes down into a cylinder and dances around on top of the piston till it becomes incandescent and preignites the charge. After a few days during which we curse the magneto and plugs, it flies out of this exhaust and suddenly the magneto and plugs work all right again. I had suspected something of the kind several times and had made examination but found nothing. This time we not only found the rivet, but also the marks of copper on top of the piston where it had been dancing. I will try to assemble the whole engine properly and end motor trouble from this on.

I had intended to come home as soon as I could train my men, but the *Daily Mail* has offered a prize of 2500 for a flight across the channel, and has offered to privately give me $7500 extra, $10,000 in all, if I will go for the prize and win it. The latter is confidential. . . . I am personally inclined to chuck the prize business and get home as soon as possible. What do you think? . . .

Maxim was here several days this week. I doubt the goodness of his purposes, and dislike his personality. He is an

awful blow and abuses his brother and his son scanda-
lously. . . .

Did I tell you I had a telegram of congratulation from the
German crown prince last week? I suspected at first that it
was a fake, but it seems to have been genuine.

I will send home some money soon. Have Kate get a year's
leave of absence and take a rest. . . .

You ought to write a letter to Leon Bollée as President of
the Aéro Club of the Sarthe, thanking it for its telegram to
you on the evening they met to drink our healths, on the
occasion of my putting the record up to an hour and a half.
They will appreciate the courtesy. Do not neglect it. Everyone inquires how you are coming on, and hopes you will be
in the air again soon.

. . . .

Wilbur Wright to Orville

Le Mans, October 24, 1908

I will get the 5000 fr. prize of the Aéro Club on Nov. 5 at
their monthly dinner which I am to attend. At the same time
they will present the gold medal which they have voted to
us, and a medal of the Academy of Sports. The Aéro Club
is really letting itself out to be decent. They offered to give
a special dinner but I preferred the other. I will have quite
a collection of gim-cracks to bring home. I told you of the
medals of the International Peace society. . . .

Last Saturday I took up on the machine one of three rich
Italians who had come up with a possible view to getting our
Italian rights. Also one of three officers sent by the French

navy department to report on our machine, and finally the Chargé d'affaires of the German embassy at Paris. . . .

I will begin at once to train operators, starting with Compte de Lambert.

I forgot to say that a couple of Spanish officers closely connected with the King's household were here on Saturday. Also an officer of the Argentine government.

.   .   .   .

Wilbur Wright to his brother Reuchlin

Le Mans, October 26, 1908

Somehow the people seem to have opened their hearts toward me and do everything they can think of to give me assistance or pleasure. All the children within a dozen miles of my camp know me and as I ride along the roads they politely take off their hats and smile and say, *"Bon jour, Monsieur Wright."* They are really almost the only ones except close friends who know how to pronounce my name. People in general pronounce my name "Vreecht," with a terrible rattle of the "r." In many places I am called by my first name, "Veelbare," almost entirely.

.   .   .   .

Wilbur Wright to Orville

Paris, November 3, 1908

I came up to Paris yesterday partly for business and partly for the banquet at which our medals and prizes are to be presented.

The *Daily Mail* offers $12,500 for a cross channel flight and half the net receipts of an exhibition of the machine at a big hall in London. If I felt sure of decent weather I would go for it as such an exhibition would practically end the necessity of further demonstrations next year, and cause all the parliaments of France, Germany & England to vote credits at their winter sessions. I understand that the French budget committee has already voted to include a big appropriation in the coming budget.

. . . .

Wilbur Wright to his father

Le Mans, November 9, 1908

On Thursday I took lunch as guest of honor with the "Autour du Monde" a club composed of many of the most prominent people of France. Among those present were Liard, president of the University, Bergson, the greatest living French philosopher; Rodin, the great sculptor; Painleve, the distinguished mathematician; Pastor Wagner, of the "Simple Life"; M. Lepine, who maintains public order in Paris, but who is a nice mild looking savant in appearance, rather than a chief of police. Many others were almost equally distinguished as editors, authors, scientists, or states-men.

In the afternoon I visited the French senate where the question of recommending an appropriation for the encour-agement of aerostation was under discussion. After adjourn-ment the Baron d'Estournelles de Constant, Senator from La Sarthe, gave a little reception in my honor in the lunch room, and introduced me to the president of the Senate and many of the senators.

In the evening I attended the dinner given in my honor by the Aéro Club at which some three hundred guests were present, the number being limited only by the size of the hall. It was held in the grand banquet room of the Automo-bile Club on the Place de la Concorde, a magnificent hall. M. Barthou, French minister of Public Works, presided, and many distinguished people were present. The gold medal of the Aéro Club and the gold medal of the Academy of Sports were presented to Orville and me. I was received very cordially.

The government had decided to confer upon me the "Legion of Honor" but on learning of it privately, I sent word that it would be impossible for me to accept an honor which Orville could not equally share.

Weiler wished to give a dinner to meet Clemenceau and other ministers and distinguished men but I thought best to decline. Mr. Henry White, the American ambassador, also wishes to give a dinner in my honor before I leave France.

The Aero Club of Great Britain has also voted a gold medal, the first in the history of the Club, to Orville and me, and wishes me to attend a special dinner in my honor in a few weeks, for the purpose of receiving it.

I was offered the honorary presidency of the new English

Aeroplane Society, but I declined it as I have declined all formal honors in which Orville was not associated. He must come over next year. . . .

. . . .

One casual remark by Wilbur in France has since been quoted all over the world. When asked to make a speech at a dinner in Paris he said, "I know of only one bird—the parrot—that talks; and it doesn't fly very high."

Wilbur Wright to his sister

Le Mans, November 10, 1908

In a week Pop will be eighty years old. "Boo-hoo-hoo." I hope you will have a nice celebration of the event. We ought to give him one more square meal before we all go to the poor house. . . . If we have a few more such years as this one Grand-pa may find himself the youngest member of the family. . . .

. . . .

Bishop Wright lived until April 4, 1917—aged eighty-nine.

Wilbur Wright to Orville

Le Mans, November 12, 1908

We have an offer of 500,000 fr. cash and 25% of the profits for our Italian business. I think we ought to take it. If we do I will probably have to spend most of the winter in Europe, as it will be important to get things along as fast as possible in order to be ready for one of the northern countries in the spring. We have made an offer to Russia to furnish 10 machines for 100,000 dollars and permit them to build additional machines for a royalty of $2,500 each. There is some prospect of business there. The first Russian patent has been allowed, quite recently. The French company will be organized as soon as the legal formalities are completed. The stock will be 800,000 fr. of which we take 250,000 fr. . . .

November 13, 1908

Today I went for the Aéro Club de La Sarthe prize for height. The conditions provided that the contestant go over a row of balloons 30 meters high. I went up to about 70 meters, or more than double the required height. Friday the 13th seemed to have an off day. . . .

.   .   .   .

Orville Wright to Wilbur

Dayton, Ohio, November 14, 1908

It is two weeks today since I left the hospital at Fort Myer, yet I am just beginning to get about the house on crutches. I sit up several hours at a time, though I suffer some from the pressure of the blood in my feet and legs, after so long a period of disuse. This is the first I have written since the accident.

I have tried to get reliable information concerning the accident, but I find most witnesses observe very little of the details of what happened.

We had made three rounds of the ground, keeping well inside of buildings, trees, etc. so that the turns were of necessity pretty short. On the fourth round, everything seemingly working much better and smoother than in any former flight, I started on a larger circuit with less abrupt turns. It was on the very first slow turn that the trouble began. Just after passing over the top of our building at a height which I estimate at 100 or 110 ft., but which Lieut. Lahm, Chas. Taylor, Furnas, and many others thought to be 150 ft., and while traveling directly toward Arlington Cemetery, I heard a light tapping in the rear of the machine. A hurried glance behind revealed nothing wrong, but I decided to shut off the power and descend as soon as the machine could be faced in a direction where a landing could be made. This decision was hardly reached, in fact I suppose it was not over two or three seconds from the time the first taps were heard, till two big thumps, which gave the machine a terrible shaking, showed that something had broken. At the time I only thought of the transmission. The machine suddenly turned to the right and I immediately shut off the power. I then discovered that the machine would not respond to the steering and lateral balancing levers, which produced a most peculiar feeling of helplessness. Yet I continued to push the levers, when the machine's sudden turn to the left, (the right wing rising high in the air) till it faced directly up the field. I reversed the levers to stop the turning and to bring the wings on a level.

Quick as a flash, the machine turned down in front and
started straight for the ground. Our course for fifty feet was
within a very few degrees of the perpendicular. Lieutenant
Selfridge up to this time had not uttered a word, though he
took a hasty glance behind when the propeller broke, and
turned once or twice to look into my face, evidently to see
what I thought of the situation. But when the machine
turned head first for the ground, he exclaimed "Oh! Oh!" in
an almost inaudible voice.

I pulled the front rudder lever to its limit, but there was
no response in the course of the machine. Thinking that,
maybe, something was caught and that the rudder was not
completely turned, I released the lever a little and gave another pull, but there was no change. I then looked at the
rudder and saw that it was bent to its limit downward, and
that the pressure of the air on the under side was bulging
the cloth up between the ribs. The first 50 ft. of that plunge
seemed like a half minute, though I can hardly believe that
it was over one second at most. The front rudder in that distance had not changed the course more than five or ten degrees. Suddenly just before reaching the ground, probably
25 feet, something changed—the machine began to right
itself rapidly. A few feet more, and we would have landed
safely. As it was, the skids hit out at the front end. All the
front framing was broken and the machine turned up on
edge just as it did in the last flight in the south.

The only explanation I have been able to work out of the
cause of the plunge for the ground, is that the rear rudder,
after the stay wire was torn loose by the propeller, fell over
on its side and in some mysterious manner was caught and
held in this position, with a pressure on its under side. . . .

I do not like the idea of your attempting a channel flight,

when I am not present. I haven't much faith in your motor running. You seem to have more trouble with the engine than I do.

. . . .

The day after the accident, the mechanics, Taylor and Furnas, brought the broken propeller and some of the other broken parts to Orville's bedside. From these parts he was able later to determine the cause of the accident. A new pair of propellers, several inches longer than any previously used, had been installed just before the flight. The trouble started when a longitudinal crack developed in one blade of the right propeller. This crack permitted the blade to flatten and lose much of its thrust, with the result that the pressures on the two blades became unequal, causing a severe vibration of the propeller shaft housing. The vibration loosened one of the stay wires that held in position the tube in which the propeller-shaft turned. Then the propeller began to swing sidewise and forward until a blade hit and tore loose the stay wire to the vertical tail, permitting the tail to take a nearly horizontal position. A pressure on the tail's underside lifted the rear of the machine, thus causing it to dart for the ground.

A surprising thing was that, despite his serious accident, Orville afterward continued to enjoy flying for the sport of the thing. Wilbur, after his first few flights, would just as soon have stayed on the ground; he flew only for business reasons.

In his later years, as a consequence of his accident, Orville's back was so sensitive to vibration, especially in landing, that he did almost no flying, even as a passenger.

Wilbur Wright to his father

Le Mans, November 24, 1908

We are arranging to establish a camp in the southern part
of France so that the men I train may continue practice during the winter. I am beginning to fear that I will not be able
to come home for Christmas, there is so much to do here. I
wish you could all make up your minds to come over here
for a while. . . .

The outdoor exercise has been very good for my health. I
now weigh a trifle over 150 lbs., about eight pounds above
my usual weight.

. . . .

Wilbur Wright to Orville

Le Mans, December 3, 1908

I fear some questions regarding the cause of the accident
can never be settled. From what you say I doubt whether
the additional length of the screws was a cause of the trouble. I understand that you were circling to the *left*. In that
case the pressure would have been on the *right* side of the
tail and the *left* propeller would have struck the wire. In
fact the right propeller was the one which broke. The machine of course turned first to the right under part of the left
propeller, and afterwards to the left on account of the *drag*
of the left propeller after stopping. It is probable that this
turn to the left was more due to the greater angle you imparted to the left wing to keep from turning to the right.

No, this is wrong. It must have been caused by the tail. It is probable that the upper tail wire wrapped up in the left screw and caused the turn to the left and the plunge. The latter may have been partly due to the broken right wire wrapping up in the right screw and pulling the rear ends of the ribs down to a greater angle. . . .

The French company had its first meeting on Monday and will organize next Monday probably. There is talk of giving the selling agency to a company headed by young Clemenceau. They guarantee to sell 25 machines per year at 25000 francs cash, and pay us 20000 francs per machine. They would pay 125,000 fr. down at signing of the contract (5,000 fr. per machine) and balance on each machine as delivered. Two automobile dealers have already ordered 10 machines each. The Clemenceau contract does not cover government business.

We will have to sell in Europe at about $5,000 per machine. In America our price ought to be about $7,500. We will have to make a special price to the government on additional machines if we get $25,000 for the first one.

.   .   .   .

Wilbur Wright to his sister

Le Mans, December 7, 1908

. . . We are looking for grounds in the south of France and may choose Pau down near the Spanish frontier. . . .

I would have liked to send a lot of little presents home for Christmas, but I can buy nothing here and I will not get back to Paris in time. Spend Twenty-five dollars for me at

Dayton. I cabled Orville to give Reuchlin and Lorin each
a thousand dollars. . . .

I am sure I told you several times to get a year's leave
of absence and take a good rest. If I go down to Pau, it would
be a good place for you to spend a few months. I know that
you love "Old Steele" but I think you would love it still better
if the briny deep separated it from you for a while. We will
be needing a social manager and can pay enough salary to
make the proposition attractive, so do not worry about the
six per day the school board gives you for peripateting about
Old Steele's classic halls.

. . . .

Wilbur Wright to his father

Le Mans, January 1, 1909

I suppose that before this letter reaches Dayton Orville
will have started for France and possibly Kate with him. I
would have been glad if all of you could have come over for
a while, but I suppose you would have found the traveling
fatiguing, and then one misses very much the little things
which he can have at his own home but which he cannot
find in hotels.

We have arranged that Orville and Kate shall have free
accommodations at the best hotels at Pau, which is one of
the great winter resorts of France. The community has built
us a house to furnish us living quarters and shop room. It is
about 50 ft. x 60 ft. and is well built. The grounds are about
8 miles from Pau and extend over a country 3 miles by 10
miles. I think it will be a very good place.

It is probable that from Pau we will go to Rome for a month before returning to America. The aeronautical society of Rome offers us $10,000 for a machine and training of an operator. The government is interested in the offer also, and will probably order some machines.

Yesterday being the last day of the year I made another try for the Michelin Prize and remained up 2 hours and 20 minutes. The distance, counting from port to port, was 124 kilometers, but the real distance was nearly 150 kilometers, about 90 miles. It was very cold and during the later part of the flight a drizzle of sleet and rain fell. After landing I prepared for another start and took M. Barthou, the minister of Public Works, for a ride. He informed me that the government had decided to confer the Legion of Honor upon both Orville and myself.

As the other men who had entered for the prize were able to do nothing, the cup and the money, $4,000, came to me, or rather the cup comes to the Aéro Club of the Sarthe of which I am a member, and a duplicate in bronze comes to me permanently. If Orville had been able to compete for it in America it would have been more interesting. I am glad, though, that the Aéro Club of the Sarthe is to have the honor of being the first holder of the cup, for it has done everything humanly possible to help me and make things pleasant for me. You will be able to realize what I mean only when I tell you that about a half dozen of them have spent probably a third of their days out at our grounds for nearly four months. People in America do not put themselves to such trouble for anyone.

I am sorry that I could not come home for Christmas but I could not afford to lose the Michelin prize, as the loss of prestige would have been much more serious than the direct loss. If I had gone away the other fellows would have fairly

busted themselves to surpass any record I left. The fact that
they knew I was ready to beat anything they should do kept
them discouraged.

.   .   .   .

Orville Wright to his brother Lorin

Pau, France, February 3, 1909

If prices in real estate should make a big dip or if any
special bargains come along, let us know. We will probably
invest our money in real estate. . . .

.   .   .   .

Under the contract between the Wrights and the French
company, one of the brothers was to train three pilots. Wilbur
had begun this at Le Mans and then when winter weather
came he continued the training at Pau. Soon after his arrival
there Orville and Katharine came over to join him. Later they
all went to Rome where a company, or "aviation club," to
buy a Wright plane had been formed. Wilbur trained two
flyers there. While in Rome the brothers made preliminary
arrangements for a Wright company in Germany. (The
final contract was closed in August, 1909.)

Wilbur Wright to his father

Pau, March 1, 1909

I am expecting to finish my work here in a couple of weeks and then go to Rome for a month before coming back to America. It will be a full year in Europe. On the whole I have had an interesting time over here, but I will be very glad to get back home again. . . .

For several weeks we have been having visits from a number of distinguished visitors. Mr. Balfour, the former prime minister of England, was here a couple of weeks ago. Then the king of Spain made a special trip to see us, and a few days later M. Barthou, one of the French cabinet ministers, came down and took a ride with me. He told me that the government would soon confer the Legion of Honor on both Orville and me. Although the camp is eight miles from Pau crowds of people come out every day and visitors flock there from all parts of Europe. The crowds are better handled than at Le Mans and give little trouble. . . .

It will not be necessary to put a mortgage on your Grant County property. We can scrape together a few dollars for you if you need it.

. . . .

Orville Wright to his brother Lorin

Paris, March 20, 1909

I am sending inclosed a draft on New York for $5797. For pity's sake don't lose it as I spent seven francs and over an hour's time getting it. Besides I had to sign a paper releasing the bank Credit Lyonais from all responsibility in case there was delay in paying it in America on account of the postal strike here, and a release from issuing a duplicate in case this is lost. Such banking methods I never heard of.

. . . .

To Wilbur and Orville Wright from their father

March 21, 1909

I am glad to notice that they credit Wilbur for Sunday observance and freedom from tobacco. It will do more good than all the worth of the money you will ever get out of your invention.

. . . .

Orville Wright to his brother Lorin

Paris, April 2, 1909

I am sending inclosed a draft on New York for $21,297.19. Please deposit it in building associations at 4 pc. I think it is best to distribute it somewhat.

. . . .

Katharine Wright to her father

Rome, *April* 14, 1909

We had J. Pierpont Morgan, his sister, daughter and a friend out to visit the camp yesterday afternoon. They were very pleasant people.

. . . .

Wilbur Wright to Octave Chanute

May 17, 1909

We reached home last Thursday after a very good trip of 15 days from Rome. . . .

The English are fitting up a very nice flying ground at Shippy Island near the mouth of the Thames and we have taken orders for about a half dozen machines which are being constructed for us by Short Brothers. We have had opportunities to close out our English business but have preferred to hold on to it for the present. We sold in France and Germany, and will probably close a contract for Italy very soon. After sailing we learned that Lt. Calderara at Rome had met with an accident but we have no reliable information regarding it as yet. I left him with greater misgivings than my other pupils, because he was a cigarette fiend, and was being very badly spoiled by the attention and flattery he was receiving. Lambert and Tissandier were splendid fellows in every respect and very trustworthy.

. . . .

Wilbur Wright to Octave Chanute

June 6, 1909

We have been very busy on a machine for Ft. Myer and as we are interrupted very much the work goes slower than we could wish but we hope to be flying before this month ends. About a week of the time will be consumed in traveling back and forth between Dayton and Washington to receive medals. The Dayton presentation has been made the excuse for an elaborate carnival and advertisement of the city under the guise of being an honor to us. As it was done in spite of our known wishes, we are not as appreciative as we might be.

.   .   .   .

About a month after their return to Dayton the city gave the Wrights a "home coming" that lasted two days. Before it was quite over, Wilbur and Orville set out for Washington to prepare for the completion of Army demonstrations, interrupted by Orville's accident.

Orville made his first flight on June 28 and finished on July 30. One of the most memorable of the flights in this series was on that final day when Orville with an Army officer, Lieutenant Benjamin D. Foulois for passenger, made the first cross-country airplane trip, a total distance of about ten miles to Alexandria and return without any suitable place to land if trouble had occurred.

The Wrights got a bonus of $5,000 more than the price agreed upon—ten per cent for each mile at speed above forty per hour—altogether $30,000 for the machine.

Almost immediately after the formal acceptance of the machine by the United States Government on August 2, Orville and Katharine set out for Berlin where he would start training two flyers for the German Wright company, after giving an exhibition arranged for on behalf of the Berlin *Lokal Anzeiger*.

Orville Wright to Wilbur

Berlin, August 19, 1909

We reached Berlin this morning. Berg had secured the best rooms in this hotel [Esplanade] for us for nothing. We have a large sitting room about 25 x 30 feet, two large bed-rooms and two bath rooms.

. . . .

Orville Wright to Wilbur

Berlin, August 24, 1909

I have just read in the papers of the filing of suits against Curtiss & Co. I think it would be a good plan to give out an interview in which announcement is made of suing all who have any connection with infringing machines.

. . . .

Wilbur Wright to Orville

August 30, 1909

I see by the papers that you and Bill [The German Emperor] had quite a confab. I advise that you move into a hotel about like the Brittania at Rome. If you stay where you are too long Swes [Katharine] will never be able to live on the salary she gets when she goes to teaching school after Christmas.

.   .   .   .

Katharine had often expressed great distaste for the hotel in Rome.

Orville Wright to his brother Lorin

Berlin, September 9, 1909

I am sending a draft for $40,000. If Will is not at home please place it in different building associations.

.   .   .   .

Orville Wright to Wilbur

Berlin, September 23, 1909

I finished on Templehofer field last Saturday with a flight for the one-man duration record. I was compelled to stop after an hour and 46 minutes on account of the water supply being exhausted. The little drive arm on the water pump had broken, and as a result the water had all boiled away. . . . I made a flight on every appointed day excepting one, and on that day a pouring rain set in just as I was ready to start. The machine was out in the rain for nearly an hour and was thoroughly soaked through. One of the glued joints in the propeller was loosened as a result. . . .

The day I made the high flight, which was very little higher than some other flights here, I circled the field once and was on the second round before I looked for the balloon, which was in the center of the field. At first I did not see it as I was looking above for it, having no idea that I was already above it. When I passed over it I was at least 50 meters above it. I then started to come down in making a small circle and passed over it again, this time with a clearance of at least 60 or 75 feet. Then I decided to climb up again and go over it at a great height. I made one circle in climbing and again passed over the balloon with a clearance of at least 50 meters. After coming down I found that the balloon had been raised to 172 meters for the third crossing, so that my real height must have been close to 225 meters.

By watching the position of the tape on the front bar, I find it just as easy to climb at great heights as when near the ground.

I had a telegram after my last flight from Sherl (*Lokal Anzeiger*) congratulating me on the series of flights. It has pleased the people here very much that I was able to fly every day in spite of the wind, which on only two days was as low as 3 meters per second, most of the time was 6 to 9 meters, and one day, they say, 12 meters. The weather the last few days has been very much warmer and the air stiller.

In the early flights in winds the machine was jerked from under me a number of times, and I would find myself sitting five or six inches up the back of the seat. I have now learned, by watching the tape, when these rolling gusts are coming and prepare for them, so that I can keep the seat much better. Saturday afternoon, however, I got caught by one that raised me 8 or ten inches off the seat. As I try to hold myself in the seat by pushing myself tight against the back I rode for quite a distance before I slipped down to the seat. I am going to tie myself to the seat with string. . . .

I have never passed through so many and such severe whirlwinds as in the flights here. But they were usually in certain parts of the field and I could keep out of the worst of them if I chose. I would be flying along very nicely when of a sudden the machine would begin to quiver, and in looking at the tape I would see it swerve to one side at an angle of over 45 degrees, and then in a few seconds, without my making any change with the rudder, it would swing an equal amount to the opposite side. . . .

The Crown Prince called me up on the telephone again yesterday and wanted to know how soon I was coming to Potsdam to do the teaching. (I have now had a half dozen or more conversations with the Crown Prince on the telephone. We are getting quite chummy!) He says he doesn't want to miss getting a ride. Everyone tells me that I had better get the consent of the Emperor before taking him, as there might otherwise be trouble.

`   .   .   .   .

During one of his flights at Potsdam, started late in the afternoon, Orville stayed up so long that darkness came on.

It was darker than he realized when he was ready to land, and many of the spectators, including members of the Emperor's family, helpfully turned on their automobile lights. It was doubtless the first night flight ever made.

Orville Wright to Wilbur

Berlin, September 24, 1909

The difficulty in handling our machine is due to the rudder being in front, which makes it hard to keep on a level course. If you want to climb you must first give the front rudder a larger angle, but immediately the machine begins to rise you must reverse the rudder and give a smaller angle. The machine is always in unstable equilibrium. I do not think it is necessary to lengthen the machine but to simply put the rudder behind instead of before.

.   .   .   .

Wilbur Wright to Orville

New York, September 26, 1909

I intend to bring suit against importers of Bleriot and Farman machines and I think the patent matter should be pushed in Europe also. The license proposition can be discussed to better advantage after we have shown our teeth a little.

.   .   .   .

Wilbur Wright to his sister

September 26, 1909

I see you in front of the crowds with the empress and princesses, etc. and not writing any letters, but all right for you. Just wait till winter comes and then you'll get the bad of it just like any other grasshopper after the festive summer season is over. I have had *one* letter since you left home more than six weeks ago. There may have been two but it has been so long ago that I cannot remember clearly any more.

. . . .

Orville Wright to Wilbur

Berlin, September 28, 1909

I am sending enclosed a draft for $8,000. This leaves me a little over $1,000 to pay bills here. . . . I haven't time now to write about the flying races here. If I had gone in them I think we would have taken everything. But I did not enter having received the telegram saying you were displeased with my competing.

. . . .

On September 16, Orville had raised the world's altitude record from 100 to 172 meters. Two days later he made a new world's record for a flight with a passenger, flying for more than one hour and thirty-five minutes.

While Orville was in Germany, Wilbur was making equally sensational flights in New York for the Hudson-Fulton Celebration.

Wilbur Wright to his father

New York, October 7, 1909

On Monday I made a flight up the Hudson to Grant's Tomb and back to Governor's Island. It was an interesting trip and at times rather exciting.

.   .   .   .

The flight up the Hudson was one of the most daring yet made in an airplane, and Wilbur had taken the precaution to buy a canoe which he roped to the lower part of the plane. The part of the canoe ordinarily open was covered with canvas to make it water-tight. Wilbur's idea was that if anything went wrong the canoe might possibly serve as a buoy, or pontoon, to keep the machine afloat.

As provided for in the Government contract, Wilbur went next to College Park, Maryland, to train as pilots Signal Corps officers. The men trained were Lieutenants Frank P. Lahm and Frederic E. Humphreys. Their instruction began on October 8 and was completed October 26. Lieutenant Lahm, who had been the first army officer ever to fly as a passenger in a plane, received the first lesson in pilotage. Humphreys made the first solo flight a few minutes before Lahm's. Wilbur also gave lessons to Lieutenant Benjamin D. Foulois.

Orville Wright to Wilbur

Berlin, October 8, 1909

I think it will be a good plan to get a practice ground somewhere in order that we can begin experiments soon after my return. Kitty Hawk will do, though it would be impossible to use wheels there. Wheels have not proved a great success in Germany, as the flying at Berlin and Spa (Belgium) have demonstrated.

. . . .

Wilbur Wright to his father

Washington, D. C., October 9, 1909

I am living at College Park, Maryland, while training the Signal Corps officers. We have a very fair ground and I hope to get through in a few weeks. I fear we will have some trouble with the crowds of sight-seers, as we have but few soldiers to police the grounds.

. . . .

Wilbur Wright to George A. Spratt

College Park, Maryland, October 16, 1909

It is quite true that before we had very seriously taken up the subject of the measurement of lifts and drifts of surfaces, you told to us your idea of balancing the lift of a surface against its drift, (as you described it,) and determining their relationship directly, instead of measuring each independently; and that later when we took up that subject we utilized the idea in a machine of different design from yours. We have not wished to deprive you of the credit for the idea, and when we give to the world that part of our work, we shall certainly give you proper credit. We believed then and believe yet that it is a more convenient method than measuring each (lift & drift) separately and then making the comparison as Langley, Lilienthal and most other experimenters had done. But while we considered the idea good I must confess that I am surprised and a trifle hurt when you say that the advice and suggestions we gave you in return "cannot be considered in any degree a fair compensation." I suppose that when two men swap stories each thinks his own story better than the other's, and it is about the same when men swap ideas. But aside from the ideas and suggestions you received from us, we also furnished you copies of our tables, not only those made on the machine of which your idea formed a part, but also on the pressure testing machine. My ideas of values may be wrong, but I cannot help feeling that in so doing we returned the loan with interest, and that the interest many times outweighed in value the original loan itself. Has your idea yielded you yourself tables as comprehensive and accurate as those you received through us?

But if you really feel that you have given more than you have received yet, I am quite ready to place at your disposal any scientific information or practical knowledge which we have gathered in ten years of investigation and practical experience.

Tell us your needs and we will help you. I learn from a

gentleman I met in New York, who said he was associated
with you, that you are experimenting with a machine on
which you expect to mount a motor. Perhaps there is some
point about which you would find our advice helpful. I will
be at College Park for a few weeks and will be very glad to
have you come down.

.   .   .   .

Wilbur Wright to his father

Washington, D. C., October 31, 1909

After a two days' trip to New York I am back in Washington again for a few days. I have practically finished my
work here and will go back to New York on Wednesday
and meet Orville and Kate who will probably land on Thursday morning. Lieutenants Lahm & Humphreys are managing the machine very well, and Lt. Foulois is also learning
rapidly.

My trip to New York was in connection with a deal to dispose of our American rights. It is proposed that we transfer
our business for U. S. and Canada to a company of which
J. P. Morgan,* Cornelius Vanderbilt, Judge Gary, George
Gould and others will be the chief stockholders. We are to
receive $100,000 in cash and one third of the stock of the
company, and also a 10 per cent royalty on the selling price
of each machine made by the company. I think the deal will
be consummated but the papers are not yet signed. . . .

When in New York last week I received another $10,000

---

* Morgan withdrew when he learned that some of the others did not
want him in the company. They knew that where Morgan sat would
be the head of the table!

from the Hudson-Fulton people, thus making a total of $12,-500 out of the $15,000 agreed upon. It is doubtful whether I ever get any more, as the treasury is about empty.

. . . .

Orville Wright to Wilbur

Berlin, Thanksgiving, November 24, 1909

De Lambert would like to organize a company to manufacture our machines on royalty. He says Tissandier would invest in it, and that there would be no trouble in getting the necessary capital. De Lambert thinks there has been a conspiracy for some time to break the company so as to turn the business over to the Astra. The whole business in France seems to have been nothing but a graft on the part of the Astra.

I saw Capt. Englehard [of German Wright company] this morning. He says that I had no more than got out of sight last year until every man in the shop was making improvements on the machine and that in a short time they had so many on that the machine couldn't carry them all.

. . . .

Wilbur Wright to Octave Chanute

December 6, 1909

We are all home again after a rather strenuous summer and autumn. Orville and my sister had a splendid time in

Germany, and Orville returned much stronger in every way than when he went away. I finished the work at Washington just as they returned. Since then we have been working very hard on the organization of our business and the preparation of our case in the suit against Curtiss & Herring. The affidavit filed by Mr. Herring is thoroughly characteristic of him. He has suddenly discovered that he invented in 1894 the method of controlling lateral balance by setting surfaces to different angles of incidence on the right and left sides of the machine and correcting the difference in their resistances by means of an adjustable vertical tail.

We have closed out our American business to the Wright Company, of which the stockholders are Messrs. C. Vanderbilt, Collier, Belmont, Alger, Berwind, Ryan, Gould, Shonts, Freedman, Nicoll and Plant. We received a very satisfactory cash payment, forty percent of the stock, and are to receive a royalty on every machine built in addition. The general supervision of the business will be in our hands though a general manager will be secured to directly have charge. We will devote most of our time to experimental work.

All of us are in very good health. Father, though in his eighty-second year, is still quite active. My own health owing to the outdoor life of the past year is better than in former years. I trust that you retain well your strength and enjoyment of life.

. . . .

Wilbur Wright to Arnold Kruckman, aeronautical editor of the New York World

December 21, 1909

We notice in the *World* of 12 December an article in which

you say of us, "Their persistent failure to acknowledge their monumental indebtedness to the man who gave them priceless assistance has been one of the most puzzling mysteries in their career."

We wish to say to you, Mr. Kruckman, that your accusation is most unjust and undeserved. We have repeatedly acknowledged our indebtedness to the Chanute double decker for our ideas regarding the best way of obtaining the strongest and lightest sustaining surfaces. But it is an absolute mistake that he "suggested the warping tip idea." We were using the warping tip long before we made Mr. Chanute's acquaintance. It was entirely original with us so far as we knew. If you will read Mr. Chanute's book *Progress in Flying Machines* on Le Bris and D'Esterno you will see that there is nowhere any mention of adjusting the right and left tips to respectively different angles to control lateral balance. On what then do you base your statement that their machines did contain such a feature?

Mr. Chanute's sympathetic interest in our work was one of the chief stimulants which kept us at work till we attained success. We therefore owe him a great debt of gratitude which we have not the least thought or wish to repudiate. Without it we might have quit and thus failed. But the impression which has grown up in some quarters that we began our work with a copy of one of his machines as a continuation of his experiments, and that we worked under his teachings and instructions, and even at his expense is quite false. Except in the matter of sympathetic interest we are less indebted to him than to Lilienthal. We of course owe something to all the experimenters whose writings we had read.

We invited Mr. Chanute to visit our camp each year in

order that we might not be without a trustworthy witness of our performances. His thorough acquaintance with our progress and the fact that most of the information regarding our work leaked out through him, led to a false impression that we were working under his direction and with his financial assistance. Many of the published stories have been very embarrassing, because if left uncorrected they tend to build up a legend which takes the place of truth, while on the other hand any attempt on our part to correct inaccuracies gives us the appearance of ungratefully attempting to hurt the fame of Mr. Chanute. Rather than subject ourselves to criticism on that score we have preferred to remain silent, but now you find fault with our silence. We, rather than Mr. Chanute, have been the sufferers from this silence so far, and we see no immediate danger that he will not receive the credit to which he is justly entitled, for his services to the cause of human flight.

Mr. Chanute is one of the truest gentlemen we have ever known and a sympathetic friend of all who have the cause of human flight at heart. For many years we entrusted to him many of our most important secrets, and only discontinued it when we began to notice that his advancing years made it difficult for him to exercise the necessary discretion. His correspondence with American and foreign experimenters has probably been greater than that of any other person and will be of priceless value to future historians. It will also show exactly what his services to us have been. But meanwhile we will continue to give him deserved credit, and avoid being forced into even the appearance of detraction by public denials of incorrect newspaper statements for which he is not responsible.

IX

THE COST OF PRE-EMINENCE

Wilbur Wright to Octave Chanute

Dayton, O., January 20, 1910

The New York *World* has published several articles in the past few months in which you are represented as saying that our claim to having been the first to maintain lateral balance by adjusting the wing tips to different angles of incidence can not be maintained, as this idea was well known in the art when we began our experiments. As this opinion is quite different from that which you expressed in 1901 when you became acquainted with our methods, I do not know whether it is mere newspaper talk or whether it really represents your present views. So far as we are aware the originality of this system of control with us was universally conceded when our machine was first made known and the questioning of it is a matter of recent growth springing from a desire to escape the legal consequences of awarding it to us.

In our affidavits we said that when we invented this system we were not aware that such an idea had ever suggested itself to any other person, and that we were the first to make a machine embodying it, and also that we were the first to demonstrate its value to the world, and that the world owed the invention to us and to no one else. The patent of Mouillard was cited as an anticipation by the German and the English patent offices, and also by the defendants' attorneys in the recent trial at Buffalo, and in each case it was decided that it did not constitute an anticipation. I have also seen Lebris and d'Esterno mentioned as having anticipated us, but the accounts in your book regarding the works and writings of these men do not contain any explanation of such a system of lateral control. Do the French documents from which you derived your information contain it, and if so can you give information as to where such documents may be obtained? It is our view that morally the world owes its almost universal use of our system of lateral control entirely to us. It is also our opinion that legally it owes it to us. If however there is anything in print which might invalidate our legal rights it will be to our advantage to know it before spending too much on lawyers, and any assistance you may be able to give us in this respect will be much appreciated, even though it may show that legally our labors of many years to provide a system of lateral control were of no benefit to the world and a mere waste of time, as the world already possessed the system without us.

.   .   .   .

Octave Chanute to Wilbur Wright

January 23, 1910

This interview, [in New York *World*] which was entirely unsought by me, is about as accurate as such things usually are. Instead of discussing it I prefer to take up the main principles at issue.

I did tell you in 1901 that the mechanism by which your surfaces were warped was original with yourselves. This I adhere to, but it does not follow that it covers the general principle of warping or twisting wings; the proposals for doing this being ancient. You know, of course, what Pettigrew and Marey said about it. Please see my book, page 97 for what d'Esterno said of the laws of flight; the 3^d being torsion of the wings and the 6 being torsion of the tail. Also, page 106, Le Bris, rotary motion of the front edge of the wings. The original sources of information are indicated in foot notes. I did not explain the mechanism because I had not the data.

When I gave you a copy of the Mouillard patent in 1901 I think I called your attention to his method of twisting the rear of the wings. If the courts will decide that the purpose and results were entirely different and that you were the first to conceive the twisting of the wings, so much the better for you, but my judgment is that you will be restricted to the particular method by which you do it. Therefore it was that I told you in New York that you were making a mistake by abstaining from prize winning contests while public curiosity is yet so keen, and by bringing suits to prevent others from doing so. This is still my opinion and I am afraid, my friend, that your usually sound judgment has been warped by the desire for great wealth.

If, as I infer from your letter, my opinions form a grievance in your mind, I am sorry, but this brings me to say that I also have a little grievance against you.

In your speech at the Boston dinner, January 12, you began by saying that I "turned up" at your shop in Dayton in 1901 and that you then invited me to your camp. This conveyed the impression that I thrust myself upon you at that time and it omitted to state that you were the first to write to me in 1900, asking for information which was gladly furnished, that many letters passed between us, and that both in 1900 and 1901 you had written me to invite me to visit you, before I "turned up" in 1901. This, coming subsequently to some somewhat disparaging remarks concerning the helpfulness I may have been to you, attributed to you by a number of French papers, which I, of course, disregarded as newspaper talk, has grated upon me ever since that dinner and I hope that, in future, you will not give out the impression that I was the first to seek your acquaintance, or pay me left handed compliments, such as saying that "sometimes an experienced person's advice was of great value to younger men."

P.S. The statement that warping in connection with the turning of the rudder was patented in 1901 was not from me. The reporter must have gotten this elsewhere.

.   .   .   .

Wilbur Wright to Octave Chanute

January 29, 1910

Until confirmed by you, the interview in the New York *World* of January 17 seemed incredible. We had never had the slightest ground for suspecting that when you repeatedly spoke to us in 1901 of the originality of our methods, you referred only to our methods of driving tacks, fastening wires, etc., and not to the novelty of our general systems. Neither in 1901, nor in the five years following, did you in any way intimate to us that our general system of lateral control had long been a part of the art, and strangely enough, neither your books, addresses or articles, nor the writings of Lilienthal, Langley, Maxim, Hargrave, etc. made any mention whatever of the existence of such a system. Therefore it came to us with somewhat of a shock when you calmly announced that this system was already a feature of the art well known, and that you meant only the mechanical details when you referred to its novelty. If the idea was really old in the art, it is somewhat remarkable that a system so important that individual ownership of it is considered to threaten strangulation of the art was not considered worth mentioning then, nor embodied in any machine built prior to ours. . . .

The patent of Mouillard, to which you refer, does not even mention the control of the lateral balance, nor disclose a system by which it is possible to attain it.* I have read several of the books of Marey, and Pettigrew, as well as what your book says on d'Esterno, LeBris, etc., but I do not find in any of them any mention whatever of controlling lateral balance by adjustments of wings to respectively different angles of incidence on the right and left sides. Have you ever found such mention? It is not disputed that every person who is using this system to-day owes it to us and to us alone. The French aviators freely admit it. No legal disclosure of the

---

* On December 30, 1903, thirteen days after the first flight at Kitty Hawk with a motor-plane, Mr. Chanute read a paper before Section D of the American Association for the Advancement of Science, in which he made mention of these flights. That he did not at that time think the Wright system of control similar to Mouillard's is evidenced by the following quotation from his address which appeared in the *Popular Science Monthly,* March, 1904. "Being accomplished mechanics, they designed and built the apparatus, applying thereto *a new and effective mode of control of their own*. . . ." (Ed.)

system prior to us has yet been produced. Unless something as yet unknown to anybody is brought to light to prove the invention technically known to everybody prior to 1900, our warped judgment will probably continue to be confirmed by the other judges as it was by Judge Hazel at Buffalo.

As to inordinate desire for wealth you are the only person acquainted with us who has ever made such an accusation. We believed that the physical and financial risks which we took, and the value of the service to the world, justified sufficient compensation to enable us to live modestly with enough surplus income to permit the devotion of our future time to scientific experimenting instead of business. We spent several years of valuable time trying to work out plans which would have made us independent without hampering the invention by the commercial exploitation of the patents. These efforts would have succeeded but for jealousy and envy. It was only when we found that the sale of the patents offered the only way to obtain compensation for our labors of 1900-1906 that we finally permitted the chance of making the invention free to the world to pass from our hands. You apparently concede to us no right to compensation for the solution of a problem ages old except such as is granted to persons who had no part in producing the invention. That is to say, we may compete with mountebanks for a chance to earn money in the mountebank business, but are entitled to nothing whatever for past work as inventors. If holding a different view constitutes us almost criminals, as some seem to think, we are not ashamed. We honestly think that our work of 1900-1906 has been and will be of value to the world, and that the world owes us something as inventors, regardless of whether we personally make Roman holidays for accident-loving crowds.

You mention as a grievance that French papers some time

ago attributed to me some disparaging remarks concerning your helpfulness to us. Without having seen the report I can not affirm or deny its correctness. But we also have had grievances extending back as far as 1902, and on one occasion several years ago, we complained to you that an impression was being spread broadcast by newspapers that we were mere pupils and dependents of yours. You indignantly denied that you were responsible for it. When I went to France I found everywhere an impression that we had taken up aeronautical studies at your special instigation; that we obtained our first experience on one of your machines; that we were pupils of yours and put into material form a knowledge furnished by you; that you provided the funds; in short, that you furnished the science and money while we contributed a little mechanical skill, and that when success had been achieved you magnanimously stepped aside and permitted us to enjoy the rewards. I can not remember that I ever spoke for publication regarding the matter. The difficulty of correcting the errors without seeming to disparage you and hurting your feelings kept me silent, though I sometimes restrained myself with difficulty. However, I several times said privately that we had taken up the study of aeronautics long before we had any acquaintance with you; that our ideas of control were radically different from yours both before and throughout our acquaintance; that the systems of control which we carried to success were absolutely our own, and had been embodied in a machine and tested before you knew anything about them, and before our first meeting with you; that in 1900 and 1901 we used the tables and formulas found in books, but finding the results did not agree with the calculations, we made extensive laboratory experiments and prepared tables of our own which we used exclusively in all of our subsequent work; that the solution of the screw propeller problem was ours; that we designed all of our machines from first to last, originated and worked out the principles of control, constructed the machines, and made all the tests at our own cost; that you built several machines embodying your ideas in 1901 and 1902 which were tested at our camp by Mr. Herring, but that we had never made a flight on any of your machines, nor your men on any of ours, and that in the sense in which the expression was used in France we had never been pupils of yours, though we had been very close friends, had carried on very voluminous correspondence, and discussed our work very freely with you.

If the remarks you complain of exceeded mere corrections of such errors, as I have enumerated above, and the mention of features peculiarly our own, such as I have cited, I can safely say that the reported remarks are not correct. We have had too much appreciation of your real helpfulness to us to wish to deny it, and have suffered much rather than risk hurting your feelings by attempting to publicly correct gross errors which did us great injustice. I can not understand your objection to what I said at the Boston dinner about your visit to Dayton in 1901. I certainly never had a thought of intimating either that you had or had not been the first to seek an acquaintance between us. You also object to my expressing an appreciation of the influence which your friendship had on our work and lives. One of the *World* articles said that you had felt hurt because we had been silent regarding our indebtedness to you. I confess that I have found it most difficult to formulate a precise statement of what you contributed to our success. General statements do not seem to be very satisfactory to you or to us. We on our part have been much hurt by your apparent backwardness in correcting mistaken impressions, but we have assumed that you too have found it difficult to substitute for the erroneous reports a really satisfactory precise statement of the truth. If such a statement could be prepared it would relieve a situation very painful both to you and to us.

I have written with great frankness because I feel that such frankness is really more healthful to friendship than the secretly nursed bitterness which has been allowed to grow for so long a time. I expect that we will always continue to disagree in many of our opinions just as we have done ever since our first acquaintance began and even before, but such differences need not disturb a friendship which has existed so long. We do not insist that friends shall always agree with us.

As for the real source of bitterness, I may say that we endured it many years in silence, before you had occasion to experience any pain on account of it. We restrained ourselves from requesting you to make a public correction of the erroneous impressions so widespread both in America and in Europe, because we appreciated how difficult and embarrassing it would be for you to modify all the things credited to you, without appearing to disclaim some things really your due. If we should ourselves attempt to make such corrections and modifications, the general effect would be the same, with the added drawback of making us appear to disparage you. We have never desired to give you less credit than you have deserved for your helpfulness to us and to other experimenters, and we have no such desire now. We do object to some erroneous impressions which have gradually grown up with regard to our relations to each other. If anything can be done to straighten matters out to the satisfaction of both you and us, we are not only willing, but anxious, to do our part. There is no pleasure to us in the situation which has existed for several years past, and a solution of the difficulties would be most welcome. We have no wish to quarrel with a man toward whom we ought to preserve a feeling of gratitude.

P.S.—I enclose a sample of the class of misrepresentations connected with your name. It just came in today. We had nothing whatever to do with ordering a machine from Lamson. Our sole connection with the matter consisted in providing you camp facilities for testing it. It was a Chanute machine. The story ought to be corrected.

. . . .

On the same day that he wrote the long letter to Chanute, Wilbur sent another letter dealing with a situation that came to be troublesome. Dr. Zahm had written the Wrights strongly hinting that he would like to be their technical adviser. A patent infringement suit against Glenn Curtiss was about to be tried. In a second letter Zahm made it clear that he had not yet become a Curtiss adviser and implied that he was still available if the Wrights wanted his services. When he learned that they were not disposed to employ him he joined Curtiss. Though he had been a great booster of the Wrights, he soon began to behave as their bitter enemy, and for many years has put out all sorts of statements in which he tried to belittle the Wrights or deny their achievements. (See letter from Orville Wright to Alexander McSurely, February 5, 1946.)

Wilbur Wright to Prof. A. F. Zahm, Washington, D. C.

January 29, 1910

Naturally we regret that you will be lined up against us even in a professional capacity as confidential adviser in the legal struggle, but we do not think that such service carried out in a spirit of fairness need interrupt the friendship which has always existed between us. It seems to be conceded that we made the system of control, which we patented, a part of the art, and that all who are using it obtained it from us. The objections to our legal claims are technical, being based on old publications which did not lead to any result, and which are now of use only as a means of depriving us of legal rights in an invention which we independently conceived, worked into shape and presented to the service of the world, at a time when effort in that line was considered a foolish waste of time and money. At present there seems to be a general tendency to concede our moral right to the invention, but to deny that we have any right to expect any monetary pay. We suppose all inventors have been compelled to meet a similar situation where the world's self-interest has been involved, and we take the matter as philosophically as possible even when we find good friends lined up against us, so far as the legal side is concerned.

.   .   .   .

Before the end of 1909 the Wrights had to take court action against patent infringers. Altogether the brothers took active part in a dozen different suits in the United States. There were also suits in France and Germany involving many infringers. Most of the suits in the United States did not go beyond the early stages, as the infringers were not disposed to continue after a preliminary injunction had been issued. But three suits were of special importance. One of these was against Louis Paulhan, French aviator, who was about to give exhibitions in the United States, using planes made in France. Another was against Claude Grahame-White, English aviator, also about to give exhibitions in the United States with planes that infringed the Wright patents. The most important suit of all was against the Herring-Curtiss Co. and Glenn H. Curtiss.

On January 3, 1910, Judge John R. Hazel of the Federal Circuit Court at Buffalo, New York, granted a temporary restraining order against the Herring-Curtiss Co. and Glenn H. Curtiss. In handing down his decision, Judge Hazel said:

It appears that the defendant Curtiss had notice of the success of the Wright machine, and that a patent had been issued in 1906. Indeed, no one interfered with the rights of the patentees by constructing machines similar to theirs until in July, 1908, when Curtiss exhibited a flying-machine which he called "The June Bug." He was immediately notified by the patentees that such machine, with its movable surfaces at the tips, or wings, infringed the patent in suit, and he replied that he did not intend to publicly exhibit the machine for profit, but merely was engaged in exhibiting it for scientific purposes as a member of the Aerial Experiment Association. To this the patentees did not object. Subsequently, however, the machine, with supplementary planes placed midway between the upper and lower aeroplanes, was publicly exhibited by the defendant corporation, and used by Curtiss in aerial flights for prizes and emoluments. It further appears that the defendants now threaten to continue such use for gain and profit, and to engage in the manufacture and sale of such infringing machine, thereby becoming an active rival of complainant in the business of constructing flying-machines embodying the claims in suit, but such use of the infringing machine it is the duty of this Court on the papers presented to enjoin.

The case was carried to the United States Circuit Court of Appeals, where the Wrights won.* They won every patent suit, both in the United States and in Europe, that was ever adjudicated.

Wilbur Wright to Octave Chanute

April 28, 1910

I have no answer to my last letter and fear that the frankness with which delicate subjects were treated may have blinded you to the real spirit and purpose of the letter. I had noted in the past few years a cooling of the intimate friendship which so long existed between us, but it was your letter of recent date and newspaper clippings to which I referred, that brought to my mind the fact that a real soreness existed on your side as well as on ours, which if not eradicated would make our friendship a mere travesty of what it once was. My brother and I do not form many intimate friendships, and do not lightly give them up. I believed that unless we could understand exactly how you felt, and you could understand how we felt, our friendship would tend to grow weaker instead of stronger. Through ignorance, or thoughtlessness, each would be touching the other's sore spots, and causing

---

* In November, 1910, the Wrights had offered to settle with Curtiss by his paying $1,000 royalty on each machine manufactured by him, and $100 for each day one of his machines made exhibition flights, the agreement to cover both past and future.

unnecessary pain. We prize too highly the friendship, which meant so much to us in the years of our early struggles, to willingly see it worn away by uncorrected misunderstandings, which might be corrected by a frank discussion. I realized that few friendships are able to stand the strain of frankness, but I believed that it would be better to discuss matters freely than to permit small misunderstandings to gradually grow into big ones by neglect. My object was not to give offence, but to remove it. If you will read the letter carefully I think you will see that the spirit is that of true friendship.

I think the differences of opinion which threaten trouble, are not so much in regard to facts, as in regard to forms of expression, and manner of statement. That is why I have suggested that a joint statement should be prepared which would do justice to both and injustice to neither. We have not the least wish that your helpfulness to us should be kept from the public, as one of the interviews attributed to you seemed to intimate. Our gratitude and our friendship are genuine. It is our wish that anything which might cause bitterness should be eradicated as soon as possible. If we discuss matters in this spirit I believe all serious misunderstandings can be removed.

. . . .

Octave Chanute to Wilbur Wright

Chicago, Ill., May 14, 1910

I am in bad health and threatened with nervous exhaustion, had to go to New Orleans for a change in March and am now to sail for Europe on the 17th of this month.

Your letter of April 28th was gratifying, for I own that I felt very much hurt by your letter of January 29, which I thought both unduly angry and unfair, as well as unjust.

I have never given out the impression, either in writing or speech that you had taken up aeronautics at my instance or were, as you put it, pupils of mine. I have always written and spoken of you as original investigators and worthy of the highest praise. How much I may have been of help I do not know. I have never made *any claims* in that respect, but I may confess that I have sometimes thought that you did not give me as much credit as I deserved.

I sent you some clippings by Mr. Knabenshue showing how the same interview which grated on you in the *World* appeared in the *Philadelphia Inquirer* and one of the foreign clippings in which you were represented as speaking disparagingly of myself. I gave the latter no credence being aware how newspaper reporters made mountains out of mole hills, yet the question arose in my mind whether there had been a mole hill. I am sure that in my own case there has never been a mole hill of disparagement of your achievements or claim that I was entitled to a part of the credit. Whatever other impressions have got abroad originated with persons who knew of our own intimate relations or others who may have felt a certain amount of jealousy at your success. I feel sure that investigation will convince you of the accuracy of the above statements.

The difference in opinion between us, i.e.: whether the warping of the wings was in the nature of a discovery by yourselves, or had already been proposed and experimented by others, will have to be passed upon by others, but I have always said that you are entitled to immense credit for devising apparatus by which it has been reduced to successful practice. [The highest courts later held that the Wrights had priority over all others in their concept of presenting the right and left wings at different angles for purposes of equilibrium.]

I hope, upon my return from Europe that we will be able to resume our former relations.*

.   .   .   .

To train pilots to handle exhibition planes for the recently formed Wright Company, Orville Wright, seeking a warmer climate, went early in 1910 to Montgomery, Alabama. The place used later became known as Maxwell Field. On his return to Dayton in May, he opened a flying school for The Wright Company at the same Huffman pasture where the brothers had experimented in 1904-5. Three flights at that time were especially noteworthy. A short one by Wilbur, on May 21, was the last as pilot that he ever made. On May 25 the brothers broke their rule against both being in the air at once, and they flew together for a short time with Orville piloting. Later that same day Orville took his father, then eighty-two years old, for his first trip in a flying machine.

Orville continued to make frequent flights until 1915, and did not make his final flight as a pilot until 1918.

---

* It seems likely that something approaching the former friendly relations might have been resumed; but Chanute continued in poor health and died in November of the same year. He was 78 years old.

Wilbur Wright to Hart O. Berg

November 16, 1910

As for the American Wright company, it has made a net profit of more than a hundred thousand dollars this year. Orville and I will take out more than fifty thousand clear for our share, so that in the past 16 months we have received about two hundred thousand dollars in cash in America: $30,000 from the Army; $15,000 from the Hudson-Fulton celebration; $100,000 from The Wright Company on organization, and a little over $50,000 from this year's dividends and royalties. . . .

I am sorry the German and French companies did not send men over to America this year to learn how to build and take care of machines and learn what real flying is. It would have paid them well.

.   .   .   .

The Wright Company had been especially profitable during the first year, when the sight of a flying machine was still a novelty and contracts for exhibition flights were numerous. Inevitably, the exhibition part of the business began to taper off and such profits as still might have come from it were reduced by the persistent illegal competition of patent infringers.

Toward the end of 1910, Orville Wright went to Europe on business related to the Wright companies in France and Germany.

Orville Wright to Wilbur

Berlin, November 27, 1910

I have about made up my mind to let the European business go. I don't propose to be bothered with it all my life and I see no prospect of its ever amounting to anything unless we send a representative here to stay to watch our interests. . . .

. . . .

Wilbur Wright to Orville

New York, December 3, 1910

I notice that an effort is being made to erect a monument to Lilienthal and to provide something for his family. If you find the business is in proper hands and their plans sensible and reasonable and the need of his family real, we might contribute anything you think best up to a thousand dollars.

. . . .

Wilbur Wright to Orville

Dayton, Ohio, December 9, 1910

I have collected $38,000 in dividends and bonus from The Wright Co. and will get the royalty money soon. . . . I think Swes [Katharine] will arrange to spend it for us if we wish! I put this in because she is looking over my shoulder.

. . . .

Wilbur Wright to Orville

Dayton, December 16, 1910

Merry Christmas.

Please do not fail to pay Bollée the money due him for gasoline, oil, and materials for derrick &c. Also decide what we will contribute to Lilienthal's family. See that most of it goes to the family and but little to monuments. . . . The Curtiss people have evidently given up the license idea since they found that if we license anyone we will license others than them. I think they fear that their business [exhibition] is about played out and that if they could escape for the profitable past they could afford to pay license on the small future, but in this also they were disappointed. . . .

We are experimenting with a rubberized cloth, with the rubber rubbed thoroughly into the fibers. It does not very materially increase the weight.

. . . .

Wilbur Wright to George A. Spratt

Dayton, Ohio, December 19, 1910

It has been quite a long time since we have had any news of you. Orville is now in Europe to help the European Companies to whom we sold our foreign business, in designing some new machines. I have been in America all year. Orville and I have been wasting our time in business affairs and have had practically no time for experimental work or original investigations. But the world does not pay a cent for labor of the latter kinds or for inventions unless a man works himself to death in a business way also. We intend however to shake off business and get back to the other kind of work again before a year is out.

You, of course, know of the death of Mr. Chanute. Orville and I were at a dinner in his honor at Boston in January, at which time he seemed in pretty good health. But in May he wrote that he was intending to go abroad for his health. He had a severe attack of pneumonia while in Germany and France which left him so feeble that he had scarcely strength to get home. There he gradually became weaker and faded away. I attended his funeral at his home on Dearborn St. Only a few invited friends were present, mostly his associates in the society of engineers. Col. Glassford of the Signal Corps was the only one of his aeronautical friends I recognized. He was buried at Peoria beside his wife.

. . . .

Wilbur Wright to Charles D. Walcott, Secretary of the Smithsonian Institute, Washington, D. C., in response to a request for an opinion.

December 23, 1910

I have often remarked to my brother that Prof. Langley was ill fated in that he had been especially criticized by his enemies for things which were deserving of highest praise, and especially praised by his friends for things which were unfortunate lapses from scientific accuracy. I should consider it both unwise and unfair to him to specially rest his reputation in aerodynamics upon the so-called Langley Law, or upon the computations which gave rise to it, as they do not seem to represent his best work. The particular computations which led him to enunciate this law are found on pages 63-67 *Experiments in Aerodynamics*. A careful reading shows that he never actually tried the experiments of which he professed to give the result. . . .

But in fact, as the context shows, he did not make the observations with the surfaces having "fair"-shaped edges, but only with surfaces having square edges giving other results. The curve is not correct except for ideal surfaces, absolutely free from edge resistance and skin friction. His error lay, first, in assuming that this ideal condition could be substantially attained in actual practice by using surfaces with "fair"-shaped edges, and secondly, in so stating his conclusions as to give the impression that the curve had been deduced directly from actual experiments. The latter error is repeated in various forms, as for instance on page 107, when he says,

"the experiments show that if we multiply the small planes which have been actually used, or assume a larger plane to have approximately the properties of similar small ones, one horse power rightly applied can sustain over 200 lbs. in the air at a horizontal velocity of over 20 meters per second."

And on page 6, he says,

"these experiments show that a definite amount of power so expended at a constant rate will attain more economical results at high speeds than at low ones . . . with an increasing economy of power with each higher speed, up to some remote limit not yet attained in experiment."

The actual observations as plotted on the chart, page 64, fail to substantiate the first statement, and actually contradict the last. His conclusions are really based upon an erro-

neous assumption regarding results which he thought might
have been attained if he had substituted "fair"-shaped edges
for square edges as actually used. It is clear from the Doctor's
statement that he never demonstrated by direct experiment
that weight could be carried at the rate of 200 lbs. per horse
power at 20 meters per second, nor that the power consumed
decreased with increase of speed up to some remote limit
not attained in experiment. He merely assumed that he
could have done it by varying the experiment a trifle, and
based the so-called Langley Law on this mistaken assumption. The law itself contains some elements of truth, but it
also contains elements of error, and the form of statement is
such that its general effect has been to mislead readers and
give them false ideas.

But while I think it would be a mistake to emphasize this
feature of Prof. Langley's work, the remaining paragraph of
your proposed inscription seems to me both proper and just.
Although the honor of the first practical demonstration of the
possibility of mechanical flight has been claimed for prior
experiments of Hargrave, Maxim, Ader, Tatin and Pénaud,
I think Prof. Langley has a stronger claim, than any of them.
His demonstration [with a model, in 1896] had a convincing
character which none of the others possessed. It had great
influence in determining my brother and myself to take up
work in this science, and without doubt it similarly influenced
others.

. . . .

Wilbur Wright to James Means, Boston, Mass.

February 2, 1911

When I was in Boston last Autumn we had a little talk about Herr Lilienthal's family and means for relieving its needs. It seems that the Germans now have on foot a project to raise a fund to provide a monument and assist the family, which it seems is in real need. My brother and I are not very strong believers in monuments, but we do think that the world owes something to Lilienthal and should not allow his widow to suffer real want.

Orville and I are ready to contribute five hundred dollars each to a fund to purchase annuities for the widow or any helpless children. Unless the German committee is willing to use its funds for the same purpose we would prefer to join in a separate movement. Do you think it would be possible to raise a general subscription for the purpose in America?

.   .   .   .

Wilbur Wright to Léon Bollée, Le Mans, France, February 11, 1911, enclosing an order for 1850 francs, which Bollée had spent in his behalf

We do not forget that you expended much time and gave yourself much trouble in order to be of assistance to us, and that you rejoiced with us in our successes and grieved with us in our troubles. For these things we do not attempt to pay with money, but we cherish them forever in our hearts.

.   .   .   .

A few weeks after Orville's return, Wilbur in the spring of 1911 took his turn in Europe to look after patent suits. Though the Wrights won every suit tried, in both France and Germany, collecting royalties from infringers proved to be much more difficult.

Wilbur Wright to Orville

Paris, May 26, 1911

In looking over the proposed plan of the new house I see that most of the rooms are smaller than in the original plans, and only the price has been enlarged. You are wasting entirely too much space on halls &c. . . . I see plainly that I am going to be put into one of the south bedrooms so I propose a new plan for them. In any event I am going to have a bath room of my own, so please make me one.

. . . .

The brothers had bought a seventeen-acre tract they named Hawthorn Hill, in the Dayton suburb of Oakwood, and had been making plans for a house there.

Wilbur Wright to his father

Paris, May 28, 1911

I caught cold about a month ago and have not been able to entirely shake it off. The Comptesse de Lambert has been giving me all kinds of medicines but as the reading of the testimonials, in order to get up one's faith, seems to be one of the principal points in the use of them, I apparently lose most of their virtue. The last one is a preparation of Dr. Doyen, a very celebrated Paris physician, and has a very interesting lot of pictures of microbes on the outside of the bottle. The story that goes with it, I understand, is that the blood contains both good and bad microbes. Instead of attacking the bad microbes directly this medicine is supposed to incite the good microbes to jump onto the bad ones and destroy them. Stripped of all technical verbiage and fancy pictures the stuff seems to be merely a tonic in plain English. I have taken a few doses of the stuff and am depending on Madame de Lambert and Tissandier to supply the faith necessary to make the treatment effective.

. . . .

Wilbur Wright to Orville

Berlin, June 28, 1911

The men who had almost finished their training when I arrived in Berlin ten weeks ago are still almost trained but cannot fly alone yet! The poor Captain cannot understand how you can train men in a week at home. He would not believe that I could carry two men with 375 turns of the propellers till I took him up and did it.

. . . .

Wilbur Wright to his sister, regarding an airplane he had seen in England

Berlin, June 28, 1911

[The builder] has added porches, attics and sheds to it till it now looks like an old farm house which has been in the family for three or four generations, and once in a while he makes a jump of a hundred or two feet. When he jams a wing into the ground and whirls around suddenly, he says he has found by experience that he can turn quicker that way than any other.

. . . .

Wilbur Wright to Orville

Berlin, June 30, 1911

If I could get free from business with the money we already have in hand I would rather do it than continue in business at a considerable profit. Only two things lead me to put up with responsibilities and annoyances for a moment. First, the obligations to the people who put money into our business, and second, the reluctance a man naturally feels to allow a lot of scoundrels and thieves to steal his patents, subject him to all kinds of troubles or even try to cheat him out of the patents entirely. So far as Europe is concerned I do not feel that we are in debt to either the French or German companies. We have not had a square deal from either of them. All the money we ever get from either of these countries will be fully paid for by future work and worries. But I hate to see the French infringers wreck our business and abuse us and then go unscathed. . . . For the good of the public and the protection of others we ought to do our share to discourage such people a little. . . . The people in the American company have treated us decently and I do not wish to see them suffer a real loss. . . .

. . . .

Wilbur Wright to his sister

Berlin, July 6, 1911

The papers report temperatures ranging from 105 to 110 degrees in America. I hope you have got poor old daddy's fan going for him all night. . . . Don't let him shut off the fan during the nights to save money. . . .

. . . .

Wilbur Wright to S. S. McClure, New York

August 15, 1911

I thank you for your kind letter. . . . However it has never been the practice of my brother or myself to give "authorized" interviews. When we have anything to say, we prefer to say it in our own way. . . .

Our views are so different from the views which recently have been controlling the exploitation of flight that we are not certain that we care really to discuss the subject at this time. So long as newspapers find it profitable to themselves to force the art into sensational and expensive channels, any protest is an useless as the warnings of Hecuba. When the excitement is over it will be found that three times as much money has been put into the business as has been taken out, and that not ten per cent of these vast sums has been spent usefully. Yet it is a fever that must run its course, I suppose, and nothing but time can cure it.

. . . .

Orville went to Kitty Hawk in 1911 to experiment with a new glider in which he made records not to be surpassed for several years.

Orville Wright to Captain Thomas S. Baldwin

November 18, 1911

Many thanks for your congratulations on our work with the glider at Kitty Hawk. Flying in a 25 meter per second wind is no snap, and I can tell you that it keeps one pretty busy with the levers. I got caught in one whirl of wind that turned my machine completely around and drove me into the hill. I didn't receive a scratch, but the machine needed the doctor pretty badly. I found that in order to fly such winds a greater control than has ever been put on any power machine would be necessary. It was not the velocity of the wind, but its sudden changes in direction that made the flying difficult.

I note what you say in regard to Professor [John J.] Montgomery. Montgomery was a hard man to understand. When Wilbur and I were at the Belmont meet Montgomery told us in perfect seriousness that the control of his machine was so great that the "boys," as he called them, were looping the loop time after time; in fact, were doing it so much that he was compelled to make the controls so that they could be operated but to a slight extent in order to prevent their doing this kind of flying all the time! Of course there was no doubt in our minds as to whether his statement should be believed, but it was hard to tell whether the statement was a result of an illusion, or whether it was simply a plain falsehood. But the poor man is dead now, and we will try to think it was the former. Montgomery had a number of admirers, but for what reason I never clearly understood, for I can not think of anything of any value which originated with him. A rather amusing incident happened when we were at Kitty Hawk last month. It seems that Montgomery was doing some gliding in California at the same time that we were experimenting at Kitty Hawk. Evidently he was not doing anything that had the least appearance of soaring, for, when the report went forth that I had remained in the air for nearly ten minutes [at Kitty Hawk in the autumn of 1911] without the use of any artificial power, one of Montgomery's staunch supporters, Victor Loughead, went all the way down to our camp in order that he could "set us right before the world." When he learned at first hand from a half dozen different persons who had been eye witnesses of the flights that the reports were really true, he skipped out without ever even seeing the machine! On his first appearance he told the reporters that he knew we must have been misrepresented in the reports, since it would be utterly impossible to remain aloft five minutes without the use of artificial power.

. . . .

With aviation becoming more practical, the Wrights were gaining wealth; not vast, but enough to enable them to look forward to the time when they might retire and work happily together on scientific research. But tragic days were ahead. Early in May, shortly after visiting the new home site with other members of the family, Wilbur was taken ill. What at first was assumed to be a minor indisposition proved to be typhoid fever. Worn out from worries over protecting in patent litigation the rights he knew were his and his brother's, he was not in condition to combat the disease. After an illness of three weeks, despite the best efforts of eminent specialists, early in the morning of Thursday, May 30, 1912, Wilbur Wright died. He was only forty-five years and forty-four days old.

In his diary for May 30, Bishop Wright wrote of Wilbur: "An unfailing intellect, imperturbable temper, great self-reliance and as great modesty, seeing the right clearly, pursuing it steadily, he lived and died." Then, in his "notes for 1912," the Bishop made this further appraisal of his son: "In memory and intellect, there was none like him. He systematized everything. He could say or write anything he wanted to. He was not very talkative. His temper could hardly be stirred. He wrote much. He could deliver a fine speech, but was modest."

In Wilbur's will, dated only twenty days before his death, he made bequests of $50,000 each to his brothers Reuchlin and Lorin, and his sister Katharine; and $1,000 to his father "to use for little unusual expenditures as might add to his comfort and pleasure."

All the residue he left to Orville "who has been associated with me in all the hopes and labors both of childhood and manhood, and who, I am sure, will use the property in very much the same manner as we would use it together in case we would both survive until old age. And for this reason, I make no specific bequest to charity."

Orville Wright succeeded Wilbur as president of The Wright Company.

Wilbur Wright to the Aero Club of America Bulletin, *a few days before his fatal illness in May, 1912. This analysis of the work of Lilienthal was published in the September, 1912, issue of the* Bulletin

When the general excellence of the work of Lilienthal is considered, the question arises as to whether or not he would have solved the problem of human flight if his untimely death in 1896 had not interrupted his efforts. . . . One of the greatest difficulties of the problem has been little understood by the world at large. This was the fact that those who aspired to solve the problem were constantly pursued by expense, danger, and time. In order to succeed it was not only necessary to make progress, but it was necessary to make progress at a sufficient rate to reach the goal before money gave out, or before accident intervened, or before the portion of life allowable for such work was past. The problem was so vast and many-sided that no one could hope to win unless he possessed unusual ability to grasp the essential points, and to ignore the nonessentials. . . . When the detailed story is written of the means by which success in human flight was finally attained, it will be seen that this success was not won by spending more time than others had spent, nor by taking greater risks than others had taken.

Those who failed for lack of time had already used more time than was necessary; those who failed for lack of money had already spent more money than was necessary; and those who were cut off by accident had previously enjoyed as many lucky escapes as reasonably could be expected.

Lilienthal progressed, but not very rapidly. His tables of pressures and resistances of arched aeroplane surfaces were the results of years of experiment and were the best in existence, yet they were not sufficiently accurate to enable anyone to construct a machine with full assurance that it would give exactly the expected results. Under such conditions progress could not but be slow. His methods of controlling balance both laterally and longitudinally were exceedingly crude and quite insufficient. Although he experimented for six successive years 1891-1896 with gliding machines, he was using at the end the same inadequate method of control with which he started. His rate of progress during these years makes it doubtful whether he would have achieved full success in the near future if his life had been spared.

. . . .

Orville Wright to his brother Reuchlin

August 16, 1912

I think it was Will's wish to have all the Wright Company interests stay in my hands. I am sure it is the desire of the other stock-holders. The stock now is in the hands of only a few persons, so that it makes it very much easier to transact the business. We occasionally wish to do things that require the consent of each stock-holder, and, of course, the more the stock is distributed, the harder it is and the more time it takes to get such consent. In drawing up his will, I think Wilbur thought that we had a little over $300,000 besides our Wright Company stock. Our profits of last year added to what we had the year before would have made our total above $300,000, but together we gave away a little over $20,000 last year, so that this reduced his share about $10,000. I do not think there is any question about our winning our patent suits, but, of course, there is no certainty in the law: but in case we should lose the suits, and in case no value were placed on the patents, Will's stock in the company ought to have an actual value of about $25,000.*

It is very generous of you to offer to take only ¼ of the property Will possessed outside of his Wright Company stock, but I am glad to have you get the full amount as he left it. The stock can hardly help but have some value, and even if it had none, I am fixed so that I will get along very comfortably.

. . . .

Bishop Wright to his son Reuchlin, in Baldwin, Kansas

Dayton, Ohio, October 13, 1912

Concerning Wilbur's will, it is his last will and testament. Every one of us wants it carried out in every particular, as if it were sacred writ. If he had made no will, it

---

* The Wright Company did win the patent suits and the stock came to be worth much more.

would have been less satisfactory. His will was that each brother and his sister should have fifty thousand dollars. All will realize just that much, unless it be Orville. He may or may not. Wilbur believed he would, and have funds for benevolences of which he spoke in his will. Orville regards the will as if sacred, and will carry it out precisely.

He made his will when he was entering a pitiless struggle with death, and it came out as he feared.

X

ELDER STATESMAN OF AVIATION

Orville Wright to Henry Woodhouse, New York, N. Y.

December 9, 1912

Your letter enclosing galley proof of your article on "The Conquest of the Air" for *Collier's* has been received. I have delayed answering until I had the opportunity of again looking over the work of several of the men mentioned in the paper to make sure that my recollection of their work was right. Your article is very good indeed, and I have but little criticism to make, and this criticism is mostly a matter of opinion.

Sir George Cayley was a remarkable man. He knew more of the principles of aeronautics than any of his predecessors, and as much as any that followed him up to the end of the nineteenth century. His published work is remarkably free from error and was a most important contribution to the science. It is a question in my mind whether one should say that he is the originator of the monoplane, since every machine proposed prior to his time was really a monoplane. As I understand the meaning of the term, monoplane is used to designate a machine in which surfaces are not superposed. Wenham was the inventor of superposed surfaces, but insofar as I can remember, he never built a biplane. His machines possessed a number of surfaces, superposed one above the other much like the slats of a window blind. Stringfellow reduced the number of planes to three. Hargrave, Lilienthal and Chanute, I believe, were among the first to use only two.

I do not think that in the light of twentieth century knowledge the "Aerial Steam Carriage" of Henson could be considered scientific for an instant. The machine was never built, but Henson's work in connection with Stringfellow deserves some notice, as they together succeeded in building a small model which drew a good deal of attention to the subject of aviation. Nothing in Henson's or Stringfellow's machine indicates that they had any comprehension of the principles of stability and their machines certainly indicate that they possessed no scientific knowledge in regard to the shapes of surfaces or the power required for flight. Stringfellow deserves a great deal of credit for the building of a very light motor, one of sufficient lightness to support a well designed aeroplane. The Stringfellow motor was far in advance of the aeroplane to which it was attached.

The stories of the experiments of Jean Marie le Bris are too absurd to be given serious consideration. It is impossible to perform any of the feats attributed to him with a structure such as he used. You are probably aware that the accounts of his experiments are all taken from a novel.

The French inventor, Alphonse Pénaud, deserves a great deal of credit. Although his experiments were confined to small models, yet he was the originator of a system of fore and aft stability that is used more or less in nearly every aeroplane of the present day. He approached the subject in a scientific manner.

I hardly think it should be said that "these early experiments (of Mouillard) laid the foundations of modern aviation." Mouillard was an enthusiastic observer of the flight of birds, but I do not think there was anything in his work that contributed scientifically to the solution of the problem. Mouillard was a poet rather than a scientist, and it was to the charm of his writings in enthusing others in the work that the world owes a debt of gratitude.

I think the work of Maxim and Langley deserves more extended notice than you have given them. The reputation that these two men already possessed in other lines of scientific endeavor probably did the most to bring to public attention the subject of aviation which was then in disrepute.

. . . .

Orville Wright to Griffith Brewer, London, England

April 22, 1913

Your letters . . . were received, but . . . late in arriving on account of the recent flood.

The water covered over half the city. At our Third Street office the water was about ten to twelve feet deep in the street, but did not quite reach the second floor. On Hawthorne Street it was about eight or nine feet deep and stood six feet on the first floor. Most of the things downstairs were ruined. We saved a few of our books and several small pieces of furniture. We might have saved almost everything had we had more notice, but Katharine and I overslept that morning and had to be out of the house within one half hour of the time we were up. The water in leaving deposited several inches of a slimy mud over everything. The gutters of the streets of Dayton for hundreds of miles are heaped several feet high with mud, furniture, etc., that has been removed from the residences and stores. In the center of the city the water was twelve to fifteen feet deep, and the entire stock of many of our merchants was destroyed. Thousands of families have lost everything they had. This is probably the greatest calamity that has ever happened to an American city, as insurance policies do not cover damage by flood.

During the time of the highest water fires broke out in the different parts of the city and nothing whatever could be done to stop them. The large buildings immediately west of our Third Street office burned, and I went to bed the first night of the flood, thinking that my office had burned, and all of the papers and data on aeronautical matters had gone with it. A constant downpour of rain while the adjoining buildings were burning probably saved the office.

Our factory was well out of the flood district, but we have not been able to do much work as yet on account of the difficulty in getting our workmen back and forth to work. We have been without regular street car service, electric light and gas for the past four weeks.

.   .   .   .

To Orville Wright a serious part of the flood loss was the damage to photographic negatives showing his and Wilbur's progress toward flight. But the famous picture of the first power flight was not much harmed.

Accompanied by his sister, Orville made his last trip to Europe in 1913 on business relating to a patent suit in Germany. At about the same time he sanctioned the forming of a Wright company in England. Before Wilbur's death there had been opportunities for a company in England, but the brothers had held back because all the offers appeared to be purely stock promotions in which the names of members of the English nobility would appear as sponsors.

Orville Wright to R. G. DuBois, Esq., East Orange, N. J.

March 18, 1914

I do not think that all of the trouble is in our patent law itself. The patent laws of all countries are a good deal alike, though I prefer the German and the French to that of America. The most serious trouble that the American inventor encounters, however, is the very high cost of litigation in America. Our patent litigation in America has cost us over ten times what it cost in either France or Germany. A big part of this is due to the many delays that are permitted in America.

. . . .

Orville Wright to Franklin K. Lane, Secretary of the Interior

March 19, 1914

The interview published in the New York *Times* of February 27th, while not altogether accurate, was unusually good for a newspaper report. I stated that inventors were poorly protected by the law, and that unless they had large financial backing to maintain their claims through long drawn-out litigation in the courts, patents were of no value to them.

I shall be pleased to accept your invitation to submit to you my views as to changes that should be made in the patent laws to make them a better protection to inventors.

. . . .

Orville Wright to T. W. MacMechen, President of the Aeronautical Society of America, New York

August 29, 1914

It does not seem to me entirely fair that the Aeronautical Societies of America should be constantly requesting licenses to permit aviators with infringing machines to fly without paying any license fee at all. All of these aviators have been offered a license on a very reasonable basis. It seems to me, in view of all the court decisions, that it is the duty of the Aeronautical Societies to urge aviators to take out a license, rather than be requesting us to let them fly free. We have often offered to give free licenses to meets run on a strictly sporting basis, in which no remuneration was to be offered the flyers. But it has never seemed to me just that the aviators should be given a free license by us in order that they can use our invention to make money for themselves.

. . . .

The decision, in the Wrights' favor, of the United States Circuit Court of Appeals in the infringement suit of Wright against Curtiss was not handed down until January 13, 1914. Curtiss made no secret of the fact that he still hoped to find a loophole to get around the Wright patent. In short, he had no compunction about helping himself to their discoveries if he "could get away with it." Since the decision of the court enjoined him from using two ailerons operating simultaneously in opposite directions, he thought perhaps he could escape penalty by using just one aileron at a time, while the other remained inoperative. This, however, was covered by Claim I of the Wright patent, if the claim were given a liberal interpretation. The Court of Appeals had held that the Wright patent *was* entitled to a broad interpretation, on account of the Wrights being the pioneers in the field of heavier-than-air flying machines. But Claim I had not been cited in the former suits, and so had not as yet been adjudicated. Anticipating a suit to settle this question, Curtiss took astounding means to prepare for combating it. If he could prove, or seem to prove, that a machine that could fly had been built before the Wrights', then they would not be the pioneers; he could weaken their claims, to his financial advantage, in the suit he expected to have to defend.

He arranged with the Smithsonian Institution to take the old Langley plane of 1903 to Hammondsport, New York. There, by making liberal use of the Wrights' discoveries, he rebuilt that plane and succeeded in June, 1914, in having it make short hops of less than five seconds. Then it was announced to the world that the *original* Langley plane had been flown! There was no hint of all the fundamental changes that had been made in the machine. One of the changes had to do with the supporting posts on the wings. Professor Langley had not known—indeed, no one knew until the Wrights' wind-tunnel experiments established the facts—where the center of the air pressure would be on a curved surface, and consequently he had failed to place his wing-trussing posts where they were most needed. In the attempts to fly the machine over the Potomac in 1903, the wing that bore the greater part of the weight had each time collapsed at the moment the apparatus left the starting platform.

Three fundamental changes were made in the design of the wings themselves: (1) The camber was greatly changed; (2) the shape of the leading edge was entirely different; (3) the aspect ratio—the ratio of span to chord—was increased. These three features are the most important characteristics in determining the efficiency of a wing. The change of the camber may of itself increase the efficiency of a wing by thirty per cent.

At the fraudulent Hammondsport tests, Dr. Zahm, who was technical adviser to Curtiss and had become a bitter enemy of the Wrights, was the official observer! It was the false reports of these tests, and the failure to correct them during many years, that caused the long Wright-Smithsonian controversy.*

After all the evidence had been taken for the second infringement suit of the Wrights against Curtiss and just before the case was to come to trial, Orville Wright sold his interest in The Wright Company to New York capitalists. Curtiss then contrived to gain delay after delay by approaching the new owners with proposals of settlement. These negotiations dragged on until the United States entered the First World War, and the Manufacturers Aircraft Association was formed for the cross-licensing of manufacturers building

---

* A detailed account of the Wright-Smithsonian controversy is in *The Wright Brothers*, by Fred C. Kelly.

machines for the United States Government. Through this cross-licensing agreement, The Wright Company received royalty on all planes manufactured for the Government. Consequently, this last case against Curtiss never came to trial.

Orville had not been happy as a business executive and without Wilbur, he was less so. Most of the stockholders in The Wright Company were Tammany men and Orville thought he saw signs of their using the company for political purposes. For example, they wanted to hire a certain lawyer because he was believed to be close to President Woodrow Wilson, not because his services were needed by the company. This annoyed Orville and his associates were irritated by him, too, because he wouldn't "play ball." So he offered to buy them out, guaranteeing that, including their dividends, they would have received one hundred per cent profit on their investment. Oddly, in buying out other shareholders he found it necessary to borrow money—the only time he ever did in connection with aviation. His borrowing was not for long, however, for he resold the company soon afterward. Since aviation as a business was showing greater promise than ever before, he made a handsome profit on the resale, and this was the source of the greater part of his fortune.

Orville Wright to Griffith Brewer, The British Wright Company, Ltd., London, England

May 9, 1917

I am just now getting my wind tunnel in working order. I do not know what I will have to do in the military work. I have been commissioned a Major in the Aviation Section, Signal Officers' Reserve Corps. It is possible that I may have to go to Washington, although General Squier told me a short time ago that they thought they would have more need of me in the laboratory.

. . . .

Orville Wright to Charles A. Moran, New York

May 11, 1917

I have your very interesting letter . . . in which you raise a question as to the accuracy of a statement in an interview with me quoted by Mr. Burton J. Hendrick in *Harper's Magazine* of April.

The statement that the "weight increases as the cube, whereas the area of the wings increases as its square," is not absolutely correct, but is practically so. . . .

You are probably aware that there is a limit, with the materials possessed at the present time, beyond which a bridge span cannot even support its own weight. The reasons for this are evident. To illustrate this: supposing one were to support a beam a foot long and an inch square at the two tips, it will support a given load, but if the beam were an inch square and ten feet long, it would weigh ten times as much, but would have only one-tenth the strength. It is evident that before long the length would be reached where the beam would break of its own weight.

Nature has never succeeded in building a large creature which could fly. I believe the Pteredactyl, which was the largest, weighed only in the neighborhood of thirty pounds, and evidently was but a poor flyer. The theory, which I state in the interview, I think, has been fully borne out by the experience of all the flying machine manufacturers.

. . . .

Orville Wright to C. H. Hitchcock, Washington, D. C.

June 21, 1917

At the suggestion of Mr. Howard Coffin, I am sending you my opinion of the program as laid out by the Aircraft Production Board.

When my brother and I built and flew the first man-carrying flying machine, we thought that we were introducing into the world an invention which would make further wars practically impossible. That we were not alone in this thought is evidenced by the fact that the French Peace Society presented us with medals on account of our invention. We thought governments would realize the impossibility of winning by surprise attacks, and that no country would enter into war with another of equal size when it knew that it would have to win by simply wearing out its enemy.

Nevertheless, the world finds itself in the greatest war in history. Neither side has been able to win on account of the part the aeroplane has played. Both sides know exactly what the other is doing. The two sides are apparently nearly equal in aerial equipment, and it seems to me that unless present conditions can be changed, the war will continue for years.

However, if the Allies' armies are equipped with such a number of aeroplanes as to keep the enemy planes entirely back of the line, so that they are unable to direct gun-fire or to observe the movement of the Allied troops—in other words, if the enemy's eyes can be put out—it will be possible to end the war. This is not taking into account what might be done by bombing German sources of munition supplies, such as Essen, which is only about one hundred and fifty miles behind the fighting lines. But to end the war quickly and cheaply, the supremacy in the air must be so complete as to entirely blind the enemy.

.   .   .   .

Orville Wright to Griffith Brewer, Esq., London, England

March 3, 1919

My argument against the very large aeroplanes was from the standpoint of their present military usefulness. Of course, when the time comes that it is desirable to drop a ton or more of explosives in a single charge, the large aeroplane would be the only one with which this could be accomplished. However, in the [recent] war, where the large planes were used, the size of the bombs was not increased but only a greater number of them were carried. I believe that for a long time to come the big machines will be at the mercy of the smaller ones.

.   .   .   .

Orville Wright to Lieutenant Colonel C. DeForest Chandler,
Washington, D. C.

December 15, 1921

Your letter enclosing copy of your article on "How Uncle Sam Bought the First Airplane" was duly received. I am sorry to have kept you waiting so long for an answer. I was extremely busy at the time so I took the paper home and read it one evening.

In reading it over at that time a number of statements in the paper did not quite agree with my recollection. . . . Mere memory, however, is not always to be trusted. I thought I would probably have papers in the office that would throw some light on these points. Having more time the last few days I have undertaken to look up some of them, but I find that to be a very big job. I will, therefore, now go hastily through the paper giving my impressions on some of the points on which our recollections apparently do not entirely agree. Where we have to depend entirely on recollection, by all means use your own, for you probably have as good or better memory than I. . . .

I will tell you confidentially that when we learned of the bid from Herring we suspected immediately, because of former experiences with him, that he had made his bid $5,000 under the price that every one knew we were going to bid, with the expectation of getting the contract and then, we having none, coming to us for the carrying out of the contract for him, Herring securing a part of the price as commission. The acceptance of the three bids put a crimp in his plans. Nevertheless he did come to us at Dayton with just the very plan we had suspected. We refused to help him

out in the matter and that is the reason he was compelled to make the ridiculous "technical delivery" of his machine.*
He never had any serious thought of delivering a machine himself. Herring was a guest in our camp at Kitty Hawk in 1902 and learned of the great advance we had made both in control and in the aerodynamic parts of the machine. When we made our first power flight in 1903 he immediately wrote a letter suggesting that he could reveal our system of control and cause us a great deal of trouble and proposing that we give him a third interest in our invention. Later he secured the controlling stock in the Curtiss Company by representing to Curtiss that he had a photograph which would defeat our patent. This was a fraud and when Curtiss discovered it he entered suit to recover the stock. I believe they have been scrapping over this ever since.

. . . .

Orville Wright to Griffith Brewer, London, England

November 13, 1923

Your suggestions with regard to the disposition of the 1903 machine have been thought over a good deal since you left. If you are right in thinking that the officers of the Museum would be keenly interested in securing this machine for exhibition in the Kensington Museum, I should be inclined to let them have it. The fire risks are too great where it is now stored and I have no better place for it.

Of course the machine ought to be in the National Museum at Washington. . . .

---

* Herring delivered parts of a plane, or motor, in a suitcase!

If I were to receive a proposition from the officers of the Kensington Museum offering to provide our 1903 machine a permanent home in the Museum, I would accept the offer, with the understanding, however, that I would have the right to withdraw it at any time after five years, if some suitable place for its exhibition in America presented itself.

. . . .

Orville Wright to Griffith Brewer, Esq., London, England

November 13, 1923

I have just written you a letter in regard to the disposal of the 1903 machine. The letter states the conditions under which I would be willing to let the machine go to the Kensington Museum. I do not feel at all easy about the machine where it is. It is not likely to have to go through another flood, but it is liable to fire. I would suggest that you sound the management of the Museum on the matter before letting them know that I have written you anything concerning it. . . .

I have only been in the office a few days since you left. While bending over the washbowl in my bath room . . . something seemed to give way in my back. I had not yet put on my belt. . . . I will hereafter be cautious about washing my face without my belt on. [After his accident at Fort Myer, he had to wear a special belt.]

. . . .

Orville Wright did not send the original airplane to the Science Museum at Kensington until 1928. He had patiently waited fourteen years from the time of the fake trials of the Langley-Zahm-Curtiss plane at Hammondsport. His replies to many letters deploring his decision to send the machine to England usually included this comment:

> In a foreign museum this machine will be a constant reminder of the reason of its being there, and after the people and petty jealousies of this day are gone, the historians of the future may examine impartially the evidence and make history accord with it.
>
> Your regret that this old machine must leave our country can hardly be so great as my own.

Orville Wright to Major General Mason M. Patrick, Chief of Air Service, War Department, Washington, D. C.

June 30, 1925

I have your letter . . . in regard to a name for the new field upon which the new buildings of the Engineering Division are to be located.

Either name, "Wilbur Wright Field," or "Wright Field," would please my sister and myself.

.   .   .   .

Orville Wright to Commander H. C. Richardson, Navy Department, Bureau of Aeronautics, Washington, D. C.

February 17, 1926

Your letter . . . asking for information as to when my brother and I first made trials with floats is received.

In 1906, after our own Government and some of the European governments had shown little inclination to take our invention seriously, we thought a way to impress them of its importance would be to make a flight over the parade of battleships to be held at the Jamestown Exposition in 1907. At that time we contemplated assembling a new machine at our old camp at Kitty Hawk, flying it from there to Jamestown, and after taking an unexpected part in the parade, flying it back to our camp at Kitty Hawk. As such a project could not be carried out safely in a single flight we decided to put hydroplanes and floats on the machine so that starts and landings could be made from the water.

As soon as the weather permitted in 1907 we began experiments with the hydroplane on the Miami River at Dayton. The enclosed print appeared in the Dayton *Herald,* March 21, 1907. The cambered steel hydroplanes, located a few inches beneath the forward and rear ends of the floats, and extending between them, do not show in the picture, as they are under water. The forward plane had a little over half the area of the rear one. The apparatus was loaded for the tests to nearly 1300 pounds, which was the estimated weight of the plane with one person aboard and the hydroplanes and floats attached. The plane, which was used later by Wilbur in his flights at Le Mans, France, had our four cylinder vertical motor of 30 to 35 horse power. In these tests on the river we used the motor, transmission and propellers from our 1905 aeroplane. That motor, when functioning properly, developed a little over 20 horse power. But the experiments on the river terminated before we succeeded in getting more than two-thirds of that power.

With 14 horse power the apparatus quickly raised until only the bottom of the floats dragged on the water. But we failed with this power to get the front edges of the planes entirely out of water and thus let the planes skim the water on their rear edges as we had expected. Just as the front edges reached the surface the planes seemed to lose a part of their lift with a consequent sinking back into the water. This was due to the loss of lift on the upper side when the water ceased to flow over the top, but we did not understand the cause of it at the time. We estimated the speed to be between 15 and 20 miles an hour, but no exact measurements of this were secured because our attention in the few trials made was directed to getting the motor tuned up. The experiments had to be suspended when one of the propellers was broken.

Immediately following these experiments, negotiations with a foreign syndicate called us to Europe, so that the project of flying at Jamestown had to be given up.

.   .   .   .

Orville Wright to R. J. Bretnall, Principal of High School, Milburn, N. J.

May 3, 1926

I have your letter asking my opinion regarding our National defense. I do not believe in a separate Air Service, thus forming three separate departments of the National defense. I can not here touch on all the reasons for this belief. One important reason is that there would be less cooperation between the Air Service and the Army and Navy under such an arrangement than there is at present.

Lack of cooperation between the Army and Navy is a serious defect in our present system. A separate independent Air Service would add to the seriousness of this defect. Air Service is more necessary to the functioning of both the Army and the Navy than are either of these two branches to each other.

Divided command does not lead to efficiency. The Air Service should be under the direction of the commanders of the Army and Navy; or the Army and Navy should be under the direction of the commander of the Air Forces; or the three, the Army and the Navy and the Air Force, should all be under the direction of one supreme command. Three separate departments each pursuing its own independent course will not furnish a strong National defense.

I would favor some system that would bring the Army, Navy and Air into closer cooperation. Whether a department of National defense would do this or whether it would do the reverse would depend upon the machinery provided for its operation.

. . . .

Orville Wright to William E. Shea, Washington, D. C.

[Shea was assisting Mark Sullivan, then at work on his history, *Our Times.*]

June 28, 1927

I must apologize for my procrastination, but it seems that I never can get any writing done until the last minute when I just must do it. . . .

Your comparison of the rudders of the aeroplane and the ship . . . is not quite correct. The principal function of the rudder of an aeroplane is that of lateral equilibrium, and not that of steering as in the case of the ship's rudder. . . . The rudder had practically no steering effect in the early types of aeroplanes, and has little more today in machines with fuselages. . . . In making a circular flight the pressure on the rudder of an aeroplane is almost always on the side towards the outside of the curve, though the rudder may be turned inward; while the pressure on the ship's rudder in making a turn is always on the inside. The rudder produces the turn . . . of the ship while the aileron generally produces the turn . . . of the aeroplane.

. . . .

Orville Wright to Merrick T. Jackson, Western Electric Company, New York, N. Y.

January 25, 1928

I believe Dr. Alexander Graham Bell's own experiments with flying machines, other than his kites, began with the formation of the Aerial Experiment Association in 1907, although prior to that time he had taken much interest in the experiments of others. He was present as a witness of the tests of Professor Langley's steam-driven aeroplane model in 1896. His account of these has often been published. Dr. Bell also seemed interested in our flights with a man-carrying aeroplane in 1903, 1904 and 1905. In a number of newspaper interviews at that time he stated quite positively that we had made such flights. Wilbur and I often wondered at this, for many at that time did not believe in them. Some years later Dr. Bell told me that this early confidence came from Professor Langley's having told him that he knew these flights to be a fact.

. . . .

Sefton Brancker, of the British Air Ministry,
to Orville Wright

[Regarding the arrival in London of the original Wright airplane.]

February 21, 1928

I am most sincerely grateful to you for your generosity in arranging that Great Britain shall possess this most interesting and highly important aircraft. . . . It will now become the most important exhibit in our national aeronautical exhibition, in Kensington.

. . . .

Orville Wright to William G. Shepherd of Collier's Weekly

August 8, 1928

I have put off writing, because I didn't see how to correct your article. You seemed to entirely misapprehend the history of aviation prior to the time we took it up, or I should say Langley's part in it. You seem to be under the impression that Langley's tables of air pressures were generally used in making calculations at that time, and that we had upset them one after another. The Langley Law was the only new theory coming from him. This law was so startling it attracted a great deal of notice, but unfortunately it was an error. Langley's chief contribution to aeronautics, outside of lending his name to an art then in disrepute, was his building with infinite care and at great expense larger flying models than had been built up to that time. They were not the first . . .

The only tables of pressures on cambered [curved] surfaces were those of Lilienthal. Lilienthal had made his measurements of cambered surfaces, also plane surfaces, more than ten years before Langley made his measurements of planes. We did not use the Duchemin formula (corroborated by Langley) in designing our early gliders. It was our measurements in our wind-tunnel that proved the Duchemin formula and Langley's confirmation of it to be wrong.

Langley did not develop a new system of stabilizing aeroplanes. He used the system invented and patented by Pénaud in 1870. Langley in his writings acknowledges this. . . .

Langley did not "discover the relations of speed and angle of inclination to the lifting power of surfaces moving in the air," as claimed on the Langley tablet and quoted by you on page 8. He tried to do this, as did Duchemin, Lilienthal and others before, but failed.

I have given you the above facts because you seem to be under the impression . . . that at the time we began our experiments practically all work in aeronautics or rather aviation was based upon Langley's measurements and theories. Langley did not show his best ability in aerodynamics. The work of Sir George Cayley, Pénaud, Lilienthal, Maxim and others displayed much more originality.

There was no race between Langley and ourselves. Langley probably did not know that we were working on a motorplane. We had heard only rumors that he was building a man-carrying machine. This did not disturb or hurry us in the least. We knew that he had to have better scientific data than was contained in his published works to successfully build a man-carrying flying machine. . . .

When we were carrying on our wind-tunnel work we had no thought of ever trying to build a power aeroplane. We did that work just for the fun we got out of learning new truths. But after we had demonstrated in a glider that our tables were correct, we saw that with this new data, not possessed by earlier experimenters, it would not be hard to design a man-carrying power aeroplane.

. . . .

Orville Wright to Waldemar Kaempffert, Director of the Rosenwald Industrial Museum, Chicago

October 9, 1928

You ask whether Chanute was the first to apply the principle of the Pratt truss* to the biplane. On this point I am not altogether certain. I think there can be no question that modern aviation owed it to Chanute, but it is possible that some of the earlier experimenters may have used it. . . .

Although Chanute may not have contributed anything new to aviation itself, still I think that his name should come within the first half dozen to whom the world owes most for the aeroplane. This is on account of the encouragement he gave to us.

. . . .

Orville Wright to A. A. Merrill, California Institute of Technology, Pasadena, California

October 23, 1928

I am in receipt of your letter of October 16th asking for information as to why my brother Wilbur and I "ignored Pénaud and substituted an idea of your own which was so bad that you had to change it a few years later." As you seem to be much distressed about this, I will hasten to answer your letter ahead of many others of some weeks' standing.

---

* Thomas Willis Pratt, bridge builder, died 1875. He invented the Pratt truss, patented 1844, for use in bridges and roofs.

I was rather surprised that such a question could be asked at this late day, for I had supposed that everyone at all versed in aerodynamics would know the advantages as well as the disadvantages of both the front and the rear elevators. As you do not seem to be informed in these important phases of equilibrium, I will here briefly state some outstanding advantages and disadvantages of the two systems:

The Pénaud system had advantages in its excellent degree of longitudinal inherent stability, and in its adaptability for use with a fuselage and single propeller. It had disadvantages in being wasteful of propeller thrust, and in being very dangerous at large angles of attack by causing the "nose dive."

The Wright system had advantages in absolute freedom from the "nose dive" and in the conservation of propeller thrust. It had disadvantages in having only a moderate degree of inherent stability and an almost altogether inadaptability to use with a fuselage and single propeller.

In the beginning of human flight the advantages of the Wright system exceeded the advantages of the Pénaud system. With the advent of powerful motors, the acquirement of skill and knowledge by pilots enabling them to avoid the "stalling engine," and the necessity of using a fuselage, the order of importance has been reversed. Yet no aeroplane today relies on the Pénaud system, as you seem to suggest. The present aeroplane is a compromise of the Pénaud system of inherent stability and a system of movable elevators relied on by us.

The fact may be significant that of those who used the Pénaud system in gliding, to any extent at all comparable with our own experiments, two lost their lives, and all the others with little success abandoned their experiments. . . .

We, on the other hand, by using another and safer system, were able to carry on experiments for years and live to see the age of man-flight realized.

The higher dynamic efficiency of the Wright system, to which I have referred . . . has been demonstrated in the small rubber-driven flying model contests. This type holds the record for endurance.

I have assumed that by the expression "ignored Pénaud" you meant to indicate failure on our part to use, rather than failure to appreciate, the work of Alphonse Pénaud. Pénaud had one of the greatest minds that ever wrestled with the problem of flight. He contributed several important inventions, one of which was his system of inherent stability. Apparently, however, among its valuable qualities he did not recognize also some qualities not so good and some actually dangerous for man-flight. Pénaud was the inventor not only of the system of inherent stability used in most flying models today, but also of the rubber band motor used in practically all of them. We have always looked upon him as the father of the modern flying models, and have repeatedly stated that our first flying toys were copied from one of his.

.   .   .   .

Orville Wright to Dr. Allen Johnson, Editor Dictionary of American Biography, Washington, D. C.

April 10, 1929

I have your letter . . . inquiring about the inspiration we received from James Means.

At a dinner in honor of Mr. Chanute in Boston in 1909 or 1910, my brother Wilbur spoke of the help received by us in our early study of the subject from the *Aeronautical Annuals*, edited by James Means and published by him in 1895, 1896 and 1897. He did not say that we were first interested in flying by these *Annuals*, but he spoke, in highest praise of them, and of the value they had been to us in gaining an understanding of the art as it existed at that time. We did not see the *Annuals* until 1899, but had been actively interested in aeronautics for several years before that time from reading of Lilienthal's experiments in Germany.

Mr. Means carried on some practical experiments with model gliders, before 1895, but nothing, I believe, of importance resulted from these. His important contribution to aeronautics was his publication of the *Aeronautical Annuals*. These *Aeronautical Annuals* of 1895-96-97 contained the best collection of reprints from the work of the earlier experimenters in aviation that had appeared up to that time. Mr. Means showed rare judgment in his selections, separating most of the good work from the mass of worthless matter which had been published.

. . . .

Though Orville Wright did not take time to reply to more than a small part of the voluminous mail he received, he had a soft spot for inventors and never failed to write a good letter in reply to anyone who told him of plans for a new gadget. This was true no matter how illiterate the writer was. One man addressed him as "Orvel Write" and enclosed what he called a "ruff scach," but he received a nice note in reply. If the inventor lived near Dayton, Orville would invite him to drop in at his office.

Orville Wright to J. K. Lux, Tampa, Florida

October 16, 1929

Having lately returned from a long vacation, my time is so taken with matters which have accumulated during that time that I can give your paper and drawings but a cursory examination.

From the limited part of it which I have read, I have the impression that your paper is based on an erroneous idea as to the behavior of air in flowing over aeroplane surfaces. The idea of offset tandem planes as described in Section 23 of your paper was advanced and published by Montgomery in 1905. We at that time saw the fallacy and danger of such an arrangement, and called the attention of Mr. Chanute to it, Mr. Chanute at that time being in correspondence with Montgomery. Chanute evidently did not report this to Montgomery, and a few weeks later the Montgomery machine, in one of its glides, went into a dive exactly as we had predicted. Maloney the pilot was killed. Your tandem arrangement not only produces an unstable condition of equilibrium, but it is dynamically inefficient as well. After the air has been deflected downward by an aeroplane wing, any attempt to secure additional lift in this downward current of air is certain to be wasteful.

You evidently are of the impression that most of the lift on an aeroplane surface is due to the impact of the air on its under side. As a matter of fact the greater part of the lift results from the partial vacuum created on its upper side. The design of the upper side of an aeroplane wing is more important than that of its lower side.

The design of plane shown in the sketch enclosed in your letter . . . would be exceedingly wasteful of power.

I infer that you have the impression that a sharp leading edge reduces the resistance of a surface. It is well known among aeronautical engineers today that this is not true. It was generally thought among the earlier experimenters that this would be so, but we learned in 1901 from our wind-tunnel experiments that it was not so, and the success of our first power machine, which flew in 1903, was due in a large measure to the design of the wings which had a much blunter leading edge than had been used by the experimenters before.

. . . .

Orville Wright to James C. E. Allum, Chicago, Illinois

March 14, 1930

I have your letter . . . with regard to Mr. Cadwallader's "magnetic motive power," and I note what you say as to Mr. Cadwallader's character. I receive letters right along from men, like Mr. Cadwallader, who honestly believe they have discovered a method of producing dynamic force out of static force. In most of these inventions the force of gravity is proposed as the motive power.

A few years ago an intelligent and ingenious inventor brought to me a design for a machine to create power out of magnetism. While I had every reason theoretically to believe the machine could not work, yet it was several days before I found the flaw in his line of reasoning.

As a rule the perpetual motion machine inventor is a hard one to deal with. He is afraid that if he shows his invention it will be stolen from him. As a result he often does not get the advice of people whose knowledge of the subject makes them competent to give an opinion.

I cannot see that there is any more prospect of getting continuous power out of magnetism, than there is of getting it out of gravity.

. . . .

Orville Wright to C. A. Carlisle, Indianapolis, Indiana

January 22, 1931

I have your letter in regard to a design for aeroplane propellers. No drawing was sent to me to illustrate the nature of your invention, but I understand from Dr. Lewis' letter to you, a copy of which you enclosed, that the blades of your propeller are set at a dihedral angle of 22½ degrees, and that the blades are flat surfaces and not cambered surfaces, as are usually used in aeroplane and propeller design. You state in your letter of August 4th that the "blades may be widened to give an area equal to 80% of the area of the circle prescribed by the tips."

Water propellers having the blades set at a dihedral angle have already been tested and used for quite a number of years. In fact, I have one on an outboard motor which I have used since 1916. I have not found this propeller as efficient as the straight blade propeller but it has the advantage of tending to clear itself of entangling weeds.

Some ten or fifteen years ago I had letters proposing the use of the dihedral angle in propellers for aeroplane use. But no propeller of this type has ever been built, so far as I know, which was equal in efficiency to the ordinary type of propeller.

From your letters I infer that you think we used flat or plane wings in our early aeroplanes, and that you think planes are as efficient or more efficient than cambered or curved wings. Plane surfaces are not nearly so efficient as cambered ones. The success of our first plane was mostly due to the highly efficient propellers and to the efficient cambered wings which we used. The propellers were designed entirely from theory—a theory of our own—and the actual measured thrust came within two per cent of the calculated thrust.

We are able to calculate in advance the width a propeller blade should be to give the highest efficiency. It is the width of the blade that determines the angle of attack. The wider the blade, the smaller the angle of attack. If the blade is too narrow, the angle of attack is too great to be efficient; and if too wide, the angle of attack is too small to be efficient. Blades covering 80 per cent of the described area could not be efficient. Some of the early marine propellers of a hundred years ago had blades covering 80 per cent or more of the described area, but they were not at all efficient. Of course, at that time the reason for this was not understood.

The propellers of aeroplanes today are quite efficient. In fact they are about the most efficient part of a flying machine. The propeller efficiency could be increased by increasing the pitch and by increasing the diameter. But you will see that the diameter must be restricted, from practical considera-

tions, and that the pitch can be increased only by gearing
the speed of the propeller down below that of the speed
of the motor.

. . . .

Orville Wright to Mrs. George H. Tomlinson,
Evanston, Illinois

January 11, 1932

I have your letter of January 5th in regard to the visit of
your friend the Japanese naval officer, to Dayton. I shall
be glad to see him . . . at any time during his visit here.

You do not remember ever having met me, but that
only shows that an old bachelor remembers meeting a pretty
young girl better than a young girl remembers meeting an
old bachelor. I once called at your home and remember
being introduced to you. This was when you were quite a
young girl.

. . . .

Orville Wright to L. J. Lesh, Chicago, Illinois

February 1, 1933

According to the newspapers there is talk of abandoning
Chanute Field. If the field is abandoned some other field of
more importance should be given the name. Nearly all of the
fields are named for men who lost their lives in the military

service. Without meaning anything derogatory to any of these, it must be said that Octave Chanute contributed much more to aviation than did any of them.

. . . .

Orville Wright to Lenox R. Lohr, General Manager,
A Century of Progress Exposition, Chicago, Illinois

April 29, 1933

After careful consideration, and after consultation with friends, I have come to the conclusion that it is not advisable to put the Kitty Hawk plane on exhibition at the Exposition. . . .

When I speak of the risks I refer to the dangers of accident in twice tearing down the machine for shipment, in twice setting it up, and in transport two ways between London and Chicago, in addition to whatever risks there may be while it is on exhibition. . . .

The plane is getting old and is of a delicate structure, nearly all parts of which are extremely inflammable. It is too bulky for shipment in one piece, and it suffers every time it is taken apart and set together again, regardless of the care taken. It suffered a breakage in getting to England after all my personal care in seeing it packed. Insurance is of no value since the plane is irreplaceable if lost.

. . . .

Orville Wright to W. E. Ericson, E. Edelmann & Co., Chicago, Illinois

May 15, 1935

I have had no experience with windmills. Any suggestion I offer will be based upon theory, not practice.

I will use the term propeller to designate a device which acts upon air; and windmill to designate a device which is acted upon by the air. The propeller consumes power, the windmill creates power.

At first glance it might seem that an efficient propeller would be an efficient windmill, and vice versa. This, however, is not a fact. A good windmill is a very inefficient propeller.

I suspect that the best design of windmill for your purposes would be one that is cheap to build, small in size, and has high r.p.m., so that the generator can be smaller.

The windmill is not limited in number and area of blades, nor in diameter, as is the propeller. Four blades will give more torque than two, six more than four, etc., up to a point where the loss due to reduction of the amount of air passing through the windmill overcomes the gain due to added blade area. Extremely high lift-drag ratio of the airfoil used is not of as great importance in the windmill as in the propeller, because the drag is overcome by the mounting. In the propeller this drag has to be overcome through the expenditure of power.

A cambered blade will produce more torque per unit of area than a flat one, especially at the smaller angles of attack. If you are using sheet steel for the blades a camber of 1/12 would increase the torque nearly fifty per cent.

Of course, the exact design, size and number of blades will be dependent upon the requirements of the generator that is to be used.

. . . .

Orville Wright to W. E. Scripps, Detroit News,
Detroit, Michigan

January 14, 1937

I have studied the photograph of the barn in Richmond [Indiana], which you sent me, but have not been able to make out definitely just what it is. The barn appears to be a little too large for the barn at the North Fourteenth Street house where we first lived in Richmond. That was the only place in Richmond, so far as I can remember, where Wilbur and I made kites. The barn on Fourteenth Street had but one door in front, while the one in the photograph seems to show three doors.

. . . .

Orville Wright to Sam H. Acheson, The Dallas Morning News, *Dallas, Texas*

January 22, 1937

The long fanciful story purporting to describe our first flights was sent out from Norfolk by Harry P. Moore of the *Virginian-Pilot*. It appeared in the *Virginian-Pilot*, the Cincinnati *Enquirer,* and some other papers on the morning of December 18, 1903.

On the afternoon of December 17, Wilbur and I had walked to Kitty Hawk four miles away from our camp to send a telegram home telling of our success. The only telegraph at Kitty Hawk was at the Weather Bureau station. Our telegram was sent over the Weather Bureau line to the station at Norfolk, and there transferred to the Western Union. . . .

While we were still in the office at Kitty Hawk word came back from the Weather Bureau man at Norfolk (James J. Gray) asking permission to give the news to a newspaper friend of his. . . . We answered "positively no." Nevertheless Gray did inform his friend Moore that we had sent a telegram to our father telling of our successful flights, but evidently he gave Moore no particulars. Moore tried to get information about the flights over the telephone but, failing, made up the fantastic story which appeared the next morning.

Father had my brother Lorin take his telegram to the Dayton representative of the Associated Press the evening of the 17th. After reading it the press man sniffed, "59 seconds; if it were 59 minutes it might be worth mentioning." So he did not mention it, and it was only after reading the Moore story in the Cincinnati *Enquirer* the next morning that the Dayton paper woke up to the fact that something really had happened. That is the reason you did not get authentic news until the second day.

Mr. J. J. Dosher was in charge of the Kitty Hawk station and telegraphed the message to Norfolk. I frequently see it stated in the newspapers that A. W. Drinkwater sent out the telegram. That is not true. Drinkwater did not come into the picture until 1908. He was in charge of the Weather Bureau at Manteo, Roanoke Island, in that year and sent out a great quantity of telegrams for the New York newspaper men who came down to watch our practice flights.

. . . .

Orville Wright had accepted the story, often repeated, that it was H. P. Moore who got the first flight report for the Norfolk paper from the Weather Bureau. But while this book was being prepared I talked with Keville Glennan, who was city editor of the *Virginian-Pilot* at the time of the flight, and he told me a different story. He distinctly remembered that he had first learned of the Wright telegram from one of his reporters, Ed Dean, who regularly covered the local Weather Bureau and had been told by a friend there. Glennan and Dean had been working for some hours, trying to obtain more facts, and had their report about ready to put into type, Glennan recalled, when Moore appeared and asked if they knew about the flight. Moore had not yet become a regular reporter and was then working in the paper's business office. Just how he had learned of the flight, Glennan was not sure.

Though the account as published was fantastically inaccurate, one must credit Glennan and the other *Virginian-Pilot* editors with recognizing how important the news was and giving it a headline clear across the front page.

Orville Wright to Wilson M. Ranck, Secretary
Serials Section, American Library Association,
Rochester, New York

March 23, 1939

I have your letter of March 16th in regard to the use of the public library by my brother Wilbur and myself in our early studies of aerodynamics and aeronautics. Some sixteen years ago I had a letter on the same matter from a Mr. Samuel H. Ranck, librarian of the Grand Rapids, Michigan, Public Library. This Mr. Ranck may have been your father. I will here quote my letter to him which I think will answer your letter.

"I have your letter inquiring as to whether my brother and I got the material for our early studies in aeronautics from the Dayton Public Library.

"In the years before 1900 we frequently used the Dayton Public Library, but insofar as I can remember we found in it no books on the subject of aeronautics. We did get some books from the library on the subject of marine engineering in the hope of finding an explanation of the theory of the screw propeller. But these did not prove to be of any assistance to us in our work; because the marine engineers at that time did not base their calculations of screw propellers on a theory, but entirely on empirical formulae.

"Aeronautics at that time was a discredited subject and consequently the libraries did not ordinarily carry books on that subject. Most of what we read was secured from abroad or from the Smithsonian Institution at Washington."

I should make a slight correction of the last sentence in that letter. We purchased the books from the publishers, the Smithsonian Institution having furnished us a list of books and the names of the publishers.

. . . .

Orville Wright to Colonel Edward A. Deeds,
National Cash Register Company, Dayton, Ohio

June 29, 1939

A further search of our old papers brings forth the names of forty-four more persons who received instruction at the old Simms Station. . . .

I do not think the [Grover C.] Bergdoll name should be omitted from the list.*

. . . .

---

* The list of names was to go on a monument overlooking the field where the Wrights practiced and where the early flyers for the Wright Company received their training. Orville insisted that Bergdoll's later record as a draft evader did not change the facts about where he learned to fly, and that to omit his name from a list supposed to be complete would distort history.

*Orville Wright to Frederick C. Pyne, Aluminum Company
of America, Pittsburgh*

December 9, 1939

I believe the body of the motor, [in first power machine],
which included the crank-case and the water jacket for the
cylinders in one piece, was the only part in that machine
which was made of aluminum. . . . I do not remember the
per cent of copper, nor whether that was the only alloy
metal used.

In our motors of 1906 we used aluminum in the case of the
water pump and in water pipes connecting the cylinders,
as well as in the crank-case and cylinder water jackets. I
believe our first use of aluminum in the aeroplane itself,
outside of the motor, was in parts for the controlling mechanism. This was in 1908.

．　．　．　．　．　．　．　．

Orville Wright to Fred C. Kelly

Dayton, Ohio, November 9, 1940

In 1904 the Wright Brothers had made 11 flights in each
of which more than one kilometer was covered; and in 1905
they made 22 such flights. These flights were witnessed by
a good number of people, but these witnesses were not "official witnesses." There was no Aéro Club of America nor any
Federation Aeronautique Internationale when these flights
were made. The *Federation Aeronautique Internationale*
came into existence only on the 14th of October, 1905, and

the Aero Club of America, on the 15th of November, 1905. Probably neither of these organizations would have come into existence except for the interest created by the Wright Brothers' flight of 1904 and 1905. Here is a great opportunity for some one (why not you?) to crowd the name of Columbus out of the pages of history. Columbus failed to have "officials" of a regular organization, created for the special purpose of homologating discoveries, on hand when he landed in America!

Our personal acquaintance with Curtiss began in 1906. In May of that year he began writing to us, and in early September of that year he visited us at our office and workshop. Captain Baldwin brought him out. Captain Baldwin at that time was giving exhibition flights in Dayton with his dirigible balloon on which he was using a Curtiss motor. The four of us were together a good deal, and when they came to our office, we showed them a number of photographs of the flights made at Simms Station in the two previous years. When Curtiss saw the photographs he remarked it was the first time he ever had been able to believe we actually had been in the air with a flying machine.

A year later, in October, 1907, the Aerial Experiment Association was organized and Glenn Curtiss became "Director of Experiments." This was the first he himself became directly connected with aviation, except as a manufacturer of light motors. Aviation still was a side issue with him for some time.

On December 30, 1907, he wrote a three-page letter to us in which he said: "I just wish to keep in touch with you and let you know that we have been making considerable progress in engine construction." After listing and describing the various engines he was building, he proposed to furnish us "gratis" one of his 50 HP engines. He also, in this letter, men-

tioned the fact that Captain Baldwin was a "permanent
fixture in this establishment." Further on he tells of Dr. Bell's
reading to the members of the Aerial Experiment Association
the Government specifications for the purchase of a flying
machine, and adds: "You, of course, are the only persons who
could possibly come anywhere near doing what is required."

When I went to Washington to make the tests of the flying
machine for the Government, Captain Baldwin was still
there teaching the Army officers to operate the dirigible,
which he and Curtiss delivered to the Government. In speaking to me of the experiments in aviation being carried on by
Curtiss and the younger members of the Aerial Experiment
Assocation at Hammondsport, he said: "They are a gang
of pirates. I hear them talking. They intend to steal everything you have."

· · · · · · ·

Orville Wright to Archibald MacLeish, Librarian,
Library of Congress

June 2, 1941

I am enclosing photostats of two . . . letters and of a page
from *Flight* of October 11, 1934, containing a letter from
A. F. Zahm, Chief of the Division of Aeronautics. These
letters pertain to three different campaigns of propaganda,
but all three campaigns were for the purpose of discrediting
the Wright Brothers.

Referring to the letter in *Flight,* Wilbur never said that
he was convinced by the flight of Langley's model that Langley's large machine could fly, as Zahm here represents. He

did say in his letter of March 2, 1906, that, "If he (Langley) could only have started it, the chances are that it would have flown sufficiently to have secured to him the name he coveted, even though a complete wreck attended the landing." This statement was made when he believed that the failure of the machine had been due to a fault in the launching apparatus, as had been reported. He did not know the machine was so frail that when one of the wings was loaded with sand of a weight less than the weight the wings would have to carry in flight the wing bent thirteen inches out of its normal shape! (*Langley Memoir on Mechanical Flight*, p. 203). Wilbur never knew, and I did not know until after the publication of the *Langley Memoir on Mechanical Flight*, that the failure of the machine in 1903 was due to faults in its structural and aerodynamic design and not to a fault in the launching apparatus. Wilbur's statement was made under a complete misapprehension of the facts. He had never seen the machine or a drawing of it. Zahm here uses something from Wilbur's letters to corroborate a statement of his own which was not true.

. . . .

Orville Wright to Henry Ford

April 22, 1942

I quite agree with you that the aeroplane will be our main reliance in restoring peace to the World. The use of a beneficial invention for diabolical purposes, as in the present war, calls to mind a story I heard related fifty years ago by a missionary back from China. The Chinese gathered their grain by seizing the grain with one hand and cutting off the stalks with shears held in the other. The missionary thought he would be making a great contribution to their welfare by introducing the use of the scythe. More grain could be cut in an hour with the scythe than could be cut in a day with the shears. So he had a scythe shipped to him from America, and invited the natives to come to see it demonstrated. The Chinese of the neighborhood turned out in a crowd. The demonstration was a great success, and the spectators were impressed and very enthusiastic. The next morning, however, a delegation came to see the missionary. The scythe must be destroyed at once. What, they said, if it should fall into the hands of thieves; a whole field could be cut and carried away in a single night. So the use of the scythe could not be adopted! Apparently it didn't occur to them that the way to avoid such a situation would be to stop the thieves instead of to stop the use of the scythe.

. . . .

Orville Wright was conservative in his estimate of the value of the airplane. At the time of the sesquicentennial anniversary of the founding of the United States Patent Office, he and a number of other scientists were asked to list the ten inventions of the last hundred years they considered the most important. He took the word important to mean usefulness in the everyday life of an average person. His list of ten inventions included the telegraph, telephone, air brake, perfecting press, linotype machine and radio—but *not* the airplane.

Franklin D. Roosevelt to Orville Wright

Washington, October 7, 1943

THE WHITE HOUSE

Dear Orville:

December 17th of this year will be the 40th anniversary of the first flight at Kitty Hawk. We all know that to you and Wilbur man-controlled flight was intended as an adjunct to peace throughout the world. We all hope that, after the war, aviation will have a commanding position in maintaining peace. That is as you would wish it and that is what we must begin thinking about.

As you will realize, I am never sure just what my engagements will be or where I will be two months ahead of time. I want you to reserve December 17th in the hope that you and I will both be able to come to a dinner in Washington on that date.

. . . .

Orville Wright to Franklin D. Roosevelt

October 16, 1943

I am greatly honored to have from the President of the United States an invitation to come to Washington on December 17th. Under the circumstances I have had no difficulty in securing releases from other obligations for that day.

I am sorry that inabilities as a speaker compel me to decline any speaking part in a program.

I believe it is time that we should be giving consideration to post-war matters; and I hope that when the time comes our people will be willing to make such sacrifices as are necessary to secure a lasting peace.

. . . .

Orville Wright to Dr. Charles G. Abbot, Secretary, Smithsonian Institution, Washington, D. C.

October 17, 1943

I have your letter of October 12th containing a suggested note to accompany your paper. The note* as given in your letter will be satisfactory to me if at its end the words "if given adequate publication" be added.

I can well understand the difficult position you found yourself in when you took over the administration of the Institution at a time when it had on its hands an embarrassing controversy for which you were not responsible; so I appreciate the more your effort to correct the record of the tests at Hammondsport in 1914 which brought on that controversy.

I hope the relations between the Institution and myself may again be as amicable as they were in Dr. Langley's administration.

. . . .

---

* The note was simply a mention that the paper had been submitted to Orville Wright and was acceptable to him.

The paper referred to in the foregoing letter is the Smithsonian brochure, "The 1914 Tests of the Langley 'Aerodrome,'" published on October 24, 1942, containing ample apologies and retractions of former misstatements. Its publication marked the end of the controversy.

Orville Wright to Henry B. Allen, Director, The Franklin Institute, Philadelphia, Pennsylvania

October 27, 1943

Henson made no contribution to the art or science of aviation worth mentioning. (We learned nothing from him and Chanute apparently did not consider him of any importance, for in a correspondence between Chanute and Wilbur covering a period of ten years Henson was not mentioned by either of them, although more than thirty others who antedated us were mentioned.) Every feature of Henson's machine had been used or proposed previously. His mere assemblage of old elements certainly did not constitute invention, because the elements were not intended to secure a new effect not contemplated by his predecessors.

. . . .

Franklin D. Roosevelt to Orville Wright

Washington, November 11, 1943

THE WHITE HOUSE

Dear Orville:

Now that the Smithsonian Institution has recognized the Wright Brothers plane, which made its first flight at Kitty Hawk, December 17, 1903, as the first airplane capable of making a sustained flight, and made proper acknowledgment in its annual report for 1942, do you not think it would be a good idea to announce at the December 17 dinner honoring you that this plane would be brought back home?

.   .   .   .

Orville Wright to Franklin D. Roosevelt

November 16, 1943

My dear Mr. President:

I think your suggestion of having the announcement of the future return of the Kitty Hawk plane made at the dinner on December 17th a good one. I had intended that the announcement be made as soon as the Smithsonian Report appeared, but I now shall have it withheld for the dinner. If you personally were to make the announcement it would be particularly pleasing to me.

.   .   .   .

Orville Wright to Colonel E. E. B. Mackintosh, Director
and Secretary, the Science Museum, London, England

December 8, 1943

I have decided to have the Kitty Hawk plane returned to America when transportation is less hazardous than at present. Later I will let you know the time for its return. I think you will not be surprised in learning of this decision, but I wish to let you know of it before a public announcement is made. President Roosevelt has asked that the announcement be made at a dinner to be held in Washington on the 17th of this month celebrating the fortieth anniversary of flight.

I appreciate the great trouble the plane has been to the Museum under war conditions, and I am grateful for the unusual care the Museum has taken for the plane's safety.

It has been suggested that I permit the plane to be retained and again to be exhibited in the Museum for six months after the war is over while a copy of it is being made. I think this will be agreeable to me. But before the construction of a copy is started I would suggest that another set of the drawings made by the Museum in 1928 be sent to me for correction. I have found in your drawings a number of structural details that need correction, especially in places where details could not be seen by the draftsman without a complete tearing down of the machine. However, one error, easily found, was made by your draftsman in assuming the machine is symmetrical from side to side. The right side actually is four inches longer than the left. A draftsman for the United States Army some years ago made this same mistake.

I have complete and accurate drawings of the engine. I

shall be glad to furnish them, if you decide to make a replica. I also have the patterns from which the engine body was cast and would be pleased to have an aluminum casting made from them without expense to you. I shall do whatever I can in helping you to get an accurate copy of the plane and motor.

. . . .

Because of wartime conditions the actual return of the plane had to be delayed.

Orville Wright to W. R. Enyart, President, National Aeronautic Association, Washington, D. C.

May 27, 1944

Your letters of May 4th and 23rd are on a matter which I consider important. My tardy answer to them is due not to lack of interest but to lack of ability as a correspondent.

In so far as I know, there is not and never has been a "Collier Trophy." The trophy which now goes under that name was founded by Robert J. Collier in 1912, and the first award was made for the year 1911. The Deed of Gift reads as follows:

"Board of Governors of the Aero Club of America:
Dear Sirs: I have the pleasure of presenting to the Aero Club of America a bronze trophy to be known as the 'Aero Club of America Trophy,' which is to be awarded annually by the Club for the greatest achievement in avia-

tion in America, the value of which has been thoroughly demonstrated by use during the preceding year.

Robert J. Collier."

You will note that the name was "Aero Club of America Trophy." It was still Aero Club of America Trophy at the time the Aero Club disbanded and the N.A.A. took over the representation of the F.A.I.* in America. Whether any formal action was ever taken by the N.A.A. to change the name from Aero Club of America Trophy to Collier Trophy, I do not know. I never knew of any such action.

To have a real understanding of the donor's object in establishing the trophy, an understanding of his character and some knowledge of his many contributions to aviation would be necessary. These are not easily found in print. Mr. Collier was a very modest man, and was not given to self-advertisement. He was one of the finest men I have ever known—one of the mildest in appearance and manner, but one of the firmest in standing for what he believed and thought was right. He was a true sportsman who never mixed sport and business. Though he was founder and owner of it, *Collier's Weekly* never had any connection with the trophy during his lifetime. The gift of the trophy was purely a personal one. Before offering the trophy Mr. Collier had consultations with Wilbur and me.

The trophy was named the "Aero Club of America Trophy" in the Deed of Gift. Unless that name has been changed by some lawful act of a competent body, the name still must be the "Aero Club of America Trophy." If that be so, and if the N.A.A. is such a competent body, I would recommend that by proper action it change the name from the "Aero

---

* *Federation Aéronautique Internationale.*

Club of America Trophy" to the "Robert J. Collier Trophy," honoring the man who established it, and who himself was one of the most generous and the most disinterested of all the pioneers in American aviation.

.   .   .   .

The award is now known as the "Robert J. Collier Trophy."

Orville Wright to Fred C. Kelly

September 26, 1944

[The first power plane] was designed to fly at 30 feet per second and as a matter of fact it could have flown at slightly less speed than that. Since the speed of the wind at the time of the first flight was 35 feet per second or more, and since the relative speed necessary for flight was not over 30 f.p.s., the take-off could have been made without any run on the rail at all. With the skill I acquired later in piloting I would not have hesitated to take that machine off the ground without using any track and without any initial forward speed whatever. But we were not so foolish as to risk trying to do that on our first flights.

.   .   .   .

Orville Wright to Major R. H. Fleet, Consolidated Aircraft Corporation, San Diego, California

October 26, 1944

. An investigation of the records reveals that no invention of Montgomery's is used in aeroplanes today; that no theory originating with him has withstood the test of time; that Montgomery's work contributed nothing to the art of flying, nor to the science of aerodynamics.

John J. Montgomery was practically unknown until 1905, when a glider designed and built by him was elevated to a height of several thousand feet by a hot air balloon, where it was freed from the balloon and made a spectacular descent to the ground with a pilot aboard. Several other similar flights were made and then on the 18th day of July, 1905, the machine turned over on its back, collapsed, and fell to the ground. Maloney, the pilot, was killed. . . .

Many explanations were given as the cause of the disaster, but I believe any aeronautical engineer, when he once understands the design and construction of the Montgomery machine, will agree with the opinion formed at the time by Wilbur and myself as to the cause.

Setting the rear wings at a greater angle than the forward ones is dangerous on any machine, but it is especially so when the wings are cambered; because on cambered wings at most of the flying angles the center of pressure travels rearward with decrease of angle instead of forward, as was supposed by Montgomery. . . . The elevator of the Montgomery machine was too small and too close to the planes to have sufficient turning force to bring the machine out of the dive. . . .

Montgomery himself, when he again took up gliding in 1911, lost his life in a tail-spin resulting from these dangerous features in the design of his machine. . . .

In 1909 a small group of men in Chicago, inspired by the power flights made in 1908 and 1909 by the Wrights in Europe and America, wished to engage in the aeroplane business, using the Wright patented inventions without having to pay royalty for them. They looked around for something that they hoped might enable them to do so. One of the leaders in this group was Victor Loughead. In 1909 he published a book entitled *Vehicles of the Air,* in which he pronounced Maloney's descent from a hot-air balloon on a Montgomery glider (nearly 17 months after the power flights at Kitty Hawk, December 17, 1903) as being "the greatest single advance in the history of aerial navigation.". . .

What fame attends the name of John J. Montgomery in aviation history is due almost altogether to propaganda put out by Victor Loughead. It is astonishing to what lengths propaganda will be used when financial interests are involved. . . .

One other question remains: Was Montgomery a real pioneer antedating Lilienthal in successful, practical gliding flights, as claimed by Loughead?* *Did Montgomery really accomplish a single glide in his early experiments?* A glance at the record in this matter is interesting. No one, Loughead nor any other Montgomery partisan, has ever claimed that Montgomery made more than one gliding flight prior to 1900 —the one flight described by Chanute in *Progress in Flying*

---

* The Court of Claims, in deciding against the Montgomery heirs in a suit they brought against the U. S. Government, said: "It seems to us idle to contend that Montgomery was a pioneer in this particular art [of aviation]."

Machines, page 248. Chanute, who got his information directly from Montgomery in 1894, says that the glide was made from the top of a hill which sloped at an angle of about ten degrees; that it was made in a sea breeze "blowing steadily from 8 to 12 miles an hour;" *that the glide started with a "jump into the air* without previous running;" that Montgomery and his machine together weighed 170 pounds; that the wings of the machine had an "area of about 90 sq.ft;" and that "the total distance of the glide was about *100 feet."*

Loughead produced a fictitious drawing of this machine, page 140, *Vehicles of the Air,* which showed the area to have been only 40 sq. ft. But taking Chanute's figures as being more nearly correct, since they were derived directly from Montgomery, while much of Loughead's informaton was derived from Loughead's fertile imagination and wishful thinking, the glider with which the 100 ft. glide was supposed to have been made would have required a very much higher relative velocity than 8 to 12 miles an hour. Today all aeronautical engineers know that a machine having only 90 ft. wing area, with camber as used by Montgomery, can not lift more than 20 pounds at a speed of 8 miles per hour, and not more than 45 pounds at 12 miles per hour—one-eighth to one-fourth of the weight of Montgomery and his machine. His two later machines, with over 50 per cent more wing area, proved to be failures, as recorded by Chanute, because no lifting effect could be obtained with them sufficient to carry the weight!! If Montgomery had been able to get sustentation with his first machine in an 8 to 12 mile wind by merely making a leap without preliminary run, why should he have added the unnecessary 50 per cent more surface to his next machines? . . .

I believe that all of the legendary stories which have crept into aviation history making Montgomery a conspicuous figure in it, if traced back to their source, *would be found to have originated with Victor Loughead.* . . . Whether it was from ignorance, from personal interests, or from a combination of the two, that he started and so zealously pushed the cause of Montgomery, I am unable to say. But I am convinced that it was he who led the Montgomery family, apparently a group of sincere and loyal members, into believing there had been a great and profound thinker in their family, and that his contributions to aviation had been unappreciated and ignored by mankind. They had been deceived by the praise heaped upon Montgomery by Loughead. I have felt sorry for them.

. . . .

Orville Wright to Fred C. Kelly

January 17, 1945

I am afraid I will not be able to make clear to you the arrangement we had at Kitty Hawk for getting simultaneously records of the time, measured with the stop-watch; the distance through the air, measured with a Richard anemometer; and the engine speed, measured with a Veedor revolution counter. I have made a diagramatic sketch which . . . may help some.

A Veedor counter *a* was mounted at the upper end of a flat steel spring *b* . . . The Veedor counter had a spear-head shaped rubber end on its shaft which the spring of the support *b* held in engagement with the end of the crank-shaft *c*. The lever *d* (shown in red) was pivoted at its center on the

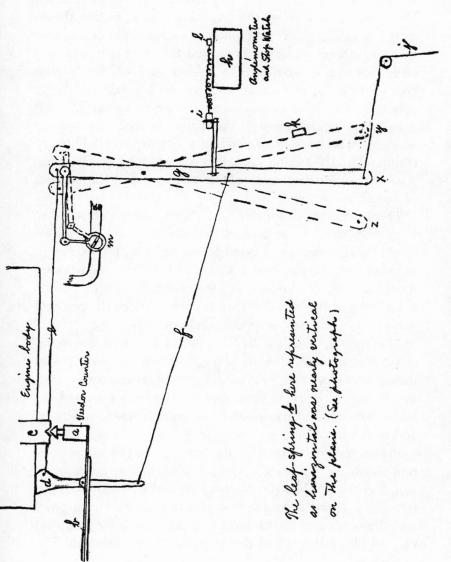

Engine body

Vixdow Counter

Anemometer and Stop Watch

The leaf spring to here represented as horizontal was nearly vertical on the plane. (See photographs.)

Diagram of the recording device used in the first flight.

revolution counter support b, with one end pressed against the side of the engine body. The end of the lever was shaped like a cam so that when the lever was in the position shown in the drawing, the revolution counter was held out of contact with the crank-shaft; but when the lever d was moved anti-clockwise it allowed the rubber end of the Veedor counter to come in contact with the engine axle and begin counting. The lever d was connected by two strings, e and f, to a lever g, as shown in the diagram. When the lever g was turned on its pivot clockwise the counter was held out of contact with the engine shaft. When it was moved anti-clockwise the counter came in contact and recorded the number of engine revolutions.

The Richard anemometer h had a stop-watch attached to it. . . . A small lever on the anemometer . . . was so arranged that when you pressed on the lever with your finger, or otherwise, the stop-watch would run and the anemometer would record the distance as measured by the little paddle wheel seen at the top of the anemometer. When the pressure was removed the two stopped simultaneously.

The lever i, attached to the upright and standing vertically, was operated by the lever g. When the lever g was moved anti-clockwise to start the revolution counter recording, it also at the same time, through the lever i, moved the little lever on the anemometer and started the anemometer and watch recording.

Before starting the engine the lever g was put in the position shown in the sketch, so that none of the instruments would record. When the machine started down the rail the string j, one end of which was attached to the starting rail and the other end to the lever g, jerked the lever g against the stop k putting all of the instruments in operation. The cord *j* was an ordinary string and broke when the lever *g* came in contact with the stop. At the end of the flight the operator struck the lever *g* with his hand, turning it clockwise, and so shut off all the instruments. At the end of the first flight I struck the lever *g* so hard it was broken and had to be repaired. I forgot to mention that a valve *m* in the gas line to the engine also was automatically closed at the same time the instruments were stopped.

The jar of rough landings set the stop-watch back to zero in all the flights. All the time records were taken with a stop-watch held by Wilbur or myself at the starting point.

. . . .

Orville Wright to W. B. Brummitt, Eastman Kodak Company, Rochester, New York

May 2, 1945

Your letter . . . inquiring as to the accuracy of the story that I made photographs from a plane in flight at the flying ground at Simms Station in 1905 is received. I assure you there is no truth whatever in the story.

I have several photographs taken in the air over Simms Station in 1912 from a Wright Model "A." I do not know who the pilot was in this case, but I suspect it was William Kabitski. The photograph was taken by the passenger.

In so far as I know, the first photographs ever taken from an aeroplane in flight were moving pictures taken at Centocelli military field near Rome in April, 1909. My brother Wilbur took up a Universal cameraman on the day the King of Italy visited our field.

. . . .

Orville Wright to D. J. Swaine, Victoria, Australia

July 30, 1945

You ask whether we found any of Hargrave's work useful. In none of our gliders, nor in any of our power machines, was anything from Hargrave used. Our first invention, a system of control for aeroplanes, could not be applied to a Hargrave kite.

.   .   .   .

Orville Wright to Henri Hegener, Bennebroek, near Haarlem, Netherlands

September 5, 1945

A reading of the European aeronautical publications from 1898 to 1902 will show that practically no serious thought was given to the aeroplane after the death of Lilienthal and after the failure of the Ader machine.

Captain Ferber was the dean and the most active of the French aviators before 1906. He has repeatedly acknowledged in print that our work was his inspiration and that he was our disciple. To give a couple of examples I would refer you to p. vii in the preface to his *l'Aviation,* published, . . . July, 1908, and to his letter to *l'Aérophile* of June, 1907, in which he tells of his emotions on first meeting my brother Wilbur in Paris. He said if it had not been for Wilbur his own experiments would never have taken place; that he himself would never have had Voisin for a student; that Archdeacon and Deutsch de la Meurthe would not have put up their prize in 1904; that *l'Aérophile* would not have quadrupled its circulation, and other special papers would not have started; that Santos-Dumont would not have turned to aviation, and that Delagrange would have continued to sculpture beautiful statues and would not have bought an aeroplane from Voisin.

A perusal of the "Portraits d'Aeronautes Contemporains" in *l'Aérophile* of those years will show that practically all of the early French aviators either started their experiments from the work of the Wright brothers or from the work of some one else whose work did begin with that of the Wright brothers. Among these will be found Ferber, Voisin, Bleriot, Delagrange, Farman, Esnault-Pelterie, etc. Of course, I know that at least one of these—Voisin—has completely forgotten that his first time in the air was on a Wright type glider!!

. . . .

Orville Wright to Alexander McSurely, Aviation News, Washington, D. C.

February 5, 1946

Thanks for the copy of *Early Powerplane Fathers*** [by A. F. Zahm]. I had not seen it before, but I had heard, several years ago, that Zahm was about to publish a "book" which would be an attack on the Wright brothers, though they would not be named specifically. I presume this is that book.

Zahm has carried on a campaign of detraction the past

---

* Published by Notre Dame University.

thirty-five years. You may wonder what has been back of his extreme bitterness against the Wright brothers. A little information about his early contacts with them may not be out of order.

Our first contact with Zahm was through a letter from him to Wilbur in March, 1902, asking for a copy of the address made by Wilbur before the Western Society of Engineers the previous September. Several letters a year then passed between them. In February, 1906, Zahm wrote a letter, which can be found in the evidence, page 689, in Wright Company versus Herring-Curtiss Company as follows:

"We have thought that when the time is opportune, it would be well for the Aero Club to pass resolutions something after the enclosed tentative form. This would be the first formal indication that your countrymen appreciate your work and are proud of it. It may also prove of historic value in showing that the specialists of your day regarded you as the inventors of the first successful flying machine."

Zahm later, after he had become a paid witness for Curtiss, discovered that he and the "specialists" of that day were perfect ignoramuses; that the Wrights were neither the inventors of the flying machine nor the first to successfully fly!! . . .

When we did not employ him as a witness, he became a witness for Curtiss, and at once was very bitter. He then wrote a book full of nasty slurs, particularly against Wilbur, who in the patent litigation was his opponent as a witness, against whom he did not appear to the best advantage.

The Wright patent, among other claims, made claim to the use of a rudder to overcome the difference in resistances of the two ailerons when one of them was turned to a greater angle of attack than the other one. Curtiss tried to maintain that ailerons did not produce a torque about a vertical axis, and that he never used the rudder for that purpose. Zahm supported him in his contention. Zahm testified as follows:

"On page 8 of the Wright Brothers' affidavit they state that in a flight made by Mr. Curtiss 'the balance was not restored by the balancing tips alone, but by the balancing tips in co-operation with the fixed vertical rudder.' This is misleading, to say the least. The lateral balancing in Defendant's machine is effected *solely by the ailerons*. The vertical rudder does not co-operate with them in *restoring balance*." (The italics are Zahm's p. 461 The Wright Company versus Herring-Curtiss Company, March 16, 1910.)

Five days after thus testifying under oath that the rudder was not needed and was not used to overcome the difference in drag of the two ailerons, Zahm applied for a patent on a device to overcome this very difficulty which he had just testified did not exist. The following is from his patent application:

"When my improvement is not employed, however, it often happens that when the ailerons are adjusted at various angles to each other, as described above, one of them will from one cause or another, receive a greater pressure than the other and thereupon produce a torque about the vertical axis of the machine and thereby tend to turn the machine from its course." (Zahm patent application, Wright Company versus Glenn H. Curtiss, et al, pp. 873 and 874.)

When we learned that four individuals had made application to the Patent Office for a patent on a device to overcome this torque resulting from use of ailerons, and that Zahm was one of these applicants, we asked for a copy of Zahm's patent application, since we knew he would state in it that there was a torque produced by the ailerons. He was ordered by the court to furnish us a copy of it. When he failed to obey the court order we went to the court again, and the judge told Zahm he would have to produce the paper or he would be in contempt. There was much mirth in the court room over Zahm's embarrassment when he tried to explain why he did not want to produce the document. As a matter of fact it would have been embarrassing to any one to be confronted with two such contradictory statements as those just quoted, both of which had been made under oath!

The [Gustave] Whitehead* story is too incredible and ridiculous to require serious refutation. Dr. John B. Crane, aided by a grant of funds from the Committee on Research in the Social Sciences of Harvard University, investigated and made a report of the claims set up for Whitehead which was published in the N. A. A. Magazine for December, 1936. His conclusions were as follows:

"1. The evidence that Whitehead made genuine, sustained, horizontal flights at any time is inconclusive.

"2. The evidence that Whitehead made short momentum flights at different times between 1904 and 1908 is conclusive.

"3. The evidence that Whitehead made short momentum flights prior to 1904 is inconclusive."

---

* Whitehead was reported, wrongly, by Zahm to have flown in Connecticut before the first flights by the Wrights.

You can find additional information on the Whitehead myth in *U. S. Air Services* for August, 1945.

. . . I have never seen the Goupil book *La Locomotion Aerienne*. My only knowledge of this book is what has come through Zahm. The reproductions, represented as designs of a flying machine proposed in Goupil's book, appear at least to be from a French publication, and probably are genuine. . . .

Goupil's proposed machine, in so far as I can remember, was never cited by the defendants in any suit in America, France or Germany. Apparently the French and Germans did not consider it as an anticipation of our patent.

The claim that Ader had made a power flight was set up after Wilbur made his first flight in France. Up to that time the French had recognized Santos-Dumont's flight on October 23, 1906, as the first flight in the history of the world in a heavier-than-air machine. However, when they saw Wilbur fly in France in 1908 the French said that no one could have made such a flight without previous experience, and they acknowledged that we had made flights at Kitty Hawk in December, 1903.

There were a few chauvinistic French who could not bear the idea of letting America get an honor in a line in which they thought France to be in the lead. Therefore, they had to look around for some Frenchman antedating Santos for whom they would try to set up a claim. The only one they could find was Ader. They then claimed that he had made a flight in 1897 with a machine financed by the French Government. We had been told by Commandant Bonel, who represented the French War Department in negotiations with us at Dayton, March-April, 1906, that he was present at the tests of the Ader machine in 1897; that those tests had

convinced him man-flight was impossible; and that he had
objected to being sent to America on a matter that would be
considered so silly as to injure his reputation. From this
we knew that if we could secure the publication of the original report of the commission appointed by the French War
Department to witness the tests, the claim would go up in
smoke. We asked the French Minister of War to make public
the report. In reply we received a letter saying that the report
would be published only on condition that we would get
Ader's consent and furnish papers from Ader, properly legal-
ized, guaranteeing that the Department would be altogether
absolved from any liability for damages. The Department,
of course, knew that we could not secure Ader's consent, and
so the report would remain secret. But Santos-Dumont had
some wealthy and influential friends. They were not going
to let Ader take an honor then accorded to Santos of being
the first in Europe to get off the ground in a heavier-than-air
machine. They forced the Minister of War to make the report
on Ader public. That report settled the claim for Ader with
everyone excepting Zahm and a few others. Zahm didn't propose to be stopped with a thing like that, and let the Wrights
get the credit of being the first in the world to fly. He just
went back six years further, and decided that Ader had
made a power flight in 1891—when no official commission
was present to contradict the claim!!

. . . .

Orville Wright to Dwight Young, The Dayton
Journal-Herald, *Dayton, Ohio*

August 20, 1946

If you are as honest as my mother was you must have had many qualms when you wrote the editorial on Orville Wright 75.

When I was a youngster five or six years old my mother paid a social visit to one of our neighbors. When the neighbor started talking about her children, praising them to the skies till mother could no longer recognize any of them, mother set in to go her one better. After her return home, she told us it was a terrible strain on her conscience, but that she didn't propose to be outdone by Mammy B—. One of Mammy B's daughters later came into our family and became the mother of a number of Wrights.

So that I can maintain my former good opinion of you, I hope you suffered as much as my mother did when you wrote the editorial.

Orville Wright to Fred C. Kelly

Dayton, Ohio, August 28, 1946

After knowing you 32 years, I think it is time we drop formal salutations. Many who have known me only a week call me Orville.

.   .   .   .

It was characteristic of Orville not to become suddenly informal without giving formal notice!

Orville Wright to Richard H. Hart, New Orleans, La.

October 9, 1946

I regret very much that I am not able to give advice that will be of value to you. After forty years' acquaintance with the ways of our departments of National defense I do not know any more about how to get them to take an interest in or to adopt valuable inventions than you do.

You probably already are acquainted with our attempts forty years ago to interest our Government in the aeroplane. That discouraging experience is in Fred Kelly's *The Wright Brothers*. In that respect Government departments are today just what they were forty years ago. In the last twenty-five years I have had the same experience with them we had in 1906.

In 1920 we developed the split flap, used in dive bombers today, applied for patent in 1921, and received a patent for it in 1924. (Patent No. 1,504,663). A description of it and our measurements of its lift and drag were sent to the Navy Department. I have the Navy report made in 1922, pronouncing it of no value. It took ten years for the Navy engineers to comprehend its value. I believe the Navy was the first to use it.

I spent nearly five years in trying to get officers in the Army to come to my office to see a device which I thought would be of use to them. I was not trying to sell something. I told them they would be free to use the idea. I later learned they had spent a lot of time in trying to develop a device for that same purpose, but getting nowhere, finally gave it up as hopeless.

.   .   .   .

To the end of his life, Orville Wright seemed boyish in his love of pranks and in his flashes of humor. One night when Griffith Brewer, then President of the Royal Aeronautical Society in Great Britain, was Orville's guest, the talk turned to how simple and easy an invention often looks after it has been made, so much so that almost anyone might think he could have done it. Then Brewer quoted a line of poetry, ". . . so easy it seemed, once found, which, yet unfound, most would have thought impossible."

"I have been trying for years," said Brewer, "to find out who wrote that line." He and Orville began to ransack books of quotations, but in vain.

By strange coincidence, in Orville's mail the next morning was a letter from a man in Spokane seeking an autograph. The writer quoted that line of poetry and gave the source; Book VI of Milton's *Paradise Lost*. Orville said nothing about this windfall because it had put into his head an idea for a practical joke. That night after dinner he located his copy of *Paradise Lost* and surreptitiously slid out a book half an inch or so on the shelf just above it to serve as a marker. Then he said to Brewer, "It looks as if we're never going to be able by ordinary research to identify the author of that line of poetry about invention—so maybe we ought to try psychic means." Brewer looked shocked.

To put Brewer into a proper frame of mind for witnessing psychic phenomena, Orville then told him the story about the time he thought that Wilbur would blow out the gas. "I'll blindfold myself," Orville went on, "and see if I can be guided by psychic means to whatever book that quotation is in." He tied his handkerchief over his eyes and began to grope along the rows of books in his library. When his hand touched the one he wanted, he said, "I feel a strong impulse to pick up this book."

When Brewer recognized the volume which Orville had selected he said, "I don't think you'll find it there. The quotation doesn't sound like Milton."

"Let's take a look anyhow," suggested Orville. "There must be some reason for my impulse to pick it up." In a few moments of thumbing through the pages he had located the lines about invention. Naturally Brewer was amazed. He wondered about this feat all the rest of his life, for Orville thought the joke too good to spoil by explanation.

Once, as a minor prank, Orville prepared a turkey in a special way for a family dinner on Thanksgiving. Nearly all his nieces and nephews preferred dark meat and this time they were surprised that, as Uncle Orv carved, the supply never gave out. One of them remarked, "This is good turkey, but do you know it tastes a little like duck." Then Orville shook with laughter as he turned the platter around to show that the turkey was only a front. Most of the dark meat *was* duck.

Contrary to the common impression, Orville loved conversation. More than one of his friends has remarked that, no matter how late at night, he was never known to yawn and never seemed to be talked out. During World War II one of his grandnephews attending Miami University, not far from Dayton, persuaded him to come and spend an evening at a fraternity house. The other boys in the group wondered how they would talk to a man of his supposed taciturnity. They soon were at ease, because Orville promptly began to do most of the talking. One of the boys, taking a preliminary course in aviation, happened to mention something in his textbook that he didn't understand. Orville looked puzzled and asked to see the book. After reading a paragraph he said, "Oh, this is wrong," and wrote a correction in the margin. Then at the student's request he added his initials. What those boys remember of that evening is not alone their contact with a keen mind, but the pleasure of having an unassuming guest who contributed wonderful conversation.

Sometimes his part in a conversation was only a surprising remark. Someone in a group raised the question of the desirability of a nap after dinner. After much discussion all agreed with the accepted medical belief of the time that a nap right after eating is not good for one's health, because more circulation of the blood is needed to aid digestion. Then came Orville's comment, "If you are correct, think what a mistake dogs have been making!"

The trait in Orville Wright that always impressed me most during a third of a century of intimate acquaintance was his aim for accuracy and precision in all he did. Instinctively a perfectionist, he was tolerant of careless statement by others, but his own had to be right. In seeking more information about his childhood, I once said to him, "One Monday morning with your face freshly washed you set out for school for the first time. Can you remember what happened that day?"

He looked at me intently for a moment and replied, "I'm not absolutely sure it *was* on a Monday."

At the laying of the cornerstone for the Wright memorial on Kill Devil Hill, all the spectators except one showed much enthusiasm. The one man who failed to catch the happy spirit of the occasion turned with a wry smile to Lindsay Warren, then representative in Congress from that district, and said something like this: "I wonder if this whole thing isn't a mistake. Fifty years from now might be soon enough to determine if this memorial should be built. To do it now seems like an imposition on the taxpayers."

The man concerned about the taxpayers was Orville Wright.

XI

BACK FROM EXILE

Orville Wright died from a heart attack at 10:30 P.M. Friday, January 30, 1948.

On December 17 of that year, the forty-fifth anniversary of the first flight, the original airplane brought back from England was formally installed in the National Museum at Washington, administered by the Smithsonian Institution.

The exhibition label includes the following:

THE ORIGINAL WRIGHT BROTHERS' AEROPLANE
THE WORLD'S FIRST
POWER-DRIVEN HEAVIER-THAN-AIR MACHINE IN WHICH MAN
MADE FREE, CONTROLLED, AND SUSTAINED FLIGHT
INVENTED AND BUILT BY WILBUR AND ORVILLE WRIGHT
FLOWN BY THEM AT KITTY HAWK, NORTH CAROLINA
DECEMBER 17, 1903
BY ORIGINAL SCIENTIFIC RESEARCH THE WRIGHT BROTHERS
DISCOVERED THE PRINCIPLES OF HUMAN FLIGHT
AS INVENTORS, BUILDERS, AND FLYERS
THEY FURTHER DEVELOPED THE AEROPLANE, TAUGHT MAN TO
FLY, AND OPENED THE ERA OF AVIATION

INDEX

Abbot, Charles G., 440

Acheson, Sam H., 429

Ader, Clement, French airplane builder, 17, 107; experiments, 380, 454, 459-460

Aerial Experiment Association, 248, 249, 250, 269, 280, 304, 370, 415, 435, 436

"Aerial Steam Carriage," 396

Aero Club of America, 172, 195, 196, 266, 434, 435, 456

Aero Club of America *Bulletin*, 389

Aero Club of America Trophy, 444, 445

Aéro Club of France, 88, 138, 160, 163, 235, 321, 325, 328

Aero Club of Great Britain, 328

Aéro Club de La Sarthe, 330, 337

Aeronautical Annuals, 95, 134, 146, 172, 421

Aeronautical Society of America, 400

Aeronautical Society of Great Britain, 98

Aérophile, 88, 170, 287, 454, 455

Aircraft Production Board, 405

Airplane (*see also* Flight, Gliders, Machine), practical value, 154; balloon and helicopter compared to, 167; Wrights' basic principles, 185; war and, 216, 405; airships, 224, 225; first cross-country trip,

342; canoe used on, 349; large *vs.* small, 406; peace restored by, 437

Alexander, Patrick Y., 98, 99, 175

Allen, Henry B., 441

Allum, James C. E., 423

American Association for the Advancement of Science, 161, 363

Archdeacon, Ernest, 137, 138, 139, 162, 166, 219, 241, 246, 251, 278, 302, 321, 454

Austrian Association of Builders, Vienna, 164

Autour du Monde, 327

Avery, William, 68, 72, 73

Baldwin, Thomas S., 386, 435, 436

Balloon, dirigible, 137, 145, 167, 224, 225, 435, 448

Barnum & Bailey Circus, 196, 236

Barthou, French minister, 328, 337, 339

Bates, Major General J. C., 148, 149

Belgium, 350

Bell, Alexander Graham, 17, 183, 248, 269, 414, 415, 436

Berg, Hart O., Flint & Co's associate in Europe, 203; Flint sends W.W. to, 204-207; character, 223; W.W. in Germany with, 225, 230, 231, 238; W.W. in Paris with,

471

240, 241, 242; W.W. in Le Mans with, 270-272; and W.W.'s first flight in France, 292, 303; buffer for W.W., 316, 318; O.W. in Berlin, 343; and Wright companies, 375

Bergdoll, Grover C., 433

Bergson, French philosopher, 327

Berlin, 229, 231, 233, 238, 239, 343, 347, 350, 383, 384, 385

Besançon, aeronautics authority, 219

Bicycle shop, see Wright Cycle Company

Bicycle, wind tunnel, 51

Birds, flight of, 35-37, 133, 134, 397; measurements of, 60; shapes of, 182

Bleriot, French aviator, 234, 271, 292, 294, 302, 347, 455

Board of Ordnance and Fortification, see U.S. Board of Ordnance and Fortification

Bolée, Leon, President of the Aéro Club of the Sarthe, 269, 270, 289, 293, 294, 321, 324, 325, 377; gratitude shown, 381; flight with W.W., 322

Bonel, Commandant, representative of French War Dept., 173, 174, 179, 242, 267, 313, 459

Borghese, Prince, of Italy, 290

Brancker, Sefton, 415

Bretnall, R. J., 412

Brewer, Griffith, British Wright Co., 403, 406, 409; O.W.'s description of flood to, 397; poetry prank, 462-463

Brinkley, W. C., 114

Bris, Jean Marie le, 355, 361, 363, 396

British Aeronautical Society, 271

British Government, 141, 142, 143, 206

Brummitt, W. B., 453

Burgess, Gelett, 5, 285

Buzzard flight, 23, 36, 37

Cabot, Godfrey Lowell, 122, 176-178, 252

Cabot, Samuel, 122, 178

Capper, Col. J. E., 142, 143, 144

Carlisle, C. A., 424

Carnegie, Andrew, 55, 56

Cartwright, Peter, quoted, 267

Cayley, Sir George, 15, 17, 134, 395, 417

Century, 119, 265, 268, 278

Chandler, Lt. Col. C. DeForest, 407

Chanute, Octave, Aero Club speech, 88, 138, 278; attempt at human flight, 17; and Carnegie, 55; congratulates Wrights, 119, 322, 323; death of, 374, 378; financial help not accepted by Wrights, 53; flight correspondence, 356-368; French conference, 173; friendship renewed, 372-374; and gliders, 66-68, 77, 78, 80; Henson not mentioned by, 441; Huffaker machine, 39, 46; lecture on gliding by W.W., 43-48; Lilienthal tables, 46; machine construction, 92, 95-97; Mouillard patent, 85; 1901 visit, 40;

1902 visit, 73-75; 1903 visit, 108, 109, 110, 111; 1904 visit, 132; 1905 visit, 144; Pratt truss, 418; *Progress in Flying Machines,* 16, 21, 23, 95, 172, 355, 448, 449; regrets U.S. Government attitude, 141, 143, 148; *Revue des Sciences,* 249; surface information, 63, 64; two planes used by, 396; views on Wright inventions, 182, 183; W.W.'s first letter to, 22; Wrights criticized by, 272, 286; Wrights' indebtedness to, 355

Chanute Field, 426

Chatterbox, The, 5

Chevelier, automobile racer, 238

Chicago Exposition, 427

Cincinnati *Enquirer,* 429, 430

Cincinnati *Post,* 150

Clemenceau, Premier Georges, 224, 328

Clemenceau Contract, 325

Coffin, Howard, 405

College Park, Maryland, 349, 350

Collier, Robert J., 269, 354, 444, 445, 446

Collier's Weekly, 263, 268, 395, 416, 445

"Conquest of the Air, The," 395

Cordley, F. R., 205, 219, 223

Cosmos Club, Wash., D.C., 296, 298-301, 322

Crane, Dr. John B., 458

Crozier, General, 177, 178

Curtiss, Glenn, acquaintance, 435, and Aerial Experiment Association, 248, 250; Commer-cial company formed, 280; flight of "June Bug," 250, 279; license offered by Wrights, 284; suit against, 304, 343, 354, 368, 370, 371, 401, 402, 408, 456; Wright machine copied by, 286

Daimler, Mercedes, 297, 298

Daniels, John T., 114, 116

Dayton *Herald,* 308, 312

Dayton *Independent,* 23, 129, 130, 272, 278

Dayton *Journal,* 118

Dayton, Ohio, early years, 5; Huffman field experiments, 130, 131, 159, 160, 193; newspaper's accounts, 164; Wrights honored by, 342; flying school, 374; flood, 397, 398; and December 17 flight, 430; photographs of flights at, 435

Dayton Public Library, 432

Deeds, Colonel Edward A., 433

Delagrange, French aviator, 212, 219, 292, 294, 302, 317, 455

Der Vogelflug, 95

Deutsch de la Meurthe, Henri, desires to form French company, 207, 219, 222, 242-244; member of French syndicate, 255; stock wanted by, 292; W.W. congratulated by, 308, 309

Deutsch-Archdeacon prize, 138, 139, 240, 454

Dickson, Captain T. C., 151

Dienstbach, Carl, 120, 153

Dirigible, 137, 224, 225, 303, 435

Dosher, Joseph J., 25, 430
Dough, W. S., 114
Drinkwater, A. W., 430, 431
DuBois, R. G., 399
Duchemin Formula, 416, 417

Early Powerplane Fathers, 455
Eastman Kodak Co., 453
Edison, Thomas A., 17, 183
Einen, Gen. von, 233
Elizabeth City, N.C., 28, 29, 32, 38, 70
Ellis, Edgar W., 153, 160
Empire of the Air, 172
England, 193, 243, 271, 272, 341, 399
Englehard, Capt., 353
English Aeroplane Society, 328, 329
English Channel, 324, 327
Enyart, W. R., 444
Ericson, W. E., 428
Esnault-Pelterie, aviator, 219, 302, 455
d'Esterno, and laws of flight, 355, 360, 361, 363
d'Estournelles de Constant, Baron, 297, 313, 328
Etheridge, A. D., 114
Etheridge Co., J. E., 28
Experiments in Aerodynamics, 94, 172

Farman, Henri, French aviator, and Deutsch-Archdeacon prize, 240; experimentation, 251; W.W. meets, 272; Wright machine wanted by, 276; patent difficulty, 347; Wright influence, 455

Federation Aéronautique Internationale, 434, 445
Ferber, Capt. Louis F., 61, 62, 87, 95, 98, 140, 144, 146, 162, 163, 170, 175, 219, 228, 231, 240, 246, 287, 454, 455
Fessenden, Reginald A., 197
Fleet, Major R. H., 447
Flight (*see also* Airplane, Gliders, Machine), possibility of human, 15; wing design, 52; successful, 114, 115, 118, 121, 301, 302, 430; power for, 133, 134; night, 154, 347; complexity of, 182-184, 189; and wind, 213; practicability of, 316
Flint, Charles R., 190-195, 203-205, 220, 223, 242, 243, 266, 305
Floats, Airplane, 349, 411
Flood, damage of, 397
Ford, Henry, 437
Fordyce, Arnold, 163-166, 173, 179, 180, 222, 230, 243, 244, 250
Fort Myer (Va.), tests at, 256, 266, 295, 296; plans for, 272; first flights, 301-306, 309; O.W.'s accident, 313-318, 321, 322, 323, 330-335; Army demonstrations completed, 342
Foulois, Lt. Benjamin D., 296, 303, 342, 349, 352
Fournier, Captain, French minister, 173
France, Chanute visits, 88, 365; W.W.'s first flight in, 291,

292; aviation information requested by, 138; option on machine, 171

France Automobile, La, 166

French aviators, 88, 89, 137, 138, 189, 190, 212, 213, 224, 225, 233, 234, 251, 363, 454, 455, 459

French Government, 159, 163, 169, 171, 206, 219, 220, 221, 228, 328

French Peace Society, 405

Furnas, Charles W., 258, 259, 264, 331, 333

Gardner, Gilson, 263

German Daimler Co., 293

German Wright Company, 338, 353

Germany, 193, 206, 220, 224, 229, 231, 327, 341, 353, 375, 384; patent suits in, 369, 382, 391, 398, 399; O.W. to train flyers, 343; Wright company formed, 338; attempts in, 245; promise of contract, 238; patents, 97, 217, 218, 360

Geyer, C. J., 312

Gillespie, Major General G. L., 136, 137

Glennan, Keville, 431

Gliders (*see also* Airplane, Flight, Machine), Lilienthal's experiments, 10, 11, 172; Wright glider, 24, 30, 32, 38, 39-43; Chanute's, 39, 66-68, 77-80; lecture on by W.W., 43-48; Huffaker's, 46; Ferber's, 61, 62; French,

137, 189, 190; patent, 175; dropped from balloon, 145; Success of 1902, 66-70, 76-84, 128, 183

Goop Book, 5

Goupil, Alexandre, 140, 459

Governments, reason to sell to, 168; lack of action from, 206; W.W. wishes regular business with, 251

Grahame-White, Claude, 370

Graphic prize, 322

Gray, James J., 430

Gross, Major, 245

Grumbach, Carrie, 17-20, 47, 112, 118-120, 124

Hammondsport, Ind., 250, 402, 410, 436, 440

Hargrave, lateral control system, 363; flight claim, 380; used two planes, 396; no use of by Wrights, 454

Harper's Magazine, 404

Hart, Richard H., 462

Hawk flight, 36, 80

"Hawthorn Hill," 382

Hazel, Judge John R., 364, 370

Hegener, Henri, 454

Helicopter, 167

Hendrick, Burton J., 404

Henson, Samuel, "Aerial Steam Carriage," 396; no contribution, 441

Herring, Augustus M., Chanute sends, 66-68, 72-74; and gliding, 78; annoying attitude of, 79; and Chanute's machine, 80; offer of, 128; company formed by, 280; claims of,

354; Chanute's machine test-
ed by, 366; at Kitty Hawk,
407, 408
Herring-Curtiss Co., 280, 370, 456
Hitchcock, C. H., 405
Hobbs, Captain, 71
"How Uncle Sam Bought the
First Airplane," 407
Hudson-Fulton Celebration flights,
349, 353, 375
Huffaker, E. C., 39, 40, 46
Huffman pasture, 130-132, 135,
152, 193, 256, 374
Humphreys, Lt. Frederic E., 349,
352
Hunaudières Course, 289
Hydroplane, 1907, 411

Ingersoll, Robert, 4
International Peace Society, 297,
325
Inventors, patents and, 150, 399,
421, 422
Italy, 243, 290, 323, 330, 338, 341

Jackson, Merrick T., 414
Jamestown Exposition, 411
Japanese Government, 220
Johnson, Dr. Allen, 420
Journal of the Western Society of
Engineers, 48, 129
"June Bug," flight of, 250, 279,
370

Kabitski, William, 453
Kaempffert, Waldemar, 418
Kapperer, aviator, 212, 213, 293,
294, 302
Kehler, Capt. von, 231, 233, 245

Kelly, Fred C., 434, 446, 450, 464:
The Wright Brothers, 402,
462
Kensington Museum, 408, 409,
410, 415
Kitty Hawk, chosen by Wrights,
24, 28, 29; W.W. reaches,
30; O.W. reaches, 32; 1900
experiments, 30-38; 1901
experiments, 40-41; 1902
experiments, 69-74, first
flight, 103-122, 430, 459;
Herring visits, 408; records
of flights, 450, 452, 453; end
of 1902 visit, 84; 1903 and
1904 flights, 153; 1908 practice, 256-265; and reporters,
264, 265; 1903 visit, 95, 99;
suitability, 130, 131; disadvantages, 139; 1911 experiments, 386
Kitty Hawk Plane of 1903, 408-
410, 415, 427, 442, 443, 469
Kruckman, Arnold, aeronautical
editor of New York World,
355

Lahm, Lt. Frank P., 235, 296, 303,
304, 306, 320, 331, 349, 352
Lahm, Frank S., 160, 235, 311,
320
Lambert, Comte de, W.W. will
train, 326; pilot, 341; wants
to form company, 353
Lambert, Comtesse de, 382, 383
Lamson, Charles, 74, 80, 368
Lane, Franklin K., 399
Langley Law, 189, 378, 380, 416
Langley Memoir on Mechanical
Flight, 437

Langley, Dr. Samuel P., experiments, 11, 17, 59, 60, 351; and Herring, 72, 79; and Kitty Hawk, 84; invites Wrights, 85, 86; flight attempts, 96, 104, 106, 108, 109, 112, 146; Chanute's opinion, 154; death of, 172; assistance to Wrights, 186, 187; lateral control system, 363; claims, 380; value of work, 397; 1903 plane, 401; 1896 airplane model, 415; W.W.'s estimate of, 436-437; 1914 tests, 441

Langley-Zahn-Curtiss plane, 410
"Late Gliding Experiments," 45
L'Aviation, 454
Legion of Honor, 328, 337, 339
Lesh, L. J., 426
Les Sports, 162, 273, 293, 321
Letellier, owner of Le Journal, 163, 222, 243, 244, 250
La Locomotion Aerienne, 459
Lilienthal, Otto, experiments, 10, 11, 16, 17, 39, 41, 46, 51-54, 59-60, 172, 351, 363, 390, 416, 417; W.W. plans stronger machine, 31; and Ferber, 61, 62; influence on Wrights, 22, 356, 421; and human flight, 389; two planes used by, 396; death, 454; greatness, 183; aid for family, 376, 377, 381; interest aroused by, 24

Lodge, Henry Cabot, 122, 300
Lowe, arms manufacturer, 219, 224, 225, 229-231, 242, 243, 245

Lohr, Lenox R., 427
Lokal Anzeiger, 343, 345
London Daily Mail, 263, 290, 322, 324, 327
London Times, 316
Lou Willis, 70, 77
Loughead, Victor, 387; Vehicles of the Air, 448, 449, 450
Louvre, 209, 211, 227
Lux, J. K., 422
Lyncker, Gen. von, 245

McClure, S. S., 385
McClure's, 23
Machine (see also Airplane, Flight, Gliders), 1903, 86, 90-92, 99, 123, 128, 130, 147, 446; government development, 170; two-man, 188, 262, 264; some who built, 396; 1903, 1904, 1905, 1907, 411-415
Mackintosh, Col. E. E. B., 443
MacLeish, Archibald, 436
MacMechen, T. W., 400
McSurely, Alexander, 455
Maloney, pilot, 145, 422, 447, 448
Manly, Charles M., 85
Manufacturers Aircraft Association, 402
Marey, writer on human flight 15, 361, 363
Margherita, Queen of Italy, 323
Matin, Le, 292, 322
Mauser gun concern, 193, 245
Maxim, Sir Hiram, interest in flight, 17; surface experiment, 60; machine lifted by, 185; Le Mans visit, 324; lateral

control system, 363; flight claim, 380; work of, 183, 397; 417

Maxwell Field, 374

Means, James, 381, 420, 421

Mercedes-Daimler Co., 292

Merrill, A. A., 418

Midgett, Captain, 258

Moltke, von, 245

Monoplane, O.W. defines, 395

Montgomery, John J., 145, 386, 387, 422, 447-449

Montgomery, Alabama, 374

Moore, Harry P., 429, 430, 431

Moore, Johnny, 114

Moore, Willis L., 24

Moran, Charles A., 404

Morgan, James Pierpont, 341, 352

Mouillard, Louis Pierre, 85, 359, 360, 361, 363; experiments of, 397; *Empire of the Air*, 172

Munn & Co., 169

National Aeronautic Association, 445, 458

Nevin, Robert M., 135, 142

New York *Evening Telegram*, 120

New York *Herald*, 165, 166, 263, 265, 266, 268, 269, 272, 292, 303

New York *Times*, 399

New York *World*, 119, 166, 355, 359, 360, 362, 366, 373

Newcomen, Thomas, 183

Newton, Byron R., 263, 265, 272

Nicholas II, Czar of Russia, 191-193

"1914 Tests of the Langley 'Aerodrome,' The," 441

Norfolk, Virginia, 429, 430

Our Times, 414

Packard Automobile Company, 312

Painlevé, member of the Institute, 323, 327

Paris, France, 209-212, 227, 276, 382

Paris *Herald*, 303

Parsons, Herbert, 197, 199

Patent suits, 369-371, 382, 388, 398, 399

Patents, English, 272, 360; European, 347; French, 97, 217, 218; German, 217, 218, 360; Russian, 330; Wright, 85, 136, 175, 266, 279, 280, 319, 364, 384, 401; questions about, 97, 150, 168, 197, 252, 361, 363, 399

Patrick, Major General Mason M., 410

Pau (France), Wrights come to, 335, 336; pilot training, 338

Paulhan, Louis, 370

Pellier, French manufacturer, 293

Pénaud, Alphonse, 15, 85, 380, 396, 416-420

Petit-Journal, 292

Petit Parisien, 292

Pettigrew, experiments of, 361, 363

Philadelphia Inquirer, 373

Phillips, human flight attempts, 17

Photographs, flight, 116, 117, 287, 398, 453

Pilcher, P. L., 23

Popular Science Monthly, 363
Potsdam, flights at, 346
Pratt, Thomas Willis, 418
Prizes, Aviation, 320, 321, 322, 324, 330
Progress in Flying Machines, 16, 21, 23, 95, 172, 355, 448, 449
Pyne, Frederick C., 434

Ranck, Samuel H., 432
Ranck, Wilson M., 432
"Red Wings," Aerial Experiment Association machine, 269
Redpath Lyceum Bureau, 87
Revue des Sciences (1903), 249
Richardson, Commander H. C., 411
Robert J. Collier Trophy, 446
Rolls, Charles S., 271, 299
Rolls-Royce automobile firm, 271
Roosevelt, Franklin D., 439, 442
Roosevelt, Theodore, 197
Root, A. I., 153
Root, Elihu, 252
Ruhl, Arthur, 263, 268, 269
Russia, 170, 191, 192, 193, 239, 291, 330

St. Louis Exposition, 58, 59, 61, 65, 88, 131, 132, 238
Ste Chapelle, 276
Santos-Dumont, Alberto, at St. Louis Exposition, 88; jumping of, 184, 185; gliding, 189, 190; gas bag experiment, 212, 213; lack of progress, 246; and Wrights, 455, 459
Sarthe, La, 310, 320, 325, 330, 337

Scientific American, 119, 168, 169, 279, 286
Scripps, W. E., 429
Selfridge, Lt. Thomas, 248, 249, 266; information given to, 279; to operate dirigible, 303, 304; death of, 313-315, 322
Shea, William E., 414
Shepherd, William G., 416
Simms Station, 130, 159, 165, 433, 435, 453
Smithsonian Institution, 11, 15, 16, 173, 378, 402, 433, 440, 442
Spain, 326, 339
Spratt, George A., visits Kitty Hawk, 39, 40; W.W. writes to, 46; testing machine of, 53; surface information, 60, 62; W.W. hopes for visit from, 73-74; character of, 81; machine, 86; W.W.'s philosophy, 89; 1903 visit to Kitty Hawk, 95, 99, 105; experiments reported to, 110, 111; congratulations of, 127; W.W. tells of new machine, 139, 147; W.W. discusses information exchanged, 350, 351, 352; W.W. tells of Chanute's death, 378
Squier, Major George O., 307
Sullivan, Mark, 414
Surcouf, aeronautical authority, 219
Swaine, D. J., 454

Taft, William Howard, 142
Tailspins, significance of, 81
Tate, Dan, 41, 71, 74-77

Tate, Capt. William J., 25, 30, 34, 41

Taylor, Charles, 104, 105, 109, 110, 229, 331, 333

Technical World, 263

Templehofer field, 344

Tissandier, pilot, 341, 353, 383

Tomlinson, Mrs. George H., 426

Tunison, Frank, 118

United Brethren Church, 3, 65, 66

U.S. Board of Ordnance and Fortification, 136, 137, 142, 148-152, 203, 208, 215, 247

U.S. Kill Devil Life Saving Station, 153

U.S. War Department, 137, 141, 255, 342

Vehicles of the Air, 448, 449

Vienna Aviation Society, 176

Vienna Exposition, 164

Virginian-Pilot, 429, 431

Voisin Brothers, aviators, 278, 302 455

Walcott, Charles D., 378

Ward, Capt. Jesse, 119

Washington, D.C., 296, 298-301, 322

Watt, James, 183

Weather Bureau, 24

Weaver, H. M., 160

Weiler, Lazare, 257, 292, 297, 308, 309, 321, 328

Wenham, F. H., 60, 395

Western Society of Engineers, 43-48, 129, 249, 456

Wilson, Woodrow, 403

White, Henry, 300, 328

Whitehead, Gustave, 458, 459

Wilhelm II, Emperor of Germany, 170, 206, 230, 231, 233, 344, 346

Woman's Home Companion, 119

Woodhouse, Henry, 395

"Wright Aeroplane and Its Fabled Performances," 168-169

Wright Cycle Company, 7-10, 23, 32, 63, 104, 133

Wright Flyer, 196

Wright, Katherine, 4, 5, 17, 18; and Chanute, 40; and her brothers, 27, 31, 47, 323; and 1902 glider, 69; first flight telegram, 118; told not to worry, 223; trip to France, 336, 338; trip to Rome, 338, 341; trip to Berlin, 343, 344, 348, 352; bequest to, 388; Dayton flood, 397; to Europe in 1913, 398

Wright, Lorin, children of, 5; visits Kitty Hawk, 77, 80, 82; and Dayton *Journal*, 108, 118, 430; W.W. sends money, 336; O.W. sends drafts, 339, 340, 344; bequest to, 388

Wright, Bishop Milton, influence and guidance, 3, 4; attempt to depose, 65-66; and son's radiators, 87; and news of 1903 flight, 118-119, 374, 430; diary, 123; warnings, 218, 232, 234, 288; comments on fame, 305, 306; sympathy, 319; W.W. wishes to see, 336; religious ideas, 340; W.W. thinking of, 385;

death, 329, 388; bequest to, 388-389; and W.W.'s will, 391

Wright Brothers, The, 402, 462

Wright, Milton, 306

Wright, Orville, as a boy, 3, 4; cooking, 7; appearance, 8; education, 10; character, 17-19; presentiment of, 20; Kitty Hawk trips, 31, 33, 40, 65-84, 103-122, 153, 256-265, 386; manner of dress, 47, 117, 118; and 1902 glider, 69; movable tail, 83; 1903 machine described, 90-92; first motor flight, 114; contributions to airplane inventions, 123, 124; Paris, 229, 230, 240, 339, 340; London and Berlin, 238; and reporters, 264, 265; W.W.'s scolding amuses, 274; at Fort Myer, 301-302; Lahm goes with, 306; accident, 313-318, 321, 322, 323, 330-335; Pau, France, 336; Rome, 338; cross-country flight, 342; Berlin, 343-348, 353, 376; night flight, 347; W.W.'s will, 389; Wright Company, 390, 391; Dayton flood, 397, 398; last trip to Europe, 398; views on licenses, 400; Curtiss case, 400-403; interest in Wright Company sold, 402-403; war and the airplane, 405-406, 437; 1903 plane, 408-410, 415, 427, 442, 443, 469; national defense, 412-413; death, 469

Wright, Reuchlin, in own home, 6; W.W. tells of French children, 326; W.W. sends money, 336; bequest to, 388; W.W.'s will, 391

Wright, Susan Koerner, mechanical ability, 4; W.W.'s care of, 5

Wright, Wilbur, as boy, 3, 4; cooking, 7, 18; appearance, 8; education, 10; writes to Chanute, 22; Kitty Hawk trips, 31, 33, 40, 65-84, 103-122, 153, 256-265, 386; Spratt visits, 39; Chanute visits, 40, 73-75, 108-111, 132, 144; Chicago lecture, 43-48; manner of dress, 47, 117, 118; wind tunnel experiment, 52, 58, 59; financial aid refused, 55, 56; philosophy of, 60, 89, 143; defends Bishop Wright, 65, 66; 1902 glider, 69; tail and wing control, 81, 82, 83; lecture offer, 87; machine control in wind, 106; first motor flight, 114; contributions to airplane inventions, 123, 124; at Huffman field, 130; and British Government, 141; U.S. Government, 143, 144, 148, 247, 255; French conference, 173; remarks on success, 183; Flint & Co's. offer, 190; to Europe, 203, 205; Berg meets, 205; Paris, 210, 232; Louvre, 211, 227; Notre Dame, 212; describes France, 217; European negotiations,

206, 222, 242-245; German promises, 233, 236, 238, 245; Berlin, 239; French company formed, 255; Le Mans, 270, 271, 277, 291, 293, 294, 310, 338, 411; Chanute criticizes Wrights, 272, 286; scolds O.W., 273, 274, 275; Ste Chapelle, 276; hurts arm, 281-282, 288; portrait, 309; La Sarthe, 310, 320, 325, 330, 337; sympathy for father, 317, 318; flies only for busi-

ness, 333; Hudson flight, 349; K.W. and O.W. met by, 352; flight correspondence with Chanute, 356-368; last flight as pilot, 374; death, 388

Young, Dwight, 461

Zahm, Albert F., 171; suggests heiress, 281, 286; O.W. and, 296; Curtiss joined by, 368, 369, 402, 436, 437, 455-460
Zens brothers, 212, 219, 302